THE FILMS OF BETTY GRABLE

544-78X

THE FILMS OF BETTY GRABLE

Ed Hulse

**Dedicated to my parents,
who've never quite understood just what it is their son
sees in all those old movies.**

Hulse, Ed
The Films of Betty Grable
ISBN: 1-880756-06-4

Cover design: Andrés Dubin, *Graphico Design*
Typesetting production: Michael Bifulco

Published by Riverwood Press, Burbank, California.
Manufactured in the United States of America.

CONTENTS

INTRODUCTION

It is probably impossible to overestimate the impact Betty Grable had on American moviegoers of the World War II era, when she was not only the number one box-office star (beginning in 1943) but the archetypal girl-next-door for millions of American G.I.s who kept her famous pin-up photo in barracks, foxholes, and backpacks during the lengthy conflict. For all her Hollywood glamour-girl trappings, Betty seemed...well, attainable. Hers was not the appeal of enigmatic beauties such as Garbo or Dietrich, nor of haughty sophisticates such as Davis or Hepburn. Grable's allure was that of a wholesome, energetic, vivacious girl with a yest for life and a healthy sexuality that manifested itself in uninhibited displays of her lithe figure.

Because most of her starring vehicles were "inconsequential" musical comedies and/or sentimental forays in nostalgia, the films of Betty Grable—like those of singing star Alice Faye, her predecessor and onetime co-star at 20th Century-Fox—never received the historical attention that they deserved. Hopefully, this book will redress that situation somewhat.

Although few contemporary critics ever acknowledged the histrionic abilities of Hollywood's musical stars (and it would be a mistake to attribute to those stars more talent than readily apparent), in retrospect we can see that carrying such patently silly stories imposed a far greater burden on the song-and-dance stars than is usually admitted. If you need any proof that starring in a musical comedy—even one bolstered by superb songs and top production values—is not something of which *anyone* is capable, just look at *At Long Last Love* or *New York, New York*.

By dint of her buoyant personality, abundant physical charms, and vigorous trouping, Betty Grable climbed the ladder of success slowly but steadily, and when she got to the top she stayed there longer than most others who made the same ascent. Her accomplishments, and her talent, should not be overlooked or taken for granted just because she specialized in providing escapist entertainment. The mere fact that her films have survived and remained in distribution—thanks to broadcast TV, pay cable, videocassette and videodisc exposure—when those of many of her contemporaries have not, speaks volumes on the timelessness of her appeal. As recent students of American popular culture have learned, much of what was once considered trash is now seen as art—and vice versa. It would be a mistake to elevate the films of Betty Grable to give them parity with, say, the westerns of John Ford or the comedies of Charlie Chaplin. But it would be no less grievous a mistake to consign them to the dustbin of pop-culture history just because they are fluffy musical comedies.

In covering Grable's films I have chosen to lavish the same attention on those in which she is barely visible as those in which she is the star. In all cases, I've compiled excerpts from contemporary reviews that appeared both in mass-market newspapers and magazines and movie-industry trade papers. Opinions expressed in the latter journals have special interest, I think, because they are geared to the motion-picture exhibitor and frequently reflect the critic's evaluation of a film's box-office potential as much as its artistic merit. In the interest of maintaining the spirit of the original reviews, I have not edited out the amusing, often arcane jargon of the trade, most of which is decipherable in proper context. I have also left intact the scriveners' punctuation.

For their invaluable aid in helping me compile the information contained herein, I must thank Linda Mehr and the staff at the Margaret Herrick Library of the Academy of Motion Picture Arts and Sciences, and the invaluable Karl Thiede, whose personal reference files are probably the most comprehensive belonging to any single scholar; Karl's diligence in compiling data on the elusive short subjects in which Grable starred merits particular commendation and thanks.

For the loan of rare and valuable stills from their private collections, I would like to thank Richard W. Bann, Robert S. Birchard, Critt Davis, Michael Hawks, Marty Kearns, Danny Schwartz, Karl Thiede, Doug Whitney, and Lou Valentino. It is well nigh impossible to find stills of Grable in her earliest film appearances as a chorus girl (indeed, to find *any* stills from those films), but every attempt has been made to uncover shots from her early featured roles—with less success than I'd hoped, even though there are many rare and interesting stills representing Grable's early movies.

Ed Hulse
May 1993

THE FILMS OF
BETTY GRABLE

BETTY GRABLE
IN PARAMOUNT PICTURES

P2001-424

BETTY GRABLE
THE GIRL WITH THE MILLION DOLLAR LEGS

T he Betty Grable story actually begins, as do a surprising number of
Hollywood success stories of the '30s and '40s, with an overly ambitious
stage mother. Lillian Rose Hoffman was born in 1889 in St. Louis, Missouri. By all accounts a beautiful child, she was also restless and headstrong, and
rebelled against the religious practices and lectures imposed on her by her strict
Quaker parents. She dreamed of becoming an actress or an opera singer.

While attending the St. Louis World's Fair in 1904, Lillian met a charismatic ticket-taker named Conn Grable. An unprepossessing man whose gruff appearance masked a gentle nature, Grable asked her out on a date—chaperoned, of
course—and the two fell in love immediately. They dated for another three years
before getting married; even then, Lillian (who had been nicknamed "Billie" by
her erstwhile lover, to whom she referred as "Bud") was still in her teens and
Grable just barely 21 years old. Conn adored his new bride, and worked feverishly
to climb the ladder of success despite little formal education. He eventually
landed in the commodities business—where, as an aggressive and personable
young man, he achieved surprising success.

Billie, on the other hand, was thankful to have escaped her stern parents,
although she chafed at the somewhat rigid mores imposed on her by married life
in Victorian-era St. Louis. Moreover, she came to resent Bud's devotion to his
large family. Persistent restlessness and still-smoldering ambition made her irritable, and the birth of their first child, Marjorie, gave her scant consolation. Bud's
instinctive business sense and relentless drive enabled him to land a prominent
position in St. Louis' first public utilities corporation, but the Grables' steadily
increasing fortunes and social position apparently meant little to Billie.

An immovable wedge was driven between the still-young couple some years later, when their second child, a son they nicknamed "Brother," died tragically. A victim of bronchial pneumonia, the infant suffocated when the family doctor misadvised Bud on a primitive home treatment. The Grable family never fully recovered from that tragedy.

By early 1916, when Billie learned that she was pregnant with her third child, the motion picture had become firmly entrenched as America's most popular form of mass entertainment. The newly established "fan" magazines were filled with glamorous stories of Hollywood movie stars, the country's new "royalty." Of course, even then many of the fan-magazine stories were largely fictitious, but they were taken very seriously by early moviegoers—including Billie Grable, who had never forgotten her childhood dreams of a career on the stage. Thanks to the burgeoning Hollywood publicity machine, the first generation of movie stars had already achieved recognition and notoriety denied all but the most famous matinee idols of the stage. Billie was intent on somehow getting to Hollywood.

Whatever aspirations she might still have harbored, though, were permanently dashed when she gave birth to a second daughter, Elizabeth Ruth, on December 18, 1916. As a young girl she had suffered from a hip ailment that was improperly treated. When the injured hip flared up during her third pregnancy, corrective surgery was ruled out by her doctors, with the result that, after Elizabeth's birth, Billie found herself permanently if not massively disabled. Her show-business hopes gone for good, Billie's resentment grew and festered.

Elizabeth, who became Betty, was an adorable infant who grew into a lovely child. Billie realized very early on that Betty was musically inclined, and insisted the child, at the tender age of four, take singing and dancing lessons, for which Conn Grable—eager to keep his wife happy and hold his family together—willingly paid. Years later, Betty recalled that during this period Billie's demands didn't seem particularly outrageous, but she never failed to remind her occasionally recalcitrant daughter that she had "sacrificed" her own ambitions to bring the child into the world.

The Grables moved from their modest but comfortable home to the reasonably lavish, well known Forest Park Hotel in 1922. Bud, whose steadily successful business endeavors made the move possible, hoped that a more extravagant lifestyle would mollify his increasingly difficult wife. Billie frequented the hotel's colorful dining room, where visiting vaudeville headliners congregated between shows. She took particular delight in trotting out her six-year-old daughter to perform for the veteran entertainers, who graciously endured the youngster's primitive song-and-dance routines. Even then Billie hoped that one of the

At eight months, with her mother Billie.

vaudevillians might "put in a good word" for Betty, and that if her daughter was cut out for a show-business career, she could act as the child's manager and thus insinuate herself into the glamorous world of which she had dreamed for so long.

Billie stepped up Betty's musical training: At various times the youngster took lessons in ballet, acrobatic, and tap dancing in addition to learning to play the piano and the saxophone. Betty longed to play with other children during her after-school hours, but Billie demanded she adhere to the intensive training program she'd devised. When Betty balked, Billie only had to remind the girl how much she'd "sacrificed" to bring her back into line.

(Years later, in an interview with *Photoplay*'s Herb Howe, Grable put the best face on her abnormal childhood: "My mother had the ambition. . .she did not force me, she gave me her boost. I have rolled along on the momentum she gave. . .I led a regulated life. Other children were playing and going to parties while I was rehearsing and going to bed at nine.")

Betty, still in grade school, began her professional show-business career as a dancer in an annual all-kiddie show at St. Louis' Odeon Theatre. Conn Grable

At age 8, in minstrel-show makeup for an amateur performance.

At age 9, in front of her St. Louis home.

At age 9, showing off her ballet skills atop the family car.

took great pride in his daughter's accomplishments, but feared that Billie's relentless drive would endanger Betty's chances for a good education. At that time, commensurate with Conn's position in the business community and the family's social prominence, the Grable girls were enrolled in the exclusive Mary Institute.

For the 1928 summer vacation, Billie talked Bud into taking the family to Hollywood. The trip only intensified her desire to move there permanently, and she saw Betty as her ticket. Back in St. Louis, she insisted that her talented daughter step up her musical training. Betty, on the verge of adolescence, was starting to develop other interests, most prominent of which was a passion for horses and horseback riding—that would prove to be lifelong. Billie promised Betty that if she was diligent about her music and dance lessons, she could take riding lessons and own her own horse. A newly motivated Betty applied herself to a tough regimen, eagerly anticipating the day her hard work would pay off. But as months passed and the horse failed to arrive, she became resentful, although she never openly confronted Billie over her duplicity.

In early 1929 Conn Grable, anxiously watching the ominous financial storm clouds that eventually burst with Wall Street's infamous stock-market crash and the Great Depression, allowed Billie to take Betty to California in pursuit of a film career. Billie's move, ostensibly undertaken to relieve Bud of some responsibility and boost the family's income potential, was in fact a shrewdly calculated tactic designed solely to achieve her long-standing goal of crashing Hollywood. A heartbroken Bud reluctantly agreed to let Billie pull Betty out of school, and he promised to look after Marjorie (who, lacking Betty's talents and beauty, apparently never occupied as prominent a place in Billie's heart).

Betty Grable was not yet 13 when she went on her first casting call, but the sight of hundreds of other girls competing for a limited number of chorus-line spots in a Fox musical proved more daunting than either she or Billie expected. The coltish Betty, heavily made up, sporting a more mature coiffure, and claiming to be 16, managed to wangle a short-term contract. She made her film debut in *Let's Go Places* (1929), barely noticable as a chorus girl in blackface.

In a 1955 interview with fan-magazine writer Aljean Meltsir, Betty described a particularly traumatic incident from her early days as a chorus girl in the movies. "When Betty's first chance for a specialty number came," Meltsir wrote, "she slipped on the steep movie steps. She picked herself up, crying.

"'Do it again,' Mrs. Grable whispered.

"Betty went back to the top of the stairs again. She slipped for the second time. She ran to the side of the stage, and Mrs. Grable followed her.

"'Go back,' she said. 'Do it again.'

"'No,' Betty said, rubbing her back.

"'Look at me,' Mrs. Grable said. 'You won't slip again. Go back.'

"Betty Grable went to the top of the stairs for the third time and danced down them."

After making a few more token appearances, Betty was fired when Fox personnel, making a routine background check, discovered she'd lied about her age. Billie then enrolled her in Lawlor's Professional School for Children, which allowed Betty to continue her education (albeit briefly and not very effectively) while enabling Billie to chat up other stage mothers and get tips about placing her daughter. With information she gleaned from virtually everybody with whom she talked, Billie pushed Betty into a seemingly unending string of one-night stands and limited engagements, including amateur nights, dance marathons, and benefit performances. Betty occasionally slipped into night-club engagements when she could fool club managers into believing she was of legal age. While Los Angeles nightlife hardly provided a healthy atmosphere for an adolescent girl, Billie encouraged her daughter to take whatever work she could get in the interest of "getting your face seen."

A 1930 casting call for producer Sam Goldwyn resulted in another contract for Betty, as one of 22 chorines selected to appear in *Whoopee!*, a lavish Technicolor musical starring Eddie Cantor, who had starred in the stage version produced by Florenz Ziegfeld. On view in the very first production number, sporting an eye-catching costume and heavy makeup necessitated by the bright lights used for early Technicolor cinematography, the leggy youngster seemed somewhat older than she actually was.

Grable, along with Lucille Ball, Virginia Bruce, and Paulette Goddard, became one of the fabled "Goldwyn Girls" who supported Cantor in his subsequent musicals for the producer. While shooting *Palmy Days* (1931), Betty met George Raft, who played a gangster in the picture, and actually went on two chaperoned dates with him before he decided, wisely, to "throw her back until she grew up," as he later recalled.

Betty's appearances in Goldwyn's high-budget, enormously popular musical comedies didn't necessarily give her very much to do; she was just one in a crowd. The ever-ambitious Billie, in direct and flagrant violation of Betty's contract, pushed her daughter into several two-reel comedy shorts. In some of these films, Betty played the ingenue role and therefore had quite a bit of dialogue, and was billed as Frances Dean. Goldwyn dropped her abruptly after *The Kid From Spain* (1932), and while no reason was given for her termination, it appears likely that the producer tumbled to Billie's unprincipled tactics and fired Betty in retaliation.

Betty's dismissal by Goldwyn apparently had little effect on her ambitious

In 1930, as a pubescent chorus girl in the movies.

mother, who continued to lobby on her behalf in even the most bizarre situations. According to Grable biographer Spero Pastos, writing in *Pin-Up: The Tragedy of Betty Grable* (G.P. Putnam's Sons, 1986), mother and daughter met actor Bert Wheeler, younger half of RKO's Wheeler & Woolsey comedy team, when a major earthquake forced all of them from their residence at the Canterbury apartment complex into an open field nearby. Pastos claims that during the night, as the Canterbury's anxious tenants camped out in fear of further tremors, Billie sang Betty's praises to Wheeler, who pulled strings to get her cast in the team's next RKO vehicle, *Hold 'Em Jail* (1932).

Although in retrospect it seems apparent that Billie had unlimited faith both in her ability to find work for Betty and her daughter's ability to make good, Betty herself probably didn't share her confidence. Moreover, she challenged Billie's insistence on constant training and practice. Painted by more than one source as the archetypal monstrous stage mother, Billie reportedly disciplined Betty harshly, grounding her often and even, according to Pastos, locking her in bedroom closets until she complied with her mother's demands. Such harsh treatment during this early phase of her career seems to have made Betty the stern taskmaster she later became, both in her private and professional lives.

Betty made her theatrical debut in a revue titled *Tattle Tales,* which starred vaudevillian and stage star Frank Fay, whose more successful wife, film actress Barbara Stanwyck, reportedly financed the show to help keep Fay happy and strengthen their crumbling marriage. The show opened in San Francisco and moved to Los Angeles shortly thereafter, presumably for fine-tuning before attempting a Broadway run. However, Fay's drinking and nasty temperament created endless problems for the company, resulting in several canceled performances and, eventually, a sizable financial loss for Stanwyck. Betty, who warbled and hoofed in a couple of numbers, was again out of work.

But not for long. Bandleader Ted Fio Rito, then looking for a female vocalist, had spotted Betty in a *Tattle Tales* performance and decided to sign her up. Fio Rito at that time enjoyed tremendous popularity, and his band toured the entire country. Billie reportedly questioned the wisdom of leaving Hollywood for weeks or months at a time, but conceded that the exposure couldn't hurt Betty's career. Grable, still a teenager, joined the band and toured with Fio Rito for nine months. Her natural vivaciousness made her a hit with live audiences, who invariably felt the energy and youthful joie de vivre she exuded.

Billie, naturally enough, accompanied her young daughter, who was attracted to several of the musicians in Fio Rito's band. Betty's mother permitted her to date them—always chaperoned—but frowned on anything that threatened to blossom into a full-fledged romance. She had too many plans for her talented daughter to be thwarted by the natural urges of a healthy teen-ager working in a glamorous business.

Grable's motion-picture appearances during 1933 consisted of supporting roles in program pictures for both the major studios and the schlocky "Poverty Row" producers. Impetuous, smart-mouthed younger sisters were a Grable specialty during this period, and she even took a small part in a quasi-exploitational sex drama portentiously titled *What Price Innocence?* In 1934 Betty earned the approving notice of some reviewers of RKO's first Fred Astaire-Ginger Rogers vehicle, *The Gay Divorcee*, in which she performed a sprightly novelty number "Let's Knock Knees," with comic relief Edward Everett Horton. RKO signed her to a term contract, giving her ingenue roles in two-reel short subjects and supporting parts in feature films. With her hair dyed peroxide blonde, she got the usual contract-player buildup by posing for innumerable publicity stills, going to various Hollywood social events, and giving her first interviews for fan magazines.

Betty invariably did her best whenever she stepped in front of the cameras, but the RKO brass never regarded her as anything more than a moderately talented, decorative chorus girl. Strange as it may seem, the potency of her appeal just never occured to anyone. Grable frequently lamented—to whomever would listen—that she wasn't "getting the breaks." Her biographer suggests that the RKO period was among the least fruitful of her whole career, and that it in fact diminished her already low self-esteem.

Grable's nadir for RKO was *Follow the Fleet*, a 1936 Astaire-Rogers vehicle for which she was promised a juicy supporting role. But the part mysteriously dwindled as production got underway, and in the final film Betty's best moments come as one of three female vocalists providing backup for Ginger in the "Pick Yourself Up" number. Grable later opined that Rogers, herself a temperamental performer under the thumb of a domineering stage mother, exerted pressure on studio brass to limit the screen time of her female supporting players.

A straight dramatic role in the gangster drama *Don't Turn 'Em Loose* (1936) probably provided Grable's detractors the straw that broke the camel's back: Critics felt she wasn't equal to the demands of the role. She was dropped shortly after the film's release.

Betty then signed with Paramount, the home of Hollywood's most successful "collegiate" comedies and musicals. The 20-year-old Grable, bright and bouncy with a dazzling smile and curvaceous figure, was an ideal co-ed type—and over the next three years she played campus cuties in a handful of programmers. Her musical abilities were utilized in some of these films, which sported stereotypical scripts and proffered stock characterizations that didn't put much strain on her limited histrionic abilities.

With Edward Everett Horton in her novelty number from *The Gay Divorcee* (1934).

Grable spent much of her time posing for publicity stills, more often than not clad in bathing suits. Based on the number of such stills that survive in private collections, one would think that she was a major Paramount star. But even though she labored mightily for the publicity department and apparently got a big buildup, Grable never attained much success, except in the studio's "B" pictures.

While under contract to Paramount, Betty, approaching legal age, managed to have a more expansive social life. She dated frequently, often with fellow Paramount contractees (although such liaisons were frequently instigated by the publicity department), and occasionally with other men she'd known from her earlier days in Hollywood. One of them, a member of Ted Fio Rito's band named Bill Carey, had joined Betty on a pleasure cruise to Catalina Island—a popular vacation spot off the California coast—when he spotted former child star Jackie Coogan on the boat and introduced him to Betty.

Coogan, who'd rocketed to international fame as the titular tyke in Charlie Chapin's *The Kid* (1921), saw his film career evaporate as he entered adolescence. A student at University of California's Santa Clara campus, Coogan hoped to launch a business career to expand the personal fortune he'd made as a child. He recognized Betty as the Fio Rito vocalist he'd admired years earlier, and was immediately attracted to her. The feeling was mutual, and over the next few months the two were seen (and photographed) cavorting all over Southern California.

Coogan was determined to regain control of the reported four million dollars he'd earned in his youth. He had recently been shocked to learn that his father—who died in a car crash—left every penny to his mother, who then married Jackie's business manager, who in turn schemed to keep the young man from getting his hands on the fortune. In the meantime, Coogan asked Betty to marry him.

The intervening half-century has obscured Grable's true motivations. She stated, repeatedly and defiantly, that she loved Coogan for who he was and not what he was worth. Even at the time of their courtship, however, there was considerable speculation (some of which made its way into print) that she relished the prospect of being married to a multi-millionaire.

The mothers of both heartily disapproved of the highly anticipated union, and Billie demanded that Betty not marry until after she'd turned 21, hoping against hope that the girl would reconsider and get on with her career. But Grable stuck to her guns, marrying Coogan on December 20, 1937—two days after her birthday. Although Coogan was no longer a screen star, he was a well-remembered figure; his past notoriety and well-publicized recent squabbles over the "inheritance" made the nuptials a front-page event. Conn Grable, by now a casualty of the Depression and an alcoholic to boot, came to Los Angeles to give Betty away.

The Coogans set up housekeeping in the fashionable Brentwood area of Los Angeles. Although Jackie was confident that his mother and stepfather would eventually relent and turn over his fortune to him, Betty grew less optimistic. She had paid for the wedding and their new home, lock, stock and barrel, and warned Coogan that unless he took legal action he might lose everything. He did finally inaugurate a lawsuit but, blithely confident that the court would rule in his favor, continued to spend Betty's money recklessly. The lawsuit made national headlines and provided fodder for gossip columnists, who fueled the flames of familial discontent by printing increasingly bitter charges and countercharges solicited from both sides.

The ever-vigilant Billie, seeing in Betty's domestic travails the stuff of a publicist's dream, stormed Paramount repeatedly and demanded that the studio either pay more attention to Betty or release her from her contract. The Paramount brass, possibly embarassed by Grable's unfortunate notoriety, dropped her from the roster of contract players. So now, as if things weren't already bad enough, Betty was out of work to boot. Billie suggested that Betty and Jackie

With fellow RKO contractee Jane Hamilton in a 1936 publicity shot.

appear together on what was left of the vaudeville circuit, reasoning that a scandal-hungry public would be delighted to see them in person—and pay for the privilege.

A humiliated Betty suffered the additional indignity of seeing herself trashed by the same columnists who, only months before, had lavished so much attention on both her career and her romance. As the Coogan lawsuit drew to a close, the press grew bolder, openly accusing Betty of being a gold digger. And to her great sorrow, an increasingly reckless Coogan—whose profligate spending, heavy drinking, and blatant if casual infidelities deeply hurt her—seemed not to care.

In a 1942 *Photoplay* article, writer Howard Sharpe told Betty's side of the

With Jackie Coogan on their wedding day in 1937.

story. "She was solidly practical and ambitious," he wrote, "aware that you never get anything for nothing. Jackie believed that as a child he had earned his living for the rest of his life, and he wanted to have fun, now.

"Thus for the brisk new house they rented. . .the first thing Jackie ordered was a record player. The first thing Betty ordered was a desk, at which to sit and keep household accounts.

"[O]ne afternoon [Coogan] borrowed five dollars. 'I'll stop by the store on my way home and get stuff for dinner with this,' he told her, shrugging into his topcoat. She watched him gun the roadster in second and saw the red wigwags on the tail lights flirting as he zoomed out of the drive, tires screeching. And she suddenly thought, *For Pete's sake, grow up! We're flat, you haven't a job and you don't get any money for another year, maybe not even then. Buy hamburger with that five, not a capon and some champagne.*"

Coogan's wake-up call came in the form of a highly unsatisfactory conclusion to the much-publicized suit: It developed that his mother, father, and stepfather had systematically squandered his fortune. (At this time, there were no laws safeguarding the earnings of child actors, although the outcome of this case led to the passage of protective legislation, which came to be known as "the Coogan law.") Jackie got exactly $126,307.50; after paying legal and other expenses, he pocketed roughly $35,000.

Grable had had enough. On January 20, 1939, she made a statement to the press announcing her separation from Coogan. Their divorce became final on November 11, 1940.

The experience scarred Betty for the remainder of her life. She deeply resented her excoriation by the press, and took great care—both during her long romance with George Raft and her later marriage to Harry James—to be wary of interviewers who claimed to be her friends and allies.

"Betty knew now," wrote Howard Sharpe in 1942, "that she had never been in love with Jackie, that she had mistaken a half-dozen lesser reactions for one real emotion; he had been a great companion and someday he would be an adult, too, and a good husband for a girl.

"A girl other than Betty—-

"Jackie had decided to sue for his inheritance. She knew what it would mean if, during a period when his mother and stepfather were trying to discount him as 'a bad boy,' she should divorce him. It would give them the case and she wanted everything for Jackie, every shred and remnant of his fortune that he could get. For him, you understand, not for herself.

"Betty Grable could take care of Betty Grable, always had and always would. She told him that. 'I don't want a red cent of whatever you win out of this

In two 1939 Paramount publicity poses, demonstrating her athletic ability and showing off her trim figure.

fight,' she said. 'I'll stick until you get it, we'll put up a front—then we'll call it quits.'

    "'If you still want to, then,' he agreed.

    "And she still wanted to."

    As painful as her marriage to Coogan must have been, it did at least provide an unexpected dividend. 20th Century-Fox production executive Darryl F. Zanuck signed her to a long-term contract late in 1939, claiming that he'd experienced an epiphany after seeing one of her old publicity photos. In retrospect, it would seem as though the studio head was being more than a little disingenuous.

    Initially, Zanuck's motivations didn't count for much, because he didn't really have a specific strategy to promote her. Fox already had one blonde musical star, the enormously popular Alice Faye, and even though Grable's exuberance set her apart from the more mature, placid Faye, Fox had only so many musicals to release in any given year.

    Fortunately, another opportunity opened up for Grable, taking the heat off Zanuck temporarily. While performing at the 1939 San Francisco Exposition, she'd been seen by theatrical agent Louis Shurr, who enthusiastically recommended her to songwriter-turned-producer B.G. "Buddy" DeSylva, then casting his lavish Broadway production of Cole Porter's *DuBarry Was a Lady*. Shurr, like others before him, had realized that the dynamic Grable, ill-used in films up to that point, projected tremendous vitality to live audiences. When DeSylva offered her the ingenue role, Betty initially appeared reluctant to accept, protesting that she had no stage experience. It's likely that she was intimidated by the prospect of appearing on Broadway and being subjected to printed lashings from the legendarily harsh New York theater critics.

DeSylva persuaded her to take the role, and she left for the East Coast on October 12, 1939, one day after filing her divorce papers in Los Angeles. Darryl Zanuck gave her his blessings, but reminded her that, as a Fox contractee, she would have to leave the show if he came up with a hot property for her. But Betty felt that was highly unlikely.

Grable showed up in New York with bandleader Artie Shaw, whom she'd started dating a short time earlier. Gossip columnists were quick to press her about the relationship, but a cautious Grable tersely stated: "We're very fond of each other, but I don't know about marrying him. My divorce doesn't become final until November 11, 1940." (Pastos claims that by this time Grable had already determined to marry Shaw, over Billie's strenuous objections.)

Betty threw herself into *DuBarry Was a Lady* with all the energy and commitment she could muster. Her infrequent chats with the New York press, as reported in both the dailies and the show-business trades, indicate that she nurtured a hope that she would succeed on stage, and was confident she could make the grade. The show's stars, Bert Lahr and Ethel Merman, were accomplished performers and seasoned Broadway veterans, but Grable felt she could keep up with them.

After playing a two-week tryout engagement in Boston, Grable looked up DeSylva. "I'm better than this," she said, referring to her part. "Better than the spot I have. Why don't you feature me?"

A puzzled DeSylva asked, "Why should I?"

"Because," Betty replied, "I'll quit if you don't."

With Grable in an expanded role, *DuBarry* moved to Philadelphia and, finally, to New York. It opened on December 6, 1939 to appreciative audiences and generally good reviews. Betty was genuinely surprised but immensely gratified by the good notices she received, especially a modestly favorable mention from *New York Times* reviewer Brooks Atkinson. Her big number, Porter's "Well, Did You Evah!", which she performed with dancer (and future choreographer and director) Charles Walter, was singled out as one of the show's best. (It was later incorporated into the score of *High Society*, MGM's musical remake of *The Philadelphia Story*, blithely interpreted by Bing Crosby and Frank Sinatra.)

THE GIRL WITH THE MILLION DOLLAR LEGS / 19

DuBarry Was a Lady made Grable the toast of Broadway and later that year landed her a *Life* magazine cover, the first of many she would grace. Bolstered by Betty's success and the restoration of her self-confidence, Billie resolved to break up her romance with Shaw. The bandleader, irritated by Billie's consistent campaigning against him, finally opted out of the relationship. And rather suddenly at that: Early in February of 1940, only a few days after their last meeting, Shaw flew to Las Vegas, where he eloped with screen star Lana Turner, whom he'd met while filming *Dancing Co-Ed* the year before.

A heartbroken Grable sidestepped reporters as long as she could, finally issuing a brief but unilluminating statement. Privately, she expressed rage and resentment. (Some sources claim there were unexpected complications to the affair's abrupt termination: a pregnant Grable had an abortion in a private Manhattan clinic.)

She remained in the cast of *DuBarry* until June, when Darryl Zanuck wired her to return to Hollywood immediately. Alice Faye had been stricken with appendicitis only days before filming was scheduled to begin on *Down Argentine Way*, a big-budget Technicolor musical in which Fox had already invested a huge amount of money. Grable, initially reluctant to leave the show in which she'd achieved her greatest success to date, finally rushed back to Fox.

Down Argentine Way, a lavish production backed by a top cast (headed by Don Ameche, a perennial Faye co-star) and sporting a sprightly score (written by top tunesmiths Mack Gordon, Harry Warren, Al Dubin, and Jimmy McHugh), effectively launched Grable as a Fox star. Freed from the restrictive conventions of the stereotypical college musicals she'd made at RKO and Paramount, Betty showed herself more than competent to topline a major production. What's more, her blonde hair, gleaming white smile, peaches-and-cream complexion, and lithe, leggy figure photographed handsomely in the garish Technicolor hues of the day. The movie industry's trade-paper reviewers, who'd virtually ignored her before, suddenly declared Grable to be the star discovery of the year.

After inexplicably teaming Grable, who'd already proven herself, with Faye in *Tin Pan Alley* (1940), an entertaining picture but one in which Betty definitely took a back seat to Alice, Zanuck decided to try out his new star in dramatic roles. Grable, who always considered herself a glorified hoofer, balked at the challenging roles in the 1941 productions *A Yank in the R.A.F.* and *I Wake Up Screaming* (originally titled *Hot Spot*), but did her best and acquitted herself handsomely. Critics thought Zanuck was trying to "bring her along too fast," however, and the studio chief must have agreed: He didn't try to spot Grable in a non-musical role for several years.

Fox publicity men had a field day with Grable, who was rapidly becoming

Dining out with new beau George Raft in 1941.

one of the studio's chief assets. In that frankly mercenary vein, they decided to promote her as the owner of Hollywood's most glorious gams. They insured her shapely legs for a million dollars with Lloyd's of London, and issued dozens of different stills featuring precise measurements of the star's limbs. During the World War II years, she would become the number-one pin-up favorite of American servicemen overseas, thanks to a particularly memorable leg shot.

Early in 1941 *Photoplay*, the most influential of the movie fan magazines, enlisted artist Paul Hesse, showman Billy Rose, Doctor Mary Halton (a prominent Hollywood physician), and costume designer Irene to select the girl with the best figure in Hollywood. Grable won hands down, leading a field that included Claudette Colbert, Ginger Rogers, Ann Sheridan, Paulette Goddard, Carole Lombard, Susan Hayward, Loretta Young, and Olivia de Havilland. Her measurements were given as 34 1/2"-24"-36", with 20" thighs, 12 1/2" calves, and 7 1/2" ankles. Her height was 5'4", and her weight was listed as 112 pounds.

In an accompanying interview, Grable explained how she kept her trim figure: "I dance anywhere from half an hour to several hours every day, at least four days of the week. . .Dancing is a good thing to help develop symmetry. You exercise just about every muscle of the body. . . ." She also confessed that "I have an excellent appetite. And—hold everything—my favorite foods are steak,

With Don Ameche, rehearsing a routine from *Down Argentine Way* (1940).

mashed potatoes, fried chicken, good old southern biscuits, and chocolate milk shakes. When I get up in the morning I drink one or two cups of coffee, with cream and sugar, and as much orange juice as I want—usually a large glassful."

As one of Hollywood's fastest rising stars, Grable fully enjoyed her new-found success, and threw herself into a vigorous social life that included brief romantic flings with Tyrone Power, Victor Mature, John Payne, Desi Arnaz, playboy Alexis Thompson, and others. Even Howard Hughes, the mild-mannered millionaire who'd already acquired a reputation for eccentricity, dated her.

During the early '40s, Betty's "steady" was actor George Raft, whom she'd dated once as a teenager, and who renewed his acquaintanceship with the girl after bumping into her at a Hollywood nightclub in late 1940. Raft squired Betty around Tinseltown and lavished expensive presents on her, much to the obvious delight of the Hollywood press corps. She was quoted as saying, "George left nothing to be desired in the way of old-fashioned gallantry and chivalry." There was one small problem, however: Raft was a married man, and his wife Grayce, from whom he'd been separated for many years, refused to grant him a divorce.

Apparently Raft was a bit *too* courteous and gallant for Grable, who eventually started seeing other men. Her obvious and genuine affection for Raft turned to resentment and frustration due to his seeming inability to reconcile his domestic problems. She spoke frankly about Raft's courtship to fan-magazine writers, who were in those days accustomed to fabricating stories about the stars, and were therefore delighted by Grable's candor and her willingness to explain the situation.

"[I]n George Raft," wrote Adela Rogers St. Johns in 1943, "[Betty] has found a man who will offer her more variety than any other one man I can think of—and a great deal of wisdom besides. The difference in some of their tastes? That's true enough. George is, for instance, an inveterate card player—a really fine bridge player among other things. The game bores Betty. Betty likes to go places and see things—so does George, up to a point, then he wants to stay home quietly. 'But,' says Betty, 'those things don't have anything to do with love. Mutual tastes and all that are fine but they're just substitutes for the real thing. If you really love somebody, everything else takes care of itself.'

"Still, she's a temperamental girl, in some ways. Quick to flare up, quick to anger, and likely, on occasion, to get annoyed if things don't happen the way she wants them to. George has a system about that. He gets out of range. When he thinks the right moment has come, he goes back—and Betty has forgotten all about it."

The highly publicized romance eventually soured, but not before Betty and George had nearly come to blows in a fashionable Hollywood night spot. Some who knew Grable claimed that Raft had in fact beaten her when they were in private, and warned her not to see other men. Warnings from Raft *meant* something, too; his underworld connections were the stuff of Hollywood legend, and people who disappointed Raft's friends often came to tragic ends. One of Grable's other suitors was bandleader Harry James, whom she first met while dancing with servicemen at the famed Hollywood Canteen (where she appeared frequently throughout the war years, at one time holding the establishment's record for continuous dancing), and whose band appeared in one of her most popular wartime vehicles, *Springtime in the Rockies* (1942). Although she still feared Raft and his explosive temper, she elected to accompany James in public. On one occasion Raft, who always kept tabs on Betty's social engagements, cornered them in a night club and hurled obscenities at them. When Betty asked him to leave, Raft responded by pasting James in the face, precipitating a raucous melee that made headlines the next day and got Grable bawled out by Fox brass.

She retaliated by calling famed columnist Louella Parsons with a "scoop": She was dumping Raft. "I would have married George a week after I met him," she was quoted as saying, "but when you wait two and a half years, there doesn't seem to be any future in romance with a married man."

Oddly enough, though, James had exactly the same dilemma. His wife Louise, a former vocalist with the band who'd borne him two sons, was content to be married in name only to one of the country's most popular (and most prosperous) bandleaders. She eventually relented, allowing James to get a quickie

With Raft at a Hollywood night spot in 1942.

divorce in Mexico. He notified Grable—who met him in Las Vegas, where his band was engaged—and they were married at the Baptist Little Church of the West on July 5, 1943, under the prying eyes of hundreds of fans and photographers (among whom were Fox photogs who had violated Grable's earnest request that her wedding not be turned into a circus by the publicity department).

Several years later Betty recalled the chaotic day. "We'd planned a quiet afternoon ceremony in a small chapel. It was dusk when the groom got off the train, both of us so relieved to see each other we could hardly speak. Immediately, we sped off to the quiet and cool of the chapel—or so we imagined. We couldn't figure out the traffic tangle until we saw the church, lit up like a Christmas tree. People were lined up for blocks, a spotlight picked out our car and a loudspeaker boomed, 'Here they come at last, folks—Betty Grable and Harry James—give the bride and groom a hand, folks!' I saw Harry's face turn white—we got out of the wrong side of the car, took hands and ran for our hotel. The minister, in answer to our pleading, performed the ceremony there.

"Afterwards, the newspapers ran editorials, the gist of which was that we 'ought to be ashamed of ourselves' disappointing people who'd driven for miles to see us. I could see their side of it—both Harry and I have been in show business too long not to appreciate and value such things.

"Nevertheless, that unexpected crowd lining the streets for our unpublicized wedding was a terrific shock. The prospect of signing autographs between our 'I do's' was something I doubt if our shaking hands could have accomplished."

By this time Betty was Hollywood's top box-office draw, a position she'd reached that year, narrowly edging out popular comedians Bob Hope and Abbott and Costello. She received an average of a thousand fan letters per week, and her pictures adorned movie-fan magazines on an almost monthly basis. Her yearly salary, which had zoomed to $125,000, made her one of the highest-paid women in Hollywood. Curiously, however, she never recorded the hit songs that were introduced in her pictures, reportedly because Zanuck thought picturegoers would shun her pictures if they could buy her songs on records.

Journalists couldn't get enough Grable news to satisfy their readers. Fox publicists were deluged with requests for information and pictures. An infatuated public gobbled up every morsel of information. Columnist Sidney Skolsky responded to many of the most frequent questions in a 1943 piece:

"She maintains a strict schedule while working. Then she goes to bed at nine and arises at six. When not working, she stays up late. However, regardless of the time she goes to bed, she insists on getting eight hours sleep. She insists that she needs it for her beauty.

"She is unlike most star actresses. She doesn't have a secretary, a personal hairdresser, or even a business manager. On the set her best friends are invariably the chorus girls and boys she dances with.

"She likes plain American cooking, but highly seasoned. The pepper pot is always near her when she's eating.

"She bathes in jig time. Five minutes is usually enough. She hates showers and likes to take a tub bath at least twice a day, one warm, one cold.

"She abhors slinky clothes, favors sport things. She looks good in a sweater, and knows it.

"She wears a nightgown to bed. She's tried pajamas, but doesn't like 'em.

"She loves to walk barefooted. She walks barefooted about the house and on the lawn."

The single most popular photo of Betty Grable—that unforgettable leg-art shot in which, standing with her back to the camera, a bathing-suited Betty smiled coyly over her left shoulder—was taken by Fox publicity photographer Frank Powolny in 1941. It's virtually impossible to calculate how many of them were distributed, but many printed sources used the figure 5,000,000. They were "hammered into the barracks walls of the Aleutians, pasted against the bulkheads

Below left: About to leave her leg prints in cement at Grauman's Chinese Theatre, accompanied by representatives of three branches of the Armed Forces, at that time her biggest boosters.

Below right: Coming out of the studio after a hard day's shooting.

With Harry James on their
wedding day 1943.

of aircraft carriers, carried in the pockets of a million American soldiers through
the mud of Okinawa and New Guinea," according to a 1946 article.

Grable gave birth to her first child, Victoria Elizabeth James, on March 3,
1944—only eight months after she'd married Harry James. The press had a field
day with the event, barging into Betty's hospital room and snapping pictures of the
beaming mother with her baby, who was instantly dubbed "the Little Pin-Up." Fox
publicity releases declared that the studio was swamped with requests for pictures
of little Elizabeth. A September, 1944 issue of *Life*, at that time a predominantly
black-and-white magazine, carried a full-color nude shot of the child.

Betty's non-stop work at the studio prevented her from spending much
time with Elizabeth for the next several years, and James' frequent tours with his
band didn't exactly make him the perfect father.

Nor, apparently, was he the perfect husband. At first Betty attributed whatever problems they had to Harry's grueling schedule, but it soon became obvious that other difficulties impaired the couple's ability to have anything resembling a normal marriage. For one thing, James was a heavy drinker, and although he refused to allow his imbibing to interfere with his performances, it certainly contributed to his occasional lapses of memory regarding his marital vows. Even more damaging was his propensity for heavy gambling, which kept him virtually impoverished throughout their 22-year marriage—despite the fact that he made enormous yearly salaries as one of the nation's top musical personalities.

Throughout the remainder of the war years, Betty juggled her film career and her marriage with considerable dexterity, maintaining her incredible popularity in a series of formulaic but vastly entertaining Technicolored musicomedies. Whenever possible she joined James while he was on tour and eventually picked up most of his bad habits: drinking, smoking, and gambling. She even persuaded Zanuck to spotlight Harry in an insipid Dick Haymes musical, *Do You Love Me?* (shot during 1945 but released 1946), which performed so poorly at the nation's box-offices that it was withdrawn from circulation only a few months after going into general release.

Grable, probably perplexed by her seeming inability to have the perfect marriage she'd so long coveted, became increasingly difficult around the Fox lot. Her own drinking and lax dietary habits added unwelcome pounds to her eye-catching figure, and while she was always able to diet them away before production began, she terrorized designers and wardrobe girls with tirades about ill-fitting costumes. She took to making excessive demands on the front office, insisting, for example, on script, director, and co-star approval. The Fox brass, increasingly irritated but willing to mollify the studio's top draw, acquiesced whenever possible.

On screen she was still America's favorite musical sweetheart, but away from the cameras she turned into a temperamental tyrant with whom some crew members dreaded to work.

Supremely conscious of the pervasive influence of the press, Betty took pains to reassure the public that hers was an ideal marriage. "My husband and I have never had a quarrel," she stated in 1946, quickly adding, "I don't expect anyone to believe this statement. Remembering the 'picky' disposition I used to have, I can hardly believe it myself. It's simply that you can't fight with Harry. He can't stand dissension—on the rare occasion he gets angry he just turns a little white and says nothing." In another interview she said, "When I started working, I thought I could not have a career and a marriage too. And marriage is all I really wanted. I am just a very lucky girl."

Right: The famous pin-up shot by Frank Powolny.

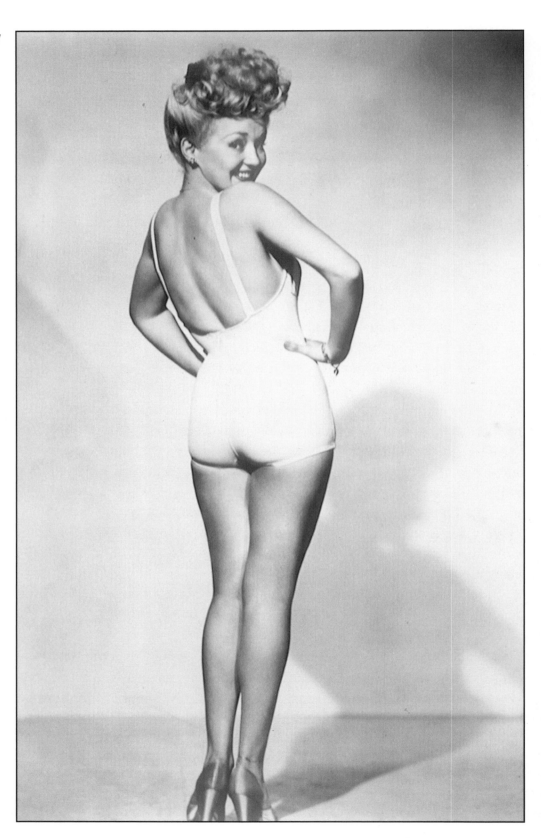

Facing page: Likenesses of Grable adorned many World War II bombers, including this one that flew over Europe.

It was inevitable that Grable's popularity would slip, and she made her first misstep at Fox with *The Shocking Miss Pilgrim* (1946), a period piece that cast her as a self-assured legal secretary carving a niche for herself in the all-male business world. An aging Grable, with her mother's blessings, had determined that she couldn't play sassy showgirls forever. Zanuck reluctantly greenlighted the film, fearing the worst but putting his faith in the star's still-potent box-office appeal. The film, a sudden and radical departure from the proven Grable formula (which didn't even give her a chance to show those million-dollar legs), elicited unfavorable reviews even from proven Grable partisans and performed poorly at the nation's box-offices.

Zanuck reasoned that *Pilgrim* failed because it wasn't a very good picture. He resolved to restore Grable to critical favor by giving her a plum dramatic role in a highly touted Fox venture: the film adaptation of Somerset Maugham's *The Razor's Edge*. But a chastened Betty declined, worried that a second miscalculation could seriously damage her standing. "I'm where I want to be now," she reportedly told Zanuck. "And I don't think [the part]'s right for me. I don't want to crowd my luck too far." Responding to published reports that she'd been offered the key female part, Betty was quoted as replying: "I'm strictly a song-and-dance girl. I can act enough to get by. Let's face it, that's the limit of my talents. If I have a good enough director he can usually pull me through the tight places. But I feel more secure if they let me do a few numbers." (Anne Baxter finally got the part, and won a Best Supporting Actress Oscar for her work.)

Mother Wore Tights (1947) returned Betty to musical comedy, albeit in period setting. Remembering her unfavorable reviews for *Miss Pilgrim*, she insisted upon wearing costumes that would flatter her figure and expose her famous legs. But well-respected designer Orry-Kelly was equally adamant on garbing her in clothes faithful to the turn-of-the-century fashions. They battled ferociously, and he won. Grable also lobbied Zanuck to co-star her with Fred Astaire or James Cagney, but he teamed her instead with Dan Dailey, an up-and-coming contract player. Fortunately, Betty took to him right off, and they worked together smoothly. The film was a big success, giving Betty's career a much-needed shot in the arm and making Dailey a star overnight.

Grable biographer Pastos claims that Grable had an affair with Dailey around this time; certainly she was very fond of him, going out of her way to defend him when *Confidential* magazine published photos of the brawny, rugged-looking actor in drag. In truth, Betty probably gravitated toward Dailey because her marriage to Harry James was foundering.

James' gambling had by now become compulsive, and Betty's was close to being the same. She genuinely shared his passion for playing the ponies, and

together they purchased a half-interest in a string of racehorses in 1947. Betty's father Conn (by this time divorced from Billie but still supported by Betty) managed the Betty J stables, which produced at least one $100,000 winner during its first few years. But while Betty—who was making $150,000 per picture— could absorb the more frequent losses, James couldn't. And the more he lost, the more he bet, hoping he'd eventually hit a jackpot.

There were other problems as well. James, a normally easygoing fellow with a casual attitude about his own infidelities, became uncharacteristically violent toward Betty when he suspected her of fooling around; reportedly he threatened Grable co-stars Dan Dailey and Dick Haymes, whom he believed were sleeping with her. Some claim that James repeatedly beat Betty during this period, but she invariably forgave her wayward husband and threw herself into her work.

The lively, frivolous backstage musicals of the war years were by now being overshadowed by more naturalistic entertainments that hewed closer to reality; the cessation of hostilities and the subsequent return of American soldiers to their families reduced the need for mindless escapism of the type in which Grable specialized. And even though she had purged herself of grandiose ambitions after the fiasco of *The Shocking Miss Pilgrim*, Betty realized that her star would soon be on the wane unless Fox could find a new direction for her.

Left: With Dick Powell on a radio program during the War.

Right: With Cecil B. DeMille after one of Betty's *Lux Radio Theatre* broadcasts.

The studio's initial attempt was *That Lady in Ermine* (1948), begun as a whimsical operetta-type story by celebrated director Ernst Lubitsch, who died of a heart attack a week into production. The film was finished by the equally celebrated Otto Preminger, who failed to maintain the tone Lubitsch had adopted and made a botch of the whole project. Amazingly enough, Betty's reviews were fairly good, possibly owing to a generosity on the part of critics who sensed that she, and Fox, were venturing into uncharted territory for her. But Zanuck was appalled by the final product and blamed its ultimate failure on Grable's limitations.

Possibly panicked by another downturn in Grable's box-office stature, Fox threw her into another backstage musical, *When My Baby Smiles at Me* (also 1948), which reteamed her with Dan Dailey and called to mind some of her earlier successes. But then, as if obsessed with killing off Grable completely, Zanuck allowed writer-director Preston Sturges to star her in *The Beautiful Blonde From Bashful Bend* (1949), a coarse, almost vulgar exercise in low comedy that flopped with a resounding thud, demolishing Sturges' reputation as a comedic genius and rendering Grable all but powerless at her home studio. "I didn't want to do it," she confessed to Louella Parsons in a lackluster attempt at damage control, "but I never interfered with my studio. I never read a script until it's ready and I always leave the selection of story, direction and cast to Darryl Zanuck—for whom I have great respect. But if he ever gives me Preston Sturges again, you'll hear Grable's voice!"

Depressed that she had lost so much ground in just a few short years, but trapped by her long-term contract, Betty inflicted her pain on everyone around her, including, some say, James and her two daughters (Jessica was born in 1947). At home she made life hell for her numerous servants, insisting on the maintenance of impossible domestic standards and brooking no dissenting views. She badgered her children, who had become dependent on nannies and were often afraid to face their domineering mother.

She countered studio-generated reports of a growing dissatisfaction with her film career by giving interviews to the fan magazines that indicated just the opposite. "I love it all," she gushed to *Photoplay*'s Diane Scott. "I always have. When I was in the chorus I was happy. I had no ambition to be a star. I just worked hard doing my job. When I was given a specialty I just worked harder.

"I'm surprised, too, every time I see my name in the top ten [box-office draws], but I'm also very grateful. That's why I work hard. If people like me that much, I *should* work hard. Musicals are right for me. People want to see me in glamorous costumes against a jeweled backdrop—a sort of backstage Cinderella, the poor working girl who makes good. They want to see me in roles they can believe in."

With James at a restaurant, perusing a 1948 magazine story about her.

Grable doggedly clung to her relationship with James, an absentee father who willingly deferred to her in all matters of parental discipline. She spent as much leisure time as possible with him, which meant that she all but moved into the Del Mar race track. Her knowledge of racing was little short of encyclopedic, and she earned a reputation as an expert handicapper. Unfortunately, her expertise didn't altogether prevent the Jameses from losing huge sums.

The burgeoning desert town of Las Vegas—developed as a modern-day Sodom and Gomorrah by organized crime figures such as "Bugsy" Siegel—was another home-away-from-home for Betty and Harry. As new casinos were built and more venues for entertainers opened up, James and his band found reasonably steady employment there. Betty would accompany him whenever possible, and the Jameses were frequently seen patrons of all the casinos, where they lost staggering amounts of money. She claimed that the desert sun was both relaxing and beneficial to her health, but the cycle of late hours, smoking, and drinking was taking a heavy toll on her appearance and attitude.

A decidedly puffy Grable, only 35 years old but looking every day of it—and then some—returned to Fox for *Call Me Mister* (1951), a smash Broadway musical that the studio figured would be an ideal vehicle for her. Dailey was also assigned to the picture; he, like Betty, was having domestic problems and hitting the bottle too much. The two stars performed their chores with little apparent enthusiasm, and the heavily reworked property, as finally released, bore little resemblance to its inspiration.

Coincidentally or not, Grable began indicating to columnists and fan-magazine scribes that she might retire. "A lot of people say you go crazy without work," she was quoted as saying. "Not me. I'd stay at home with the kids. I'd go with Harry once in a while when he's on the road. I'm sure [my career] will all be over in a heap when it happens."

It's not clear whether or not Betty had tongue in cheek while dishing out such stories, but to those who knew her, the ring of truth just wasn't there. Betty was perfectly content to leave the children in the care of day nurses, and in fact

Betty, here with the jockey of one of her favorite horses, was an expert handicapper who spent most of her leisure time at the Del Mar racetrack.

THE GIRL WITH THE MILLION DOLLAR LEGS / 35

frequently mistreated them (according to Elizabeth, interviewed years later), especially when she was annoyed with Harry. Also, talking of retirement would theoretically soften the blow when, as she believed would happen, Fox forced her out of the studio.

The sad fact was that Betty needed the work. Not only was Harry losing money hand over fist at Del Mar and Las Vegas, but the Jameses' stable had become a money pit thanks to Conn Grable's mediocre management. She determined to stick out her contract as long as possible, while secretly preparing for the worst. More difficult and demanding than ever, she completed *Meet Me After the Show* (1951) only after alienating cast and crew with her constant complaining. The generally unfavorable reviews revealed that she had finally worn out her welcome with critics, some of whom tactlessly commented on her avoirdupois and observed that the usual Grable energy was conspicuous by its absence.

A furious Betty raged incessantly, blaming everyone but the studio janitor for the failure of her latest effort and, in a fit of pique, refused to appear opposite June Haver (who had been her co-star in *The Dolly Sisters*) in *The Girl Next Door*. Fox management reluctantly put her on suspension, which lasted for ten months before a humbled Grable agreed to star in *The Farmer Takes a Wife*, a lame, musicalized remake of a rural romance previously filmed with Janet Gaynor. Never concealing her lack of enthusiasm for the project, she retreated to her dressing room whenever possible, surreptitiously boozing and calling her bookies between takes. The Fox legal department, apparently under orders to find any excuse to terminate Grable's contract, kept tabs on her activities and scrupulously recorded her every transgression. Studio publicists, who once fawned over Grable and begged her to cooperate with them, all but ignored her; they did only what was absolutely necessary to promote the picture.

Once again, Betty took it upon herself to refute studio-leaked horror stories about her. She claimed that her behavior on the set of *Meet Me After the Show* was due to overwork and exhaustion. "I was so tired my whole nervous system was upset," she told columnist Maxine Arnold. "I was cross with Harry and the girls at home. I was jumpy at the studio, flying off at people all the time. That isn't natural with me. I knew I *had* to have a vacation, or I wouldn't be any good to my family, my studio, or anybody. I just wanted two or three months' vacation. I've had a good long rest now. . . ."

Betty was suspended again, this time for eight months, when she refused to take a dramatic role in *Blaze of Glory*, which would have cast her as a prostitute. A defiant Grable swore that to accept the part would have been tantamount to destroying her career. The project, somewhat reworked, was filmed and released as *Pickup on South Street* (1953).

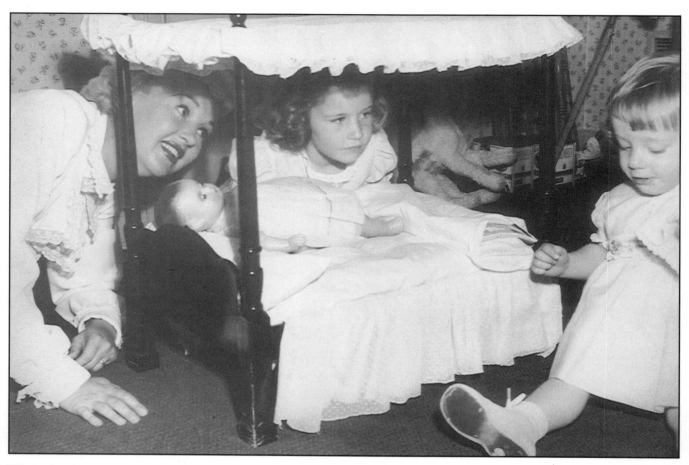

With daughters Vicki (center) and Jessica in 1949.

Darryl Zanuck believed that the best way to launch a new star personality was to team him or her with a well-established draw. He'd used Alice Faye to help boost Grable, and he'd used Grable to help boost June Haver. While Zanuck had little confidence in Grable's ability to carry *How to Marry a Millionaire*, he believed her presence would bolster its chances for box-office success and help solidify the career of Marilyn Monroe, Fox's burgeoning star property. The script had special resonance for Grable: It was patched together and rewritten from two plays by Nunnally Johnson. Grable had appeared in the 1932 adaptation of one, *The Greeks Had a Word for Them*, and in the 1941 adaptation of the other, *Moon Over Miami*.

The starring triumverate of Grable, Monroe, and Lauren Bacall initially worried the Fox brass, which feared that three star egos might make production a living Hell for the crew. To everyone's great surprise, however, there were no major conflicts, and Betty even befriended Monroe, perhaps seeing in the dedicated but insecure girl a mirror image of herself at an earlier age. They even appeared together, sans husbands (Monroe was then married to former baseball great Joe DiMaggio), at the film's premiere.

How to Marry a Millionaire performed admirably at the nation's box-offices, thanks largely (as Zanuck had suspected) to the top-billed Monroe. Nonetheless, the studio announced shortly thereafter that Grable's contract had been terminated. Betty claimed she would spend more time with her family and perhaps seek work in nightclubs, but in truth she had played out her string at Fox; Zanuck's tolerance of her obnoxious behavior had been exhausted. Upon leaving the Fox lot for what she thought would be the last time, Grable found herself surrounded by reporters. What would she do first? "If Harry wants me," she was quoted, "I'll join his band. But he's the boss. We've been so happy for ten years, he might think it wouldn't be good for us to work together. Whatever he says goes."

Grable did join her husband, but not as part of the act. She accompanied him to most of his engagements in Nevada, where gambling was legal. During one trip to Lake Tahoe, Betty was shocked to see Harry squiring leggy showgirls

The Jameses' newly purchased manor house, supposedly imported brick by brick from Scotland, and furnished with its own ghost (whom the Jameses never met).

around the casinos. She challenged him publicly, and he delivered an ominous warning, urging her to leave him alone. They occasionally brawled in private, and on more than one occasion Betty was photographed sporting discolored bruises.

Depending upon whom one chooses to believe, Grable herself engaged in some extramarital activity during this time, although if so she appears to have been more discreet than James. Pastos claims that Betty even entertained one-night johnnies at her home while Harry was away on tour.

The Jameses took up ranching, buying a 24-acre property in Calabasas, a somewhat extravagant purchase in lieu of the fact that Betty was out of work and Harry's gambling debts kept them cash-poor. Harry offered to let Betty's father manage the ranch, a somewhat quixotic gesture given Conn's lackluster handling of the Betty J stables. The elder Grable's drinking, which made him somewhat unreliable, finally took its toll early in 1954. After collapsing one night at the ranch, he lapsed into a coma while Betty raced him to a hospital. The emergency room staff refused to admit him until Betty finished the admissions forms, and the old man died in a wheelchair before he could be treated. A heartbroken Betty, traumatized by the baldfaced tragedy of her father's demise, never forgave the hospital personnel and retained a bitterness toward doctors for the rest of her life. But she mourned Bud's passing just the same, and even Billie—who by this time was living in a modest but handsome house in Beverly Hills, paid for by Betty during her peak years at Fox—expressed her regrets.

The Jameses' mounting debts eventually forced them to sell the ranch, and Betty eagerly accepted an offer from Columbia Pictures to star in an old-fashioned musical called *Three for the Show* (1955). Heartened by the chance to strut her stuff before the cameras once again, she dieted strenuously and performed energetically. But the film fell far short of her better Fox musicals, and its lukewarm reception dashed Betty's hopes for a comeback.

Grable returned to her old studio one final time that same year. Ironically, Marilyn Monroe engendered Zanuck's wrath by refusing to star in *How to Be Very, Very Popular*, a musical comedy designed to launch his latest star hopeful, Sheree North. Monroe, who had been training at the prestigious Actors Studio in New York, balked at appearing in such fluff. In desperation, Fox turned to Grable, a proven hand in such matters. She gratefully accepted the role and shot the picture without incident, hoping against hope it would be successful enough to restore her to favor with Zanuck. Although she won top billing, it was North who got the film's best scene: a spirited dance to "Shake, Rattle and Roll," the first rock 'n' roll number included in a Hollywood movie.

Grable finally threw in the towel, abandoning Hollywood and picturemaking for once and for all. She moved to Las Vegas, enrolled her daughters in a private

With Dorothy Lamour, her husband Bill Howard, and James in 1954 at a Hollywood restaurant.

school, and began travelling with a solo nightclub act, which invariably played to large and appreciative crowds. Her Las Vegas home, situated behind the Tropicana Hotel, cost a reported $100,000 but was modestly decorated, with none of the movie-star elegance of the Jameses' Coldwater Canyon residence, which had been decorated at least partially for the benefit of fan-magazine photogs who regularly shot pictorial features of Betty at home.

Betty described her new routine for the few journalists who still sought her out for interviews: up at six a.m., out on the golf course early in the morning (to beat the broiling desert sun), lunch with local friends, cards in the afternoon, dinner, attending shows at the casino lounges in the evening. She also found time to bowl, and even won a trophy in one local tournament. With the girls away at school, her mother safely ensconced in Beverly Hills, and Harry frequently gone as well, Betty enjoyed total freedom for the first time in her life.

Unfortunately, this lackadaisical lifestyle took a heavy toll on the James family. With Betty retired, the financial pressure of Harry's gambling debts gradually mounted to the point at which she found it difficult to make ends meet. She elected to go back to work, choosing to stage a revue-style version of *Guys and Dolls,* a favorite show of hers. (Grable had earlier lobbied to play the role taken by Vivian Blaine in the 1955 film version.) Old friend Dan Dailey joined her at the Dunes Hotel engagement, and while the reviews were polite at best, Las Vegas residents and tourists were delighted to see their old favorite singing and dancing again.

Grable built up the family finances to little avail, however; the family itself was crumbling. Youngest daughter Jessica shocked Betty by getting pregnant during her first year in college, and even though she married the baby's father— and suffered a miscarriage besides—Betty threw her out of the house. Shortly afterward, in 1965, she divorced Harry after 22 years of marriage, citing extreme cruelty as the grounds. James' massive debt burden precluded any possibility of alimony payments, and Grable waived her rights to collect them.

New York Journal-American columnist Dorothy Kilgallen got an exclusive interview from Betty regarding the breakup. "It was completely amicable," the former Mrs. James was quoted as saying. "Harry and I agreed that neither of us would talk to reporters. We'd been living in Las Vegas for seven years, and most of the time I was just a housewife. I even watched afternoon TV. It really wasn't a sudden thing. I thought it over for a long time and I talked it over with Harry. Our children are grown now with lives of their own. There was no reason to stay together for their sake."

Betty opined that she had no desire to marry again, and that Harry probably felt the same way. She was proved wrong in 1968, when James wed a former Las Vegas showgirl some 24 years his junior. Although he didn't even invite Betty to the wedding, James subsequently asked her for money to help relieve his financial pressures.

Around this time Billie Grable died, and while Betty had frequently resented her mother's omnipresent, even stifling influence on her, she keenly felt the loss of Billie, coming so soon after her divorce from Harry and her estrangement from Jessica. As she had in the past, Betty coped with personal tragedy by hurling herself into her work.

Grable was enlisted by theatrical impresario David Merrick to play the lead in a Las Vegas production of the Broadway hit *Hello, Dolly,* which was originally written for Ethel Merman but had subsequently starred several Broadway and Hollywood favorites. Ginger Rogers, Grable's old bete noire, was Vegas' first Dolly, but left the show after squabbling with Merrick. Dorothy Lamour briefly took the role before Betty was hired.

Years of undisciplined retirement had sapped much of her energy, con-

stant smoking had affected her voice, and the desert sun had made her skin dry and leathery. But Grable worked feverishly to master the show's songs and dances, and sweltered beneath the period costumes, wigs, and heavy makeup. She appeared almost every night in *Dolly* for nine months, delighting audiences who generously overlooked her vocal shortcomings to enjoy the still-famous gal with the million-dollar legs.

One of *Dolly's* dancers, Bob Remick, became a Grable confidant and eventually left show business to become a secretary (and constant companion) to the star. Based on the success of the Vegas engagement, Merrick decided to bring Grable to New York to replace his current Dolly: Ginger Rogers, much happier on Broadway than she'd been in Las Vegas. A quarter-century had elapsed since Betty's triumph in *DuBarry Was a Lady,* and she expressed her nervousness to close friends. How would she fare with the Great White Way's tough audiences and tougher critics?

Grable was pleasantly surprised by her reception, just as she'd been some 25 years before. *New York Times* critic Vincent Canby appraised her favorably: "At fifty, Miss Grable looks great. The dimples in the Pretty Girl are intact. The outlines of the Pretty Girl figure have filled in a bit—those appendages that Dad used to call gams are still magnificent from the occasional glimpses we get beneath the turn-of-the-century gowns." He even reviewed the opening-night audience, which itself gave "an extraordinary performance by any standard, noisy, hysterical, charged with emotion . . . rooted in the effulgent memories of *Down Argentine Way* and *Moon Over Miami*."

Despite the fact that she wasn't basically suited to play the character of boisterous busybody Dolly Levy, Grable essayed the role not only on Broadway but in a national tour as well. Bolstered by favorable reviews (more often than not forgivingly tinged with nostalgia), she became increasingly difficult, frequently quarreling with Merrick, who kept a stiff upper lip and mollified his temperamental but successful star. Betty's constant smoking weakened and hoarsened her voice, hastening her departure from the show. Her *Dolly* had been very profitable for Merrick, but show-business columnists hinted that he wasn't heartbroken to see her go.

Grable returned to Las Vegas with Remick, by now an indispensible aide and supporter. After giving her overworked throat a long rest, she accepted offers to star in several touring-company productions of nostalgic Broadway hits, including her beloved *Guys and Dolls*. She even played London's West End, albeit in a dismal, short-lived musical version of *Belle Starr,* adapted from a 1941 Fox movie starring Gene Tierney. The show was produced by one of Grable's former co-stars, Rory Calhoun, whose wife named Betty in a subsequent divorce action.

With Harry during the Las Vegas years.

Back in Las Vegas, she effected a partial reconciliation with Harry James, thawing the deep freeze in their relationship dating back to his 1968 wedding to former showgirl Joan Boyd. She even loaned him money—the lengthy engagement in *Hello, Dolly* had replenished her bank account—and was seen with him in Las Vegas restaurants and casinos.

Betty's last major public appearance was one of the most memorable in her long and distinguished career. In 1972, producer Howard W. Koch, who'd known Grable at Fox, asked her to present one of the Oscars at the 44th Annual Academy Awards ceremony. A flattered Betty, upon learning she'd appear with old friend and former co-star Dick Haymes, eagerly accepted.

She was tremendously gratified by the thunderous ovation which greeted her that night. Somewhat puffy and tired-looking, her voice raspy from years of heavy smoking, she still charmed the audience and was warmly received at the Beverly Hills Hotel's post-ceremony party. She graciously declined invitations to

Dancing with Desi Arnaz on the Feb. 3, 1958 episode of *The Lucille Ball and Desi Arnaz Show*, one of her infrequent TV appearances.

A number from *Hello, Dolly* on TV's *Hollywood Palace*.

Betty's last major public appearance at the 44th annual Academy Awards ceremony in 1972. She presented the Oscar for Music Scoring (adaptation) to John Williams for *Fiddler on the Roof.*

Photo © copyright Academy of Motion Picture Arts and Sciences

remain in Hollywood and mingle with the town's social set. In truth, she'd always eschewed Tinseltown's social scene, and was just as happy to get back to Las Vegas.

Another attendee of that year's Academy Awards ceremony was Jackie Coogan, who came to see special honoree Charlie Chaplin, for whom he'd played "The Kid" a half-century before. He didn't see Betty at all during the evening.

Returning to the desert, Grable prepared for her next theatrical engagement, an Australian tour with *No, No, Nanette,* another nostalgia-driven vehicle for the former Hollywood star. A routine medical checkup revealed that she had cancer. Doctors learned from Grable that she had experienced abdominal discomfort several times over the last few months but thought nothing of it. Exploratory surgery determined that the cancer had spread to her lymph glands. She underwent radiation therapy and was prescribed cortisone to help relieve her pain.

In the fall of 1972 Grable was admitted to St. John's Hospital in Santa Monica, where she underwent surgery to remove tumors in her lungs and intestines. The operation was successful, but doctors warned her that the cancer was spreading inexorably throughout her body. With only her work to sustain her, Betty accepted an offer to appear in a Jacksonville, Florida production of *Born Yesterday.* She managed to complete the engagement, but it drained what little strength she had left, and by April 1973 she was back in St. John's.

Old friends Dorothy Lamour and Alice Faye frequently visited Betty and spoke with her on the phone, as did her sister Marjorie, from whom she'd been estranged for many years. Betty's daughters Jessie and Vicki were also on hand, as was the loyal Bob Remick. Her condition steadily deteriorated, and she finally succumbed on July 2, 1973.

Media outlets around the world duly noted Grable's passing, but their reporting conveyed the impression that she'd become little more than a quaint relic from a bygone era. The movie musical itself was moribund, the genre consigned to film history books and trivia contests. But Betty's pictures remained in distribution, appearing on TV, occasionally on big screen in revival houses, and later on videotape and laserdisc. And her memory was kept alive by millions of fans, many of whom hadn't even been born when she was in her prime. Not a bad legacy for someone who thought of herself as "strictly a song-and-dance girl."

As a young contract player for Paramount.

THE FILMS OF BETTY GRABLE

LET'S GO PLACES
(Fox Film Corp., 1930)

Credits: Presented by William Fox. Director, Frank Strayer; screenplay-dialogue, William K. Wells; based on the story by Andrew Bennison; camera, Conrad Wells; editor, Al De Gaetano; songs, Sidney Mitchell, Archie Gottler and Con Conrad; Cliff Friend and Jimmy Monaco; Joe McCarthy and Jimmy Monaco; Johnny Burke and George Little.

Cast: Joseph Wagstaff (Paul Adams); Lola Lane (Marjorie Lorraine); Sharon Lynn (Virginia Gordon); Frank Richardson (J. Speed Quinn); Walter Catlett (Rex Wardell); Dixie Lee (Dixie); Charles Judels (Du Bonnet); Ilka Chase (Mrs. Du Bonnet); Larry Steers (Ben King); Betty Grable (Chorus Girl).

Songs: "Parade of the Blues," "Hollywood Nights," "Reach for a Rainbow," "Out in the Cold," "Um, Um in the Moonlight" (Conrad-Mitchell-Gottler), "Snowball Man" (Hanley-Brockman), "The Boop-Boop-a-Doopa-Doo Trot" (Little-Burke), "Fascinatin' Devil" (McCarthy-Monaco), and "Let's Go Place" (Friend-Monaco).

Release Date: February 2, 1930. *Running Time:* 71 minutes.

SYNOPSIS

New York-based singer Paul Adams takes a desperate chance by assuming the name of operatic tenor Paul Du Bonnet in his bid for a Hollywood career. While heading west to take advantage of a movie offer received by Du Bonnet, he meets Marjorie Lorraine, a beautiful girl who falls in love with him. Once in Hollywood he successfully carries out his impersonation, occupying the famous singer's mansion and ingratiating himself at one of the movie studios. By the time Du Bonnet finally arrives, Paul has successfully launched his film career, though he has lost Marjorie: She has learned that Du Bonnet is married and plans to join him in Hollywood. Eventually they all converge, and Paul's deception is exposed—at which time Du Bonnet discovers Paul to be his long-lost nephew, and everything ends happily.

REVIEWS

"This film is a frivolous affair, with brighteners helping out the bromidic stretches. The usual good fortune and also periods of anxiety pop up during the adventure, and as there are scenes in a Hollywood studio it has been easy to give a long stretch of dancing girls presumed to be in a kind of Antarctic cafe, where the beauties suddenly appear from gigantic snowballs and are ready to trip the light fantastic for the applauding multitude." (*New York Times*)

"Because of its Hollywood angle and snappy atmosphere this picture may be a money maker, but any future copies of the idea will not take long to convince customers it's the backstage yarn all over again. Absence of drawing names is a handicap . . . Practically all credited players are from the stage, and cast exploitation possibilities are therefore negligible. Frank Strayer rates credit for squeezing the comedy into a succession of close-packed laughs. The Wells dialog furnished a good foundation. Photography is sometimes erratic." (*Variety*)

PRODUCTION NOTES AND COMMENTS

The plot of *Let's Go Places*, as *Variety*'s review perceptively indicates, was already old hat when this picture was made. However, that doesn't seem to have troubled moviegoers of the day, who willingly absorbed cliched musical-comedy conventions for the novelty of seeing lavish production numbers on the screen. Eventually the public tired of such formulaic entertainments (which were legion in the 1929-32 period), which seemed like antiques to audiences of just a few years later, by then taken with the Busby Berkeley-influenced musicals from Samuel Goldwyn and Warner Bros. Grable made her film debut, although virtually invisible as a chorus girl, in this programmer; she was only 13 years old when it was released.

HAPPY DAYS
(Fox Film Corp., 1930)

Credits: Presented by William Fox. Director, Ben Stoloff; Screenplay, Edwin Burke, from a story by Sidney Lanfield; photography (35mm), Lucien Andriot, John Schmitz; photography (Grandeur), J. O. Taylor; editor, Clyde Carruth; songs, Con Conrad, Sidney Mitchell, Archie Gottler, L. Wolfe Gilbert, Abel Baer, James Hanley, James Brockman, Joseph McCarthy, Harry Stoddard, Marcy Klauber.

Cast: Charles E. Evans (Col. Billy Batcher), Marjorie White (Margie), Richard Keene (Dick), Stuart Erwin (Jig), Martha Lee Sparks (Nancy Lee), Clifford Dempsey (Sheriff Benton), Janet Gaynor, Charles Farrell, Victor McLaglen, El Brendel, William Collier, Sr., Tom Patricola, George Jessel, Dixie Lee, Nick Stuart, Rex Bell, Frank Albertson, Sharon Lynn, "Whispering" Jack Smith, J. Farrell MacDonald, Will Rogers, Edmund Lowe, Walter Catlett, Ann Pennington, Warner Baxter, Paul Page, the Slate Brothers, George Olsen and His Orchestra (guest stars), Betty Grable (chorus girl).

Songs: "Mona," "Snake Hips," "Crazy Feet" (Conrad-Mitchell-Gottler), "Minstrel Memories," "I'm on a Diet of Love" (Gilbert-Baer), "We'll Build a Little World of Our Own," "A Toast to the Girl I Love," "Dream on a Piece of Wedding Cake" (Hanley-Brockman), "Whispering" (McCarthy-Hanley), "Vic and Eddie" (Stoddard-Klauber).

Release Date: February 14, 1930. *Running Time:* 84 minutes.

SYNOPSIS

Margie is a soubrette on Col. Billy Batcher's Mississippi riverboat, and though she is in love with Dick, the colonel's grandson, she longs to seek her fortune in New York City. When the showboat is in danger of going broke, Margie goes to the city to call on the star troupers who formerly served their apprenticeship under the colonel and asks their aid. All the stars agree to stage a benefit in Memphis, and when they gather for the event Margie is reunited with her sweetheart.

REVIEWS

"Revue type of picture on wide angle film with a thin story background. Has big scope in names and is on an enormous production scale; impressive beauty and scenic magnificence, excellent comedy and at least three numbers of popular hit prospect. All these elements are in addition to the fact that it opens up the big screen technique which would alone mark it for distinction at the box office. The sum total is a release of big money and an epochal enterprise in the industry." (*Variety*)

PRODUCTION NOTES AND COMMENTS

One of a handful of Fox films shot and released in the "Grandeur" widescreen process, *Happy Days* followed other major-studio revues (MGM's *The Hollywood Revue of 1929* and Warner Bros.' *The Show of Shows*) designed to showcase the musical and comedy talents of its contract players. Fox's offering went the others one better by tying the individual "acts" together with a perfunctory plotline.

The Grandeur process, which utilized 70mm film for wider frame and sharper image, made for spectacular presentation, but only a few showcase theaters could afford to install the wide screens and special projection equipment needed for it; most small-theater managers were still grappling with the technical challenges of outfitting their houses for sound. Fox voluntarily retired the process in 1931, and it was another two decades before Hollywood again turned to wide-screen spectacle (and only then due to competition from television).

Happy Days presented a full-scale minstrel show, with four tiers of people—86 in all—making up its ensemble. There were several highlights, including a comedy duet by the then-popular team of Victor McLaglen and Edmund Lowe, a jazzy tune called "Snake Hips," sung by Sharon Lynn and supported by stage star Ann Pennington's energetic hoofing, and the elaborate production number "Crazy Feet," sung by Dixie Lee. Grable was one of 32 chorus girls who backed her up in a fast-stepping display of taps.

NEW MOVIETONE FOLLIES OF 1930
(Fox Film Corp., 1930)

Credits: Presented by William Fox. Director, Ben Stoloff; associate producer, Al Rockett; screenplay, William K. Wells; camera, L. W. O'Connell; editor, Clyde Carruth; songs, Jack Meskill, Con Conrad, James Brockman, James Hanley, Cliff Friend, Jimmy Monaco.

Cast: El Brendel (Alex Svenson); Marjorie White (Vera Fontaine); Frank Richardson (George Randall); Noel Francis (Gloria De Witt); William Collier, Jr. (Conrad Sterling); Miriam Seegar (Mary Mason); Huntley Gordon (Marvin Kingsley); Paul Nicholson (Lee Hubert); Yola D'Avril (Maid); Betty Grable (Chorus Girl).

Songs: "You'll Give In," "I Wanna Be a Talking Picture Queen" (McCarthy-Hanley), "Cheer Up and Smile," "Doin' the Derby," "Here Comes Emily Brown" (Meskill-Conrad), "I Feel a Certain Feeling Coming On," "Bashful" (Friend-Monaco).

Release Date: May 4, 1930. *Running Time:* 84 minutes.

SYNOPSIS

Axel Svenson is valet to Conrad Sterling, a rich man's wastrel nephew who fancies himself irresistible to show-girls. Despite Axel's best efforts, Conrad continually embroils himself in unsavory affairs. His latest flame is stage star Mary Mason, whom he tries to impress by passing himself off as a wealthy lumber baron from the Northwest. Axel, eager to help his boss, impersonates his millionaire pal. Conrad's uncle, meanwhile, threatens to discontinue his allowance unless he behaves himself. The young wastrel, trying to both rehabilitate his image and further his romance with Mary, hires her troupe to stage a benefit show for war veterans at his uncle's estate over the weekend. Before long the impersonations are discovered, but all ends happily, with Conrad getting Mary and Axel getting movie-struck showgirl Vera Fontaine.

REVIEWS

"[S]martly produced, wise-cracking affair, which . . . achieved its purpose in creating gusts of laughter. It [has] handsome scenes and both bright and trite lines. There are several catchy melodies in this attraction [and] many lavish scenes with dancing girls, but, unfortunately, there is little idea of sound perspective; for when a person is at a distance from the camera or close to it the singing is of the same volume." (*New York Times*)

"Hybrid rich boy-virtuous chorus girl meller and a hodge podge of musical revue stuff . . . . It is a poor picture that evidences no excuses for its budget except for a few clowning sequences . . . . William Collier, Jr. and

Miriam Seegar are as listless as the story and direction are flat and bromidic. Before the happy ending [there are] the usual choral and hoofing numbers. None of the girlies is of the smart and brisk type, resplendent in several other picture revues. El Brendel gets in a lot of funny cracks and mannerisms, including two of the song numbers with the hottest lines." (*Variety*)

PRODUCTION NOTES AND COMMENTS

Assembled by the same creative team responsible for *Let's Go Places*, *New Movietone Follies of 1930* wasn't nearly as enjoyable, owing to its hackneyed story and stereotypical characters. Most contemporary critics agreed that the best lines went to Swedish comic El Brendel, a mainstay at Fox during the early talkie period, whose dialect humor today seems forced and decidedly unfunny. Betty Grable was among the chorus girls seen in the musical numbers staged at the country estate.

WHOOPEE!
(United Artists, 1930)

Credits: Producers, Samuel Goldwyn and Florenz Ziegfeld; director, Thornton Freeland; screenplay, William Conselman, based on the musical play *Whoopee!* by William Anthony McGuire, itself adapted from the play *The Nervous Wreck* by Owen Davis; camera, Lee Garmes, Ray Rennahan, Gregg Toland; editor, Stuart Heisler; dance director, Busby Berkeley; musical director, Alfred Newman, songs, Walter Donaldson and Gus Kahn; Edward Eliscu and Nacio Herb Brown.

Cast: Eddie Cantor (Henry Williams); Eleanor Hunt (Sally Morgan); Paul Gregory (Wanenis); Jack Rutherford (Sheriff Bob Wells); Ethel Shutta (Mary Custer); Spencer Charters (Jerome Underwood); Chief Caupolican (Black Eagle); Albert Hackett (Chester Underwood); William H. Phibrick (Andy McNabb); Walter Law (Judd Morgan); Marilyn Morgan (Harriet Underwood); Barbara Weeks (Dancer); The George Olsen Band (Themselves); Betty Grable, Virginia Bruce (Goldwyn Girls).

Songs: "Stetson," "Making Whoopee," "My Baby Just Cares for Me," "A Girl Friend of a Boy Friend of Mine" (Kahn-Donaldson), "I'll Still Belong to You" (Eliscu-Brown).

Release Date: September 27, 1930. *Running Time:* 93 minutes.

SYNOPSIS

Henry Williams is a world-class hypochondriac who, despite the assurances of his doctors that there's nothing wrong with him, travels out west for his health. He boards

In foreground, with the Goldwyn Girls in a production number from *Whoopee!*

at Judd Morgan's ranch, attended to by Mary Custer, a feisty, tart-tongued nurse who comes to love him. Morgan's daughter Sally has long loved Wanenis, an Indian boy who lives near her father's ranch, but she is obliged to become engaged to the sheriff while Wanenis is away being educated in the white man's schools. Unwilling to go through with the marriage, Sally prevails upon Henry to take her away in his old flivver. They hide out with a nearby family, and Henry, disguised in blackface, pretends to be the cook. Later, having narrowly escaped detection and capture by the sheriff, Henry and Sally take refuge in an Indian reservation. Sally's father finally catches up to her and demands she go through with the wedding. But it is soon discovered that Wanenis is actually a white man, abandoned at birth and brought up by Indians. Thus informed, Judd Morgan gladly sanctions a union between Sally and Wanenis. Henry, meanwhile, hooks up with the long-suffering Mary.

REVIEWS

"*Whoopee!* has everything a laughable high class musical comedy should have . . . . Here Technicolor makes a magnificent picture of an impressive spectacle, which *Whoopee!* becomes several times, with its groupings, costuming and 'western' backgrounds . . . . With Sam Goldwyn on this production was Flo Ziegfeld. The Ziegfeldian dame touch all through and the Goldwyn production hand [are apparent]. Cantor has never been funnier on the stage than in this talker. [There is] superb photography, nifty number staging by Busby Berkeley, inclusive of one fine overhead shot on the girls, besides the Lady Godiva stuff of the gals riding down the trail astride horses. Best musical comedy . . . to date." (*Variety*)

"In this production Mr. Cantor's clowning transcends even Mr. Ziegfeld's shining beauties, the clever direction and the tuneful melodies. And this is saying a great deal, for there is much for the eyes to feast on in the various scenes. Messrs. Ziegfeld and Goldwyn have had the wisdom to permit humor to hold sway and this results in this film being a swift and wonderfully entertaining offering. The Technicolor work is of the best, there being only a few scenes in which the images are apparently out of focus." (*New York Times*)

PRODUCTION NOTES AND COMMENTS

A runaway hit that certainly deserved the praise lavished upon it by critics, *Whoopee!* came to the screen with many of its original cast members reprising their stage roles. Surprisingly, only one song—the title tune—was used from the original score, although tunesmiths Walter Donaldson and Gus Kahn supplied several memorable melodies for the movie version. Over one million dollars was lavished upon the production, which earned a whopping $1,637,000 in domestic film rental for Goldwyn.

Betty Grable got her first big closeup—in glorious two-color Technicolor, no less—in *Whoopee!*'s opening number, which spotlighted the gorgeous Goldwyn Girls hand-picked, it is said, by the producer himself. Many contemporary sources give credit for choosing the leggy lovelies to Ziegfeld himself, befitting his reputation as a promoter of femine pulchritude, but the legendary stage producer actually had little to do with the filming of his hit stage show. Goldwyn and he had formed a corporation with the express purpose of bringing talkie versions of Ziegfeld shows to the screen, but they squabbled continually (especially over billing) and Goldwyn successfully barred him from the sound stages during filming.

Dance director Busby Berkeley, in his first Hollywood outing, introduced many of the oddly angled, kaleidoscopic shots of dancing girls that became his screen signature. Given complete freedom to stage production numbers, he rose to the challenge magnificently, revitalizing a screen genre already beginning to show signs of stagnation.

KIKI

(United Artists, 1931)

Credits: Producer, Joseph M. Schenck; writer-director, Sam Taylor; based on the play by David Belasco, from the French play by Andre Picardi; assistant director, Earle Brown; camera, Karl Struss; editor, Allen McNeil.

Cast: Mary Pickford (Kiki); Reginald Denny (Victor Randall); Joseph Cawthorn (Alfred Rapp); Margaret Livingston (Paulette Valle); Phil Tead (Eddie); Fred Walton (Bunson); Edwin Maxwell (Doctor Smiley); Betty Grable (Girl).

Release Date: March 14, 1931. *Running Time:* 96 minutes.

SYNOPSIS

A hoydenish Parisian girl named Kiki harbors aspirations to stage stardom. She wangles a job as a chorine but loses it after fighting with another girl. Desperately clinging to her "career," Kiki nags show impresario Victor

In *Kiki*, Grable was both a chorus girl and a stand-in for star Mary Pickford, seen here with Joseph Cawthorn.

Randall into taking her back, becoming smitten with him in the process. Randall is divorced from his actress wife, who still stars in his productions. During the opening-night performance of "The Broadway Revue," Kiki spots Randall in the theater and loses her place in the chorus line. She attempts to rejoin her fast-stepping sisters and falls into the orchestra pit, crashing into the bass drum and convulsing the audience with laughter. She's fired again, but this time Randall takes pity on her and allows her to move into his apartment temporarily. Kiki, determined to win the showman's heart, pretends to fall into a cataleptic state to forstall her eviction, and gradually earns Randall's affections.

REVIEWS

"Mary Pickford's name, coupled with the well-known play, should prove a big drawing attraction and the picture deserves it—it's good . . . . Director Sam Taylor has taken the plot and made it into an uproarious slapstick comedy featured by the good acting of a fine cast . . . . The dialogue is fast and snappy. The photography is good and the sound excellent." (*Motion Picture Herald*)

"If Mary Pickford is the whole show in *Kiki* . . . it is more a tribute to the inexhaustible energy and verve of that comedienne than any dubious quality in the rest of the film. Sam Taylor has produced a smooth, merry and up-to-date version of the Belasco comedy with the aid of a thororughly good supporting cast headed by Reginald Denny, and Miss Pickford has done the rest. It does seem a bit too long, running to nearly an hour and a half." (*New York Times*)

"An intermediate feature despite the Pickford name, which indicates that it will do business. A rough-house farce with everything on the surface. Neither depth nor punch to send it across for more than ordinary money at best. Film has been given an imposing background of sets, besides being well cameraed and recorded. Miss Pickford looks and plays it well in her own way. But what was to have been a cocktail has turned out to be a soda." (*Variety*)

PRODUCTION NOTES AND COMMENTS

If nothing else, *Kiki* marked the beginning of the end for silent-screen superstar Mary Pickford: a box-office failure, it demonstrated once again that the dimension of reality offered in talking pictures worked against her characterizations. The illusory quality of her performances, so dependent upon the elaborate pantomimic acting style of the silents, dissipated with the addition of sound. (In this particular case, the fact that her French accent was inconsistent throughout the movie didn't help, either.) Largely panned by critics, *Kiki* was a big money-loser for Pickford (costing $811,000 to make but only earning $427,000 in domestic film rental), who made just one more film—1933's *Secrets*, another flop—before retiring from the screen. Betty Grable, seen as one of the chorus girls in "Broadway Revue," also served as a stand-in for Pickford, according to some sources.

PALMY DAYS
(United Artists, 1931)

Credits: Producer, Samuel Goldwyn; director, A. Edward Sutherland; story and screenplay, Eddie Cantor, Morrie Ryskind, and David Freedman; photography, Gregg Toland; editor, Keene Thompson; songs, Ballard MacDonald and Con Conrad; Cliff Friend; Eddie Cantor, Benny Davis and Harry Akst.

Cast: Eddie Cantor (Eddie Simpson); Charlotte Greenwood (Miss Martin); Spencer Charters (A. B. Clark); Barbara Weeks (Joan Clark); George Raft (Joe the Frog); Paul Page (Steve); Harry Woods (Plug Moynihan); Charles B. Middleton (Yolando); Betty Grable (Goldwyn Girl).

Songs: "Bend Down Sister," "Goose Pimples" (MacDonald-Conrad), "There's Nothing Too Good for My Baby" (Cantor-Davis-Akst), "My Honey Said Yes, Yes" (Friend).

Release Date: October 3, 1931. *Running Time:* 77 minutes.

SYNOPSIS

The mammoth, state-of-the-art bakery owned by A. B. Clark is dedicated to the glorification of the American doughnut. In addition to maintaining his ultra-modern baking equipment, Clark ensures that the comely young ladies who work for him get the best in employee benefits, including regular physical workouts supervised by Miss Martin, a long-legged gymnastic instructor. Eddie Simpson, the shill of phony mystic Yolanda, turns up at the bakery just in time to be named Clark's new efficiency expert. His affection for Clark's daughter Joan prompts Eddie to thwart Yolanda's robbery of $24,000 from the baker. Miss Martin helps him outfox the heavies. After several misadventures—during which time the stolen money is hidden in a loaf of bread and taken away—and a lengthy chase, Yolanda and his henchmen are captured, and Eddie returns the cash to a grateful Clark. He clinches with Miss Martin for a happy ending.

REVIEWS

"Better than *Whoopee!* was the verdict of a preview audience on Eddie Cantor's new picture . . . just about the right proportions of story, comedy and music . . . . A chorus of girls out-Ziegfeld the best set of Follies girls for pulchritude and dancing talent . . . . Busby Berkeley and the girls do the best dance ensembles ever seen on the screen." (*Motion Picture Herald*)

"It is quite a good entertainment, this *Palmy Days*. There are two or three inconsequential melodies and a great deal to gaze, including pretty damsels from the Pacific Coast and effectively photographed groups of dancers. The wit may not be as nimble as Mr. Cantor's image, but it is good enough to make one laugh heartily several times." (*New York Times*)

"The mingling of comedy with the severe meller drama, the chases, the villains, the tricks and the hoke, all go to provide a comedy meller-drammer Eddie Cantor will pull across with his personality, which is on the screen as on the stage. Other point to be noted is the dance staging by Busby Berkeley. That came with the very first number and kept on with the others, with each overhead camera view especially liked [by the audience]. Then the girls, though but in shadow, the best looking bunch of choristers yet on the screen." (*Variety*)

Seated in foreground with the Goldwyn Girls in *Palmy Days*.

PRODUCTION NOTES AND COMMENTS

While not quite as elaborate as *Whoopee!*, *Palmy Days* was an unqualified success for Eddie Cantor, who in his Goldwyn pictures transferred his stage persona to the screen virtually intact. Made for approximately $764,000, it netted over $1,158,000 in domestic film rental. Given bright one-liners to deliver, catchy tunes to sing, and talented supporting players to play off, Cantor solidified his position as the talkies' first true musical-comedy star. As always, he found an excuse to get into blackface for a musical number, and he gaily cavorted with the Goldwyn Girls—including Betty Grable, fetchingly clad in exercise togs.

THE GREEKS HAD A WORD FOR THEM
(United Artists, 1932)

Credits: Director, Lowell Sherman; screenplay, Sidney Howard, based on the play by Zoe Akins; gowns by Chanel; camera, George Barnes; editor, Stuart Heisler.

Cast: Madge Evans (Polaire); Joan Blondell (Schatze); Ina Claire (Jean); David Manners (Dey Emery); Lowell Sherman (Boris Feldman); Phillips Smalley (Justin Emery); Sidney Bracey (Waiter); Betty Grable (Girl).

Release Date: February 13, 1932. *Running Time:* 77 minutes.

SYNOPSIS

Three cynical young women—Polaire, Schatze, and Jean—have decided that the one sure way to beat those Depression blues is to land a millionaire . . . and they're even prepared to marry one, if absolutely necessary. The three gold diggers learn that each, unbeknownst to the other, has had an affair with a recently deceased individual named "Pops," who has left his will on a phonograph record. Thinking she's due for a wad of money, Jean turns up at the lawyer's office in deep mourning, only to discover that she wasn't in the old man's favor when he

Greeks' Evans, Claire, and Blondell, surrounded by admirers.

made up the will. More determined than ever to land sugar daddies, the girls are prepared to do anything it takes to get their pots of gold at the end of the rainbow. The hard-boiled Schatze has a heart of gold, and Polaire secretly loves playboy Dey Emery, but Jean—the most predatory of the girls—fancies herself a sure thing. She sets her sights on renowned pianist Boris Feldman—who has wagered his friends that he can make her fall for him just by playing the piano for her. The three gold diggers get themselves into plenty of trouble, but all is straightened out by the final fadeout.

REVIEWS

"The censors must be Sam Goldwyn's only fear as far as the fate of *Greeks* is concerned . . . . Nothing smarter has been done in Hollywood . . . . Slick and effortless perfection of performance. Story values are slight and general effect is episodic, but it has speed, high elan, and the dramatic quality of constant and reiterated surprise." (*Motion Picture Herald*)

"A riot of fun emanates from the screen shadows. There is beauty, too, lavish settings and good acting. Miss Evans is pretty and quite capable. Miss Blondell and Miss Claire keep the merriment bright. Mr. Sherman gives a smooth performance and adds to the general gaiety of the piece." (*New York Times*)

"It's an interesting experiment on the screen in that it's one of the first attempts to put over a smart bit of wit for feature length. Belief is that the picture will register better than satisfactory on its shrewd play for feminine interest in its subject matter and exploitation. Wit of the dialog may be a bit polished for the proletariat, but the basic human humor of these three lilies of the field in rivalry, in battle and in comradeship will register universally. The screen hasn't seen a neater bit of cast teamwork in many a moon . . . ." (*Variety*)

PRODUCTION NOTES AND COMMENTS

Based on a hit play by Zoe Akins, *The Greeks Had a Word for Them* won rave reviews from most metropolitan critics, who singled out Sidney Howard's polished adaptation and Lowell Sherman's urbane direction. As *Variety*'s review predicted, the glossy, sophisticated comedy did particularly well in urban theaters, but not so good in small-town and rural venues, where patrons not only missed some of the humor but objected to the amoral behavior of the protagonists (especially Ina Claire's character). As a result, the $555,000 production only returned $398,000 in domestic film rental to United Artists.

The basic story of *Greeks* obviously appealed to Darryl F. Zanuck, who bought a similar play written by Stephen Powys years later for 20th Century-Fox. By then, with the restrictive Motion Picture Production Code firmly in place, the blatant gold-digging aspects had to be toned down significantly, and Fox's adapters created an essentially new property, calling it *Three Blind Mice* (1938); Loretta Young, Pauline Moore, and Marjorie Weaver played the millionaire-hunting opportunists. Betty Grable, who appears briefly in *Greeks* glamorously gowned by Chanel, starred in the 1941 remake of *Three Blind Mice*, *Moon Over Miami*, and then in the "official" remake of *Greeks*, *How to Marry a Millionaire* (1953), in which she played Loco (the corollary character to this version's Jean).

PROBATION
(Chesterfield, 1932)

Credits: Director, Richard Thorpe; screenplay, Edward T. Lowe, based on the story by Arthur Hoehl; camera, M. A. Anderson; editor, Richard Thorpe.

Cast: Sally Blane (Janet Holman); J. Farrell MacDonald (Judge Holman); Eddie Phillips (Alan Wells); Clara Kimball Young (Mrs. Humphreys); Betty Grable (Ruth Jarrett); David Rollins (Alec); Mary Jane Irving (Gwen); Matty Kemp (Bert); David Durand (The Kid).

Release Date: April 1, 1932. *Running Time:* 62 minutes.

SYNOPSIS

Society girl Janet Holman, bored with a seemingly neverending string of wild parties attended by her social set—well-to-do, directionless young people—complains to her father, a night-court judge, that she doesn't have any idea what to do with herself. The judge suggests that she see another side on life by accompanying him in court. Janet agrees, and gets quite an education from the collection of motley unfortunates on whom her father passes sentence. She is particularly impressed with young Alan Wells, whom she believes to be a basically decent fellow cursed by bad luck. Judge Holman agrees and, instead of sentencing Alan to jail, puts the youth on probation and offers him a job as Janet's chauffeur. Alan's rough edges make it tough for him to mingle with the girl's spoiled, snotty set, but he more than justifies the judge's faith in him by extricating Janet, from a potentially scandalous situation at great risk to himself.

REVIEWS

"Moderately received at a New York nabe situation, this independent effort centers its attention upon a rather simple story . . . well-executed in treatment and satisfactorily performed by the players." (*Motion Picture Herald*)

"Good program picture for the lighter second runs and others and ideally spotted in second place for double-feature policies. Story contains little that is new, but capable direction and cast make the production fairly smooth and acceptable entertainment." (*Variety*)

PRODUCTION NOTES AND COMMENTS

Handsomely produced by Poverty Row standards, *Probation* didn't offer anything startlingly original in melodrama, but pleased chiefly by virtue of earnest performances from Sally Blane, Eddie Phillips, and J. Farrell MacDonald. Betty Grable was briefly seen as one of the wild youngsters whose reckless ways are frowned

Contemplating some mischief in *Probation.*

With silent-star Clara Kimball Young in *Probation*.

upon by the moralizing screenplay. Blane once again proved that she was much better than the cheapie material usually offered her.

HOLD 'EM JAIL
(RKO Radio, 1932)

Credits: Executive producer, David O. Selznick; associate producer, Harry Joe Brown; director, Norman Taurog; screenplay, S. J. Perelman, Walter DeLeon, and Eddie Welch, based on the story by Tim Whelan and Lew Lipton; art director, Carroll Clark; music director, Max Steiner; camera, Len Smith; editor, Artie Roberts.

Cast: Bert Wheeler (Curley Harris); Robert Woolsey (Spider Robbins); Betty Grable (Barbara Jones); Edgar Kennedy (Warden Elmer Jones); Edna May Oliver (Violet Jones); Roscoe Ates (Slippery Sam Brown); Paul Hurst (Coach); Warren Hymer (Steele); Robert Armstrong (Sports Announcer); John Sheehan (Mike Maloney); Jed Prouty (Warden Charles Clark); Spencer Charters (Governor); Monty Banks (Timekeeper); Lee Phelps (Spike); Ernie Adams, Monte Collins (Referees); Ben Taggart (Doorman).

Release Date: September 16, 1932. *Running Time:* 74 minutes.

SYNOPSIS

Bidemore Prison houses some of the toughest criminals in the state, but warden Elmer Jones handles them with ease, rewarding well-behaved prisoners with spots on his convict football team, the apple of his eye. As the story gets underway, he seems hard pressed to find new "talent" for the team. Before long, he's saddled with Curly and Spider, two dim-witted salesmen who've been fooled into helping rob a night club and taking the rap. Assigned to work in the prison blacksmith shop, they have several misadventures before winning the warden's confidence—and positions on the team. Curly also wins a spot in the heart of the warden's daughter, Barbara. When Jones makes a thousand-dollar wager that his team can beat the rival team at Lynwood Prison, the boys see an opportunity to get into his good graces. Spider sneaks a bottle of chloroform from the doctor's bag onto the playing field and uses it to slow up the opposition—but also slows up Curly, trying to score a game-winning touchdown before the final quarter ends. Fortunately he makes it, winning the game and the day. Better yet, the boys are cleared of the robbery for which they've been incarcerated, paving the way for Curly and Barbara to tie the marriage knot.

With Bert Wheeler in a publicity pose for *Hold 'Em Jail*.

REVIEWS

"Made some time ago, but held back until the approach of a new football season, Wheeler and Woolsey go through their usual nonsensicalities with a rather doubtful score. It is one of those pictures which is either a negative hit or a big grosser, according to the reception of these stars by the patrons. Where they are liked, it will be a howl. In other spots the laughs will be scattering and the results dubious. The production has been expensively staged, but the photography and sound are not good. The direction centers too much on the getting of the laughs and overlooks the necessity for knitting those together." (*Variety*)

"Wheeler and Woolsey at their nuttiest . . . roaring with belly laughs, rippling with smiles from start to finish. Betty Grable [is] a pleasing eyeful for love interest . . . . The kids will eat it up and the grownups will go out raving about it." (*Motion Picture Herald*)

"In this noisy, fractious offering Bert Wheeler and Robert Woolsey indulge in their usual energetic nonsense . . . there is little rhyme or reason to the incidents, which are always set forth in a bludgeon-like fashion . . . . Messrs. Wheeler and Woolsey are not nearly as funny as they have been in one or two of their other comedies. Betty Grable plays the Warden's daughter, who falls in love with [Wheeler]." (*New York Times*)

PRODUCTION NOTES AND COMMENTS

In her biggest role to date—and her first outing as an ingenue—Grable looked pretty and perky but had relatively little to do, overshadowed by a supporting cast of veteran screen funsters including Edgar Kennedy, Edna May Oliver, Roscoe Ates, Paul Hurst, and Warren Hymer. *Hold 'Em Jail* was her first film for RKO, where she would soon begin appearing in two-reel shorts, and later in big-budget features.

Wheeler and Woolsey, the former Ziegfeld stars who first appeared on screen in RKO's 1929 adaptation of their stage hit *Rio Rita*, were by this time beginning to wear out their welcome with movie fans. Although the team still had several very entertaining movies ahead of them (including another with Grable, *The Nitwits*), *Hold 'Em*

With Edna May Oliver and Wheeler in *Hold 'Em Jail*.

Jail—which cost approximately $420,000 to make—was indifferently received by critics and audiences alike; soon afterward RKO began cutting budgets on their pictures.

THE KID FROM SPAIN
(United Artists, 1932)

Credits: Producer, Samuel Goldwyn; director, Leo McCarey; screenplay, William Anthony McGuire, Bert Kalmar, and Harry Ruby; songs, Kalmar, Ruby, Irving Caesar, Harry Akst; choreography, Busby Berkeley; camera, Gregg Toland; editor, Stuart Heisler.

Cast: Eddie Cantor (Eddie Williams); Lyda Roberti (Rosalie); Robert Young (Ricardo); Ruth Hall (Anita Gomez); John Miljan (Pancho); Noah Beery (Alonzo Gomez); J. Carroll Naish (Pedro); Robert Emmett O'Connor (Crawford); Stanley Fields (Jose); Paul Porcasi (Border Guard); Walter Walker (The Dean); Julian Rivero (Dalmores); Theresa Maxwell Conover (Martha Oliver); Ben Hendricks, Jr. (Red); The American Matador (Himself); Betty Grable, Paulette Goddard, Toby Wing (Goldwyn Girls); Edgar Connor (Bull Handler); Leo Willis (Robber); Harry C. Bradley (Man on Line); Harry Gribbon (Cop); Eddie Foster (Patron).

Songs: "The College Song," "In the Moonlight," "Look What You've Done" (Kalmar-Ruby), "What a Perfect Combination" (Kalmar-Ruby-Caesar-Akst).

Release Date: Nov. 17, 1932. *Running Time:* 96 minutes.

SYNOPSIS

Eddie Williams is a generally mild-mannered college student with a curious malady: Whenever he hears a whistle he flies into an uncontrollable rage and attacks whomever is closest to him. After mistakenly invading the girls' dormitory, Eddie is brought to the dean's office to explain, but upon hearing a whistle he accosts the official and is expelled. His pal Ricardo also leaves the school, and Eddie joins him in his travels. While waiting in his car for Ricardo, Eddie falls prey to bank robbers, who make him their getaway driver. The ex-student tries desperately to get himself arrested, but for his efforts is merely identified as one of the bandits.

Fleeing the country with Ricardo, Eddie pretends to be a Mexican bullfighter named Don Sebastian and eventually gets across the border. A blonde bombshell named Rosalie attaches herself to him, and he seems content to maintain the illusion—until he learns that he's to participate in a bullfight the following week. Pursued by bandits and police alike, Eddie has no choice but to prove his prowess. To this end he arranges to have an old, feeble, trained bull substituted for the fiery beast intended for

Ruth Hall (left), Eddie Cantor, Lyda Roberti, and Robert Young in *The Kid From Spain*.

him. Naturally, there's a mixup and Eddie finds himself in the ring with the ferocious animal. Nonetheless, he manages both to escape and to clear himself with the authorities. Ricardo winds up with his lady love, Anita Gomez, and Eddie winds up with the tempestuous Rosalie.

REVIEWS

"[A]n astutely arranged combination of fun and beauty, with such effective groupings of dancing girls that these scenes themselves aroused applause. This film keeps Mr. Cantor busy most of the time and there is no objection to this, for he makes the most of his painful experiences, especially those in a closing episode . . . . On several occasions the director, Leo McCarey, takes advantage of the graceful girls in this film to give it a musical-comedy angle." (*New York Times*)

"It's a swell flicker, and as such . . . it'll get a lot of money. Still, there's so much room for cutting that 118 minutes that it should shape up even better. Sub-billed with Lyda Roberti are the Goldwyn Girls, a galaxy of lookers that require no lines other than their physical ones for international comprehension." (*Variety*)

"Comedy that is always laugh-provoking is the highlight of *The Kid From Spain* . . . . Similar to an extravagant stage musical comedy, picture only hazily follows the main plot—with a series of interlude specialties that whirl story from one sequence to another . . . . There is enough funny entertainment to please grown-ups and discounting the ocassional risque dialogue, songs and action sequences, it is more than satisfactory as juvenile amusement." (*Motion Picture Herald*)

Busby Berkeley surrounded by his Goldwyn Girls between scenes for the *The Kid From Spain*. Although this film is routinely listed among Grable's credits, finding her in the publicity stills is all but impossible. Could that be her sitting on the bottom step at far left?

PRODUCTION NOTES AND COMMENTS

The biggest boxoffice musical of the year, *The Kid From Spain* took in over $2,777,000 in worldwide film rental, more than tripling Goldwyn's negative-cost expenditure of $890,000. Boldly released during 1932's slump in musicals, it garnered enthusiastic reviews, more than a few of which commented on the picture's two-hour length. Initially released in the major cities as a "road show" attraction (playing the big movie palaces at two dollars per ticket), it was subsequently cut to 96 minutes for general release and reissue. Existing TV prints reflect the shorter running time.

This was Grable's last appearance as a Goldwyn Girl, as the producer dropped her shortly thereafter. Nonetheless, she's prominently seen as a comely co-ed in the opening number set in the college.

CHILD OF MANHATTAN
(Columbia, 1932)

Credits: Director, Eddie Buzzell; screenplay, Gertrude Pur-

cell, based on the play by Preston Sturges; song, Elmer Colby, Maurice Abrahams; camera, Ted Tetzlaff.

Cast: Nancy Carroll (Madeleine McGonegal); John Boles (Paul Vanderkill); Warburton Gamble (Eggleston); Clara Blandick (Aunt Sophie); Jane Darwell (Mrs. McGonegal); Gary Owen (Buddy); Betty Grable (Lucy); Luis Alberni (Bustamente); Jessie Ralph (Aunt Minnie); Charles Jones (Panama Kelly); Tyler Brooke (Dulcey); Betty Kendell (Louise).

Release Date: February 4, 1933. *Running Time:* 73 minutes.

SYNOPSIS

Taxi dancer Madeleine McGonegal, a "good girl" from a poor family, chafes at the thought of remaining a "Loveland" hostess until her looks fade. One night she's engaged by millionaire playboy Paul Vanderkill, who has come to the dance hall on a lark. He immediately becomes infatuated with Madeleine, but pegs her for someone he can "buy" with fancy clothes and jewels—both of which

With Nancy Carroll and Jane Darwell in *Child of Manhattan.*

he showers her with. Madeleine, who genuinely loves Paul, doesn't want to lose her one chance at happiness, even though she's ostracized by her own highly judgmental family.

When Madeleine gets pregnant, Paul realizes his responsibility and marries her. She loses the baby sometime thereafter and, believing Paul only married her as a generous gesture, flees to Mexico for a quickie divorce. Unbeknownst to Madeleine, her Mexican lawyer wangles a large alimony settlement from Paul, who bitterly believes that she was after his money all along. Brokenhearted, Madeleine offers to marry Panama Kelly, a roughhewn but faithful American who's struck it rich. But Paul tracks her down before the fateful wedding day and convinces her to return to him.

REVIEWS

"Here is a neat little romance-drama to which have been added several deft comedy touches and all made coherent by a novel suspense angle . . . . Nancy Carroll's acting is much more colorful than any of her most recent pictures." (*Motion Picture Herald*)

"Although *Child of Manhattan*, based on the Preston Sturges play, is a title with dash and spirit, [it] has nothing new to report on the whirligig of metropolitan life. Nancy Carroll invests her role with flashes of good acting, but her performance is an individual triumph in a tiresome and routine film." (*New York Times*)

"Program fodder, except that there's more simplicity than purity. It should go to fair results and ought to hold up well in the nabes. Film is from a stage play by the same name, with a suspicion on all sides at the time the play was produced that it was intended for pictures. It's that kind of picture. So implausible and so obviously manufactured for the screen that it loses half of its appeal immediately. It's hoke, baby shoes and all, plus the Cinderella yarn brought to a 10-cent dance joint. Eddie Buzzell on the direction did as well as anyone could and smartly sacrificed a number of scenes for laughter. His megging calls for a bow." (*Variety*)

Nancy Carroll and John Boles in *Child of Manhattan*.

PRODUCTION NOTES AND COMMENTS

It's likely that Columbia bought screen rights to Preston Sturges' play before it even opened on Broadway; Sturges' *Strictly Dishonorable*, a huge hit on the Great White Way, had just been adapted to film—with impressive results—by Universal. Unfortunately, however, the stage version of *Child of Manhattan* failed to achieve its predecessor's success, limping through a mere 87 performances. Interestly, the part of Panama Kelly, interpreted on screen by Columbia's resident cowboy star, Charles "Buck" Jones, was played on stage by veteran heavy Douglas Dumbrille.

As adapted for the screen, *Child of Manhattan* offered nothing that hadn't already been seen on screen dozens of times. Then, too, since it wasn't anything more than a routine soap-opera, *Child* didn't show any of the comedic brilliance Preston Sturges displayed in his other plays and film scripts. Nancy Carroll, then just beginning her long slide to cinematic obscurity, gave a competent, occasionally moving performance as Madeleine, but critics complained that leading man Boles was wooden and supporting lead Jones out of place away from the prairie. Betty Grable had a very small part as Carroll's bratty younger singer; she wasn't even mentioned by most reviewers. With a domestic film rental of $277,000, it could hardly be considered a hit for Columbia.

CAVALCADE
(Fox Film Corp., 1933)

Credits: Producer, Winfield Sheehan; director, Frank Lloyd; screenplay, Sonya Levien, and Reginald Berkeley, based on the play by Noel Coward; assistant directors, William Cameron Menzies, William Tummel; song, Coward; choreography, Sammy Lee; camera, Ernest Palmer; editor, Margaret Clancy.

Cast: Clive Brook (Robert Marryot); Diana Wynyard (Jane Marryot); Ursula Jeans (Penny Bridges); Herbert Mundin (Aldred Bridges); Una O'Connor (Ellen Bridges); Merle Tottenham (Annie); Irene Browne (Margaret Harris); Beryl Mercer (Cook); Frank Lawton (Joe Marryot); John Warburton (Edward Marryot); Margaret Lindsay (Edith Harris); Tempe Piggott (Mrs. Snapper); Billy Bevan (George Grainger); Desmond Roberts (Ronnie James); Frank Atkinston (Uncle Dick); Ann Shaw (Mirabelle); Adele Crane (Ada); Stuart Hall (Lt. Edgar); Mary Forbes (Duchess of Churt); Lionel Belmore (Uncle George); C. Montague Shaw (Major Domo); Bonita Granville (Fanny, age 7-12); Sheila MacGill (Edith, at 10); Douglas Scott (Joey, at 8); Dick Henderson, Jr. (Edward, at 12); Claude King (Speaker); Pat Somerset (Ringsider); Betty Grable (Girl on Couch); Brandon Hurst (Gilbert and Sullivan Actor).

Release Date: April 15, 1933. *Running Time:* 110 minutes.

SYNOPSIS

On New Year's Eve, 1899, young marrieds Robert and Jane Marryot drink their customary toast and prepare to usher in the new century. Robert is to leave the next day for South Africa as an officer in the Boer War, in which Jane's butler currently serves. Jane, who hates war and even dislikes seeing their two young boys playing with toy guns and soldiers, fears for her husband, but he returns hom safely some months later.

The Marryot family thrives during the early years of the 20th century, as does the family of Alfred Bridges, the Marryots' faithful butler, who opens his own pub and makes it a profitable establishment. But tragedy and trauma follows them all, beginning with the death of England's beloved Queen Victoria, and including the accidental death of Bridges and the loss of young Edward Marryot and his new bride in the sinking of the Titanic, on which they had taken a honeymoon cruise.

The indomitable Marryots perservere, however, even after their other son, Joe, is slain in battle during World War I. They follow the career of Fanny Bridges, the daughter of their old butler and friend, who becomes a famous entertainer of the Jazz Age. The film ends as Jane and Robert, now middle-aged, drink their customary New Year's Eve toast—some 30 years after we've first seen them—and look forward to a peaceful, and hopeful, future.

REVIEWS

"Here's a big, brave and beautiful picture. It's pretty certain and solid road show material. It'll call forth all the adjectives the critical boys in the dailies can think up. It'll bring Fox and Frank Lloyd all sorts of eulogies and artistic praise. And once in the first run houses in the keys it should be a boxoffice cinch. At first thought it would seem too foreign a matter for American consumption, but it's the first big historical epic on England that means something over here." (*Variety*)

"[W]ithout having seen the original [stage production], one senses the genuine quality of the film and also the advantages that have been taken of the camera's far-seeing eye . . . . One sees England, merry and sad, belligerent and peaceful, an England with the characters speaking their minds. The atmosphere of London and elsewhere has been reproduced in a masterful fashion. In all its scenes there is a meticulous attention to detail, not only in the settings . . . but also in the selection of the players. Clive Brook, Diana Wynyard and Frank Lawton give conspicuously fine performances . . . ." (*New York Times*)

"It is the mea culpa of Civilization recited in a sweep of spectacle, pageantry and drama for which the motion picture is the only capable medium." (*Motion Picture Herald*)

PRODUCTION NOTES AND COMMENTS

The Oscar-winning Best Picture of 1933 (it also earned Academy Awards for director Frank Lloyd and its picture-perfect art direction), *Cavalcade* was something of a Hollywood rarity: a film about England and Englanders, acted (with just a couple of exceptions) by English performers, and produced with such incredible attention to detail in period sets, costumes, and furnishings that several of the British players felt during the filming that they were indeed back in Victorian-era England.

Noel Coward's London stage hit was "opened up" somewhat for the screen, but American reviewers almost unanimously agreed that Fox's film treatment enhanced the original story. Clive Brook and Diana Wynyard, as Robert and Jane Marryot, were uniformly feted for their brilliant performances, and many other cast members—including Una O'Connor, Irene Browne, and Merle Tottenham, reprising their roles from the original Drury Lane production—were also singled out for praise. Betty Grable, seen for the first time in period gown, appeared briefly as a girl setting on a couch in a party scene.

As expected, *Cavalcade* became one of Fox's top moneymakers in the lucrative foreign markets, especially—and naturally—the United Kingdom. It's $1,500,000 in foreign film rentals, added to domestic totals of $1,200,000, more than justified the picture's $1,300,000 negative cost.

In her brief scene from *Cavalcade*.

Clive Brook and Diana Wynyard in *Cavalcade*.

Diana Wynyard and Frank Lawton in *Cavalcade*.

MELODY CRUISE
(RKO Radio, 1933)

Credits: Executive producer, Merian C. Cooper; associate producer, Louis Brock; director, Mark Sandrich; screenplay, Sandrich and Ben Holmes; additional dialogue, Allen Rivkin and R. G. Wolfson; art directors, Van Nest Polglase and Carroll Clark; songs, Will Jason and Val Burton; camera, Bert Glennon; editor, Jack Kitchen.

Cast: Charlie Ruggles (Pete Wells); Phil Harris (Alan Chandler); Greta Nissen (Ann Von Rader); Helen Mack (Laurie Marlowe); Chick Chandler (Hickey); June Brewster (Zoe); Shirley Chambers (Vera); Florence Roberts (Miss Potts); Marjorie Gateson (Mrs. Wells); Betty Grable (Stewardess).

Songs: "I Met Her at a Party," "He's Not the Marrying Kind," "Isn't This a Night for Love," "This Is the Hour" (Burton-Jason).

Release Date: June 23, 1933. *Running Time:* 76 minutes.

SYNOPSIS

Two well-to-do pals, Pete Wells and Alan Chandler, embark on a steamship bound from New York to California. Chandler feels that, as one of the country's most eligible bachelors, he may be targeted by gold diggers while on board ship, and he connives to have Wells run interference for him. Pete, happy to be taking a trip without his suspicious wife, worries that his efforts to help Alan might be misconstrued by society friends on board, whom he believes would alert his wife that he's misbehaving. Naturally, he's apoplectic when he discovers two drunken girls, Zoe and Vera, are sleeping in his stateroom: They got soused while seeing a friend off and missed the last call for guests to go ashore.

Phil Harris and Helen Mack in *Melody Cruise.*

Realizing he can't hide the girls indefinitely, Pete introduces them as his nieces to an old family friend. Alan, meanwhile, successfully dodges his old flame, Anna von Rader, and falls in love with beautiful, young Laurie Marlowe. There are inevitable complications, but the cruise ends happily, with Alan and Laurie together, and Pete reunited with his wife—who has found out everything.

REVIEWS

"Novelty in idea, construction and presentation is the outstanding characteristic. The show is colorfully glamorous, music catchy, settings modernistic . . . bevies of charming girls accentuate the color . . . . The picture is clean and clever, smart and colorful, so should be appreciated by all classes of trade . . . . " (*Motion Picture Herald*)

"An adroit mixture of nonsense and music which makes for an excellent Summer show. The story is a conventional farce and the humor is invariably of the fractious variety . . . . It is, however, not the singing or the clowning that makes this a smart piece of work, but the imaginative direction of Mark Sandrich, who is alert in seizing any opportunity for cinematic stunts. [T]here are moments when it has a foreign aspect and there is some extraordinarily clever photography." (*New York Times*)

"Fair diverting consignment of music and girl fluff with its moments of gayety, spice and humor, but just about staying the limit of its welcome in an hour and a quarter. Ought to be a moderate grosser for summer entertainment. Story and playing lack genuine spontaneity. It's just a well-rehearsed musical trifle, padded out unmercifully with incidentals, atmosphere and other embroideries. The meat isn't there for the players and they seem to feel it in their work." (*Variety*)

PRODUCTION NOTES AND COMMENTS

To the extent that it could be called a "triumph" of any kind, *Melody Cruise* was a triumph of style over substance. Burdened with a wafer-thin storyline, and with only a few songs to brighten it up, Sandrich pulled out all the stops to make the $163,000 B-picture look more interesting and elaborate then it was. He started with the script, having it revised so that the characters spoke in rhyme (although this conceit wasn't followed through; halfway into the picture the rhyming dialogue is dropped). Then he staged various sequences with specific optical effects in mind, so that on-screen movements of the cast could be matched up with a plethora of inventive wipes and dissolves, quickening the pace and offering a continual treat to the eye. Finally, he cut the picture with almost mathematical precision, creating a rhythm that complemented his visuals.

Melody Cruise is a charming and innocuous little film, although some flashes of updraped femininity and snatches of racy dialogue clearly mark it as a product of pre-Production Code Hollywood. Phil Harris, in his first feature-film starring role, is, as *Variety* put it, "something of a stuffed shirt," but the always-delightful Charlie Ruggles more than compensates for Harris' stiffness. Betty Grable had a small, unbilled bit as a stewardess.

WHAT PRICE INNOCENCE?
(Columbia, 1933)

Credits: Director-screenplay, Willard Mack; camera, Joseph A. Valentine; editor, Arthur Hilton.

Cast: Willard Mack (Dr. Dan Davidge); Minna Gombell (Amy Harper); Jean Parker (Ruth Harper); Betty Grable (Beverly Bennett); Bryant Washburn (John Harper); Ben Alexander (Tommy Harrow); Beatrice Banyard (Mrs. Bennett); Louise Beavers (Hannah).

Release Date: June 29, 1933. *Running Time:* 64 minutes.

SYNOPSIS

Kindly old Dr. Dan Davidge, a fixture in his small community, likes to keep tabs on all his patients and their families. He takes especial interest in the teenagers he has brought into the world, who grapple with emotional and physical changes wrought by adolescence. Davidge is particularly worried about Ruth Harper, a beautiful, basically wholesome girl who has gotten deeply involved with Tommy Harrow, a boy several years older. Tommy plainly desires a level of physical intimacy that Ruth isn't entirely comfortable with, even though she realizes that many of her friends—including Beverly Bennett—seem much more comfortable with such activities. Ruth looks to her mother for information and advice, but Mrs. Harper flatly refuses to discuss some matters with her young daughter. Unfortunately, Ruth finally succumbs to temptation—and when unexpected complications arise, she becomes panicked. Tommy, unwilling to accept responsibility, betrays her, and an ashamed, remorseful Ruth kills herself.

With Beatrice Banyard in *What Price Innocence?*

REVIEWS

"[A] professional field day for Willard Mack, who figures in it as writer, director, and actor, but a puzzling entertainment for the casual [moviegoer]. The picture can hardly be intended for general circulation, and as an item for the Broadway area it assumes the unhappy appearance of attempting to commercialize the subject of sex education. Judged on general entertainment standards, it is an embarrassing film, [although it] is presented with a certain blunt skill and is produced with a certain sincerity." (*New York Times*)

"[G]oes to an extent beyond the pale, discoursing of things physiological, psychological and pathological, with reference to sex, but with restraint . . . . The exhibitor will find nothing of vulgarity or cheapness; instead, a straightforward manner which is at once disarming and convincing." (*Motion Picture Herald*)

"Nothing unclean or unwholesome about *Innocence*, and exploitation that infers otherwise will be misleading. From the standpoint of entertainment, [it] could be categoried as visual education for adolescents, particularly girls, and for parents who are a bit abashed at the thought of initiating their offspring into an understanding of what's what. Dialog is so much domestic prattle and the action is slow [except for] a few flashes of elementary osculation." (*Variety*)

PRODUCTION NOTES AND COMMENTS

Although it was released by Columbia—not yet a major studio, but several notches above the Poverty Row production companies—*What Price Innocence?* had most of the earmarks of the independently produced exploitation films that were relatively common during the '30s and '40s. Most of them had to do with sex or drugs, and they straddled the fence of respectability by playing urban "scratch houses" (which advertised them most titillatingly) and neighborhood schools, churches, and social clubs alike. Since these films were invariably produced on the cheap, they were primarily staffed—both behind and in front of the camera—with bottom-of-the-barrel Hollywood types, which accounts for the bewildering frequency with which players and technicians almost exclusively associated with B-Westerns popped up in their credit listings.

Jean Parker, already an established screen ingenue who'd appeared in major studio productions (though usually in bits), won all the acting honors, such as they were, but Betty Grable had a solid supporting role, logging more screen time and delivering more dialogue than usual for this phase of her career. However, her performance went unnoticed by the film's reviewers.

SWEETHEART OF SIGMA CHI
(Monogram, 1933)

Credits: Producer, William T. Lackey, director, Edwin L. Marin; screenplay, Luther Reed and Albert DeMond, based on the story by George Waggner; songs, Waggner, Ed Ward, Byron D. Stokes, F. Dudleigh Vernor; camera, Gilbert Warrenton; editor, J. Edwin Robbins.

Cast: Mary Carlisle (Vivian); Buster Crabbe (Bob North); Charles Starrett (Morley); Florence Lake (Dizzy); Eddie Tamblyn (Coxswain); Sally Starr (Madge); Mary Blackford (Bunny); Tom Dugan (Trainer); Burr McIntosh (Professor); Major Goodsell (Coach); Grady Sutton (Pledge); Purnell Pratt (Doctor); Franklin Parker (House Prexy); Ted Fio Rito and His Orchestra, including Leif Erickson, Betty Grable, Bill Carey, Muzzy Marcelino, The Three Midshipmen and The Blue Keys (Themselves).

Songs: "Fraternity Walk," "It's Spring Again" (Waggner-Ward), "Sweetheart of Sigma Chi" (Stokes-Vernor).

Release Date: October 15, 1933. *Running Time:* 76 minutes.

SYNOPSIS

Rawley College, a co-educational institution, has more than its fair share of happy-go-lucky students who are more interested in extracurricular activities than they are in their studies. Vivian, a platinum-blonde bombshell who's the campus flirt, has collected more fraternity pins from members of the Sigma Chi fraternity than any other girl in college history, and it's become something of a game for her. She sets her sights on a new member, Bob North, a serious student who also strokes for the Rawley crew. Certain she can make Bob fall for her, Vivian makes a bet that she'll get his fraternity pin before the big race between Rawley and Stanton College. Just prior to the race, Bob learns about the wager and angrily confronts Vivian—giving Morley, whom he replaced as crew stroke and his rival for her attentions, the perfect excuse to move in. Although the confrontation distracts him, Bob snaps out of his funk in time to stroke his crew to victory. Later, he patches things up with Vivian, who has by now realized that she really loves him.

REVIEWS

"*Sweetheart of Sigma Chi* is not overburdened with intelligence, but the glimpses of the rowing contest between Rawley and three other colleges are depicted admirably. Mr. Crabbe's part is not as well suited to him as his wilder roles in other films. His acting ability is limited, but he has an ingratiating personality. Mary Carlisle does moderately well as Vivian and Charles Starrett is equal to the demands of the role of North's rival." (*New York Times*)

"An excellent indie which should be able to stand alone . . . on its appeal to adolescent patronage. Unlike the average undergraduate theme there is nothing rough here. Were it not for the music and smooth direction, as well as a group of good-looking youngsters who are not part conscious, *Chi*, thematically at least, could have easily been far too mild." (*Variety*)

"A lively, sparkling collegiate yarn, bubbling over with the hectic spirit of youth—fraternity boys and sorority girls. Novelty in idea and treatment sets it apart from the formula rah-rah stories, giving it an atmosphere of naturalness that eliminates any semblance of forced theatrics." (*Motion Picture Herald*)

PRODUCTION NOTES AND COMMENTS

Poverty Row seldom ventured into the realm of musical comedy for obvious reasons: Pecunious independent producers couldn't (or wouldn't) duplicate the elaborate production numbers found in major-studio musicals. Nor did the indies generally have the services of top tunesmiths, gag writers, stage-trained funnymen, or former Broadway stars. Even so, *Sweetheart of Sigma Chi* turned out pretty well, according to most trade reviewers and small exhibitors. It couldn't compete with such as Paramount's *College Humor* (also 1933) in the big cities, but in the small towns and rural areas that generally played independent product, *Sweetheart* acquitted itself handily, becoming one of Monogram's top grossing films that year.

Betty Grable, by now performing with Ted Fio Rito's popular band, was seen in one of the orchestra's numbers.

STUDENT TOUR
(Metro-Goldwyn-Mayer, 1934)

Credits: Director, Charles Reisner; screenplay, Philip Dunne and Ralph Spence, based on the story by George Seaton, Arthur Bloch, and Samuel Marx; songs, Nacio Herb Brown, Arthur Freed, James Durante; camera, Joseph A. Valentine; editor, Frank Hull.

Cast: James Durante (Hank); Charles Butterworth (Lippy); Maxine Doyle (Ann); Phil Regan (Bobby); Florine McKinney (Lilith); Douglas Fowley (Mushy); Monte Blue (Jeff); Betty Grable (Cayenne); Fay McKenzie (Mary Lou); Bobby Gordon (Jakie); Mary Loos (Dolores); Pauline Brooks (Peggy); Herman Brix (Hercules); Nelson Eddy (Student); Mischa Auer (Sikh Cop); Arthur Hoyt (Assistant to Dean); Dave O'Brien, Dale Van Sickel, June Storey, Bryant Washburn, Jr., Joan Arlen, Mary Jane Irving, Maxine Nash, Edna May Jones,

Dixie Dean, Clarice Wood (Students); Helen Chan (Sun Toy); Eddie Hart (Stewart); D. Slickenmeyer (Officer); Nick Copeland (Waiter).

Songs: "A New Moon Is Over My Shoulder," "From Now On," "By the Taj Mahal," "The Snake Dance," "The Carlo," "Fight 'Em" (Brown-Freed), "I Just Say It With Music" (Durante).

Release Date: October 5, 1934. *Running Time:* 87 minutes.

SYNOPSIS

Hank, the trainer of a college rowing team, is distraught by the failure of his boys to pass their philosophy exam, thus jeopardising a proposed world tour that would climax in a European rowing championship. Good-natured but eccentric Professor Lippincott (affectionately referred to as "Lippy") generously offers to accompany the students on their lengthy cruise, tutor them in philosophy, and give them a make-up test. Lippy brings along his niece Ann, a shy, bespectacled girl who blossoms during the ocean voyage, eventually falling for crew-team captain Bobby. The student tour takes the

With Phil Regan in *Student Tour*.

With Phil Regan in *Student Tour*.

Americans to Shanghai, India, and Monte Carlo before they participate in the climactic contest on the Thames river. Ann herself winds up substituting for the coxswain, spurring the boys to victory with a rousing song.

REVIEWS

"Shed a tear for James Durante and Charles Butterworth, who went down with the good ship *Student Tour*. To mix the figures of speech, they were outnumbered by the scenario department. Mangled almost beyond recognition, Mr. Durante was still on his feet at the end. Throughout the picture he took his dialogue like a gentleman . . . . The photoplay does contain two good songs, but otherwise it possesses the sparkle and the wit of a performing elephant and the headlong speed of Mr. Stepin Fetchit." (*New York Times*)

"Music, dances, youth, comedy flashes and collegiate romancing are the ingredients here in a musical story mixture that fails to satisfy. In spots it is rather entertaining, but on the whole the 80 [*sic*] minutes running time is tedium, largely brought on by stretches in story construction and numbers which are boringly slow. The comedy of Durante and Butterworth is aided in saving the picture from total failure by some good song number touches, in which Phil Regan and Maxine Doyle figure, together with some production background with dancing." (*Variety*)

PRODUCTION NOTES AND COMMENTS

Despite the wealth of talent involved in its making, *Student Tour* failed to impress either critics or audiences, and although it brought $400,000 in worldwide film rental back to MGM, it still lost money (negative cost, minus prints, advertising, and distribution expenses, was $411,000). The songs by Nacio Herb Brown and Arthur Freed—whose previous MGM hits included "Singin' in the Rain"—were probably the poorest that talented team ever turned out, and not even the spirited rendition of "The Carlo" by baritone Nelson Eddy raised eyebrows.

Most of the critical brickbats were directed at the poor script, lackluster production numbers, and listless performances by the supporting cast. Newcomer Maxine Doyle, thrust into the ingenue's role, did her best with a stereotyped character and weak dialogue, but her inexperience plainly showed. Even the personable Phil Regan, who would appear in several Warner Bros. pictures and later become a star at Republic, seemed at a loss. Betty Grable, playing a co-ed named Cayenne, was much in evidence throughout, but had no real opportunities in which to shine.

THE GAY DIVORCEE
(RKO Radio, 1934)

Credits: Producer, Pandro S. Berman; director, Mark Sandrich; screenplay, George Marion, Jr., Dorothy Yost, and Edward Kaufman, based on the novel and play *The Gay Divorce* by Dwight Taylor; music adaptation, Kenneth Webb and Samuel Hoffenstein; music director, Max Steiner; choreography, Dave Gould; songs, Cole Porter, Mack Gordon and Harry Revel; Con Conrad and Herb Magidson; camera, David Abel; editor, William Hamilton.

Cast: Fred Astaire (Guy Holden); Ginger Rogers (Mimi Glossop); Alice Brady (Aunt Hortense); Edward Everett Horton (Egbert Fitzgerald); Erik Rhodes (Rodolfo Tonetti); Eric Blore (Waiter); Betty Grable (Dancer); Charles Coleman (Guy's Valet); William Austin (Cyril Glossop); Lillian Miles (Guest); George Davis, Alphonse Martell (French Waiters); E. E. Clive (Chief Customs Inspector); Paul Porcasi (French Headwaiter); Charles Hall (Call Boy at dock).

Songs: "Night and Day" (Porter), "The Continental," "Needle in a Haystack" (Conrad-Magidson), "Let's K-nock K-nees," "Don't Let It Bother You" (Gordon-Revel).

Release Date: Oct. 19, 1934. *Running Time:* 107 minutes.

SYNOPSIS

Well-known musical comedy star Guy Holden complains to his friend, attorney Egbert Fitzgerald, that he's tired of working and would like to take a vacation. Fitzgerald confesses that he expects to meet a client, Mimi Glossop, at a French resort hotel. She's trying to get a divorce, and the lawyer has arranged to set her up with a hired co-respondent; their phony "liaison" will enable Mimi to secure her divorce on grounds of infidelity. Guy agrees to meet Egbert at the hotel, where they'll begin their vacation.

Arriving on the continent at the same time as Mimi and her aunt Hortense, Guy encounters the young lady and is immediately smitten. She regards him as a pest. Later on, after seeing Guy at her hotel, Mimi mistakenly leaps to the conclusion that he is her co-respondent. The arrival of Tonetti, the real co-respondent, creates more confusion, but Mimi eventually learns Guy's real identity and all ends happily.

REVIEWS

"This musical has everything for audience satisfaction [and] will establish a new marquee satellite, Fred Astaire.

Dancing to "Let's K-nock K-nees" with Edward Everett Horton while Fred Astaire watches in *The Gay Divorcee.*

Fred Astaire and Ginger Rogers in *The Gay Divorcee.*

This picture unquestionably will set the musical comedy star for the celluloid firmament. Besides his stepping he sings well and handles dialog excellently. All through the picture there's charm, romance, gayety and eclat. There's a dash of Continental spice in the situation of the professional male co-respondent who is to expedite Ginger Rogers' divorce." (*Variety*)

"Last season it was the Carioca which persuaded the foolhardy to bash their heads together. Now the athletic RKO-Radio strategists have created the Continental, an equally strenuous routine in which you confide your secret dreams to your partner under the protective camouflage of the music . . . . Both as a romantic comedian and as a lyric dancer, Mr. Astaire is an urbane delight, and Miss Rogers keeps pace with him even in his rhythmic flights over the furniture." (*New York Times*)

PRODUCTION NOTES AND COMMENTS

Following their success as a team (albeit in support) in *Flying Down to Rio* (1933), Astaire and Rogers were reunited in this modestly budgeted ($520,000) adaptation of *The Gay Divorce*, a stage hit both on Broadway and London's West End. Astaire starred in both productions, which sported a sprightly score by Cole Porter, whose classic "Night and Day" was the only song from the show to be retained in the movie version. (The Hollywood bluenoses implementing the Motion Picture Production Code objected to RKO using the show's original title, by the way, on the grounds that divorce was not a subject to be taken lightly.)

The Gay Divorcee brought a staggering $2,792,000 in worldwide film rental to RKO, guaranteeing further Astaire-Rogers vehicles. Moreover, the film's success

boosted the stocks of most of its participants—including a bouncy, bubbly Betty Grable, who sang and danced Gordon and Revel's "Let K-nock K-nees" with Edward Everett Horton. Although she disappeared from the movie immediately following completion of the number, Grable won kudos for her peppy contribution to the show. *Variety*, for example, tersely noted: "Blonde kid number-leader in 'K-nock K-nees,' in that Brighton-by-the-sea setting, shows lots of promise."

BY YOUR LEAVE
(RKO Radio, 1934)

Credits: Producer, Pandro Berman; director, Lloyd Corrigan; screenplay, Allan Scott, based on the play by Gladys Hurlbut; camera, Nick Musuraca, Vernon Walker; editor, William Morgan.

Cast: Frank Morgan (Henry Smith); Genevieve Tobin (Ellen Smith); Neil Hamilton (David Mackenzie); Marian Nixon (Andrea); Glenn Anders (Freddy Clark); Gene Lockhart (Skeets); Margaret Hamilton (Whiffen); Betty Grable (Frances Gretchell); Lona Andre (Miss Purcell); Charles Ray (Leonard).

Release Date: Nov. 9, 1934. *Running Time:* 82 minutes.

SYNOPSIS

Middle-aged Henry Smith, who's grown increasingly restless in recent months, frets that he has allowed his youth to slip away without having the romantic exploits that other men have had. He'd like to be a Don Juan for a little while, but doesn't know how to go about it. But a determined Henry persuades his devoted wife Ellen that they should go on separate vacations for a week, then return to each other with no questions asked. Ellen is initially reluctant but finally agrees. Henry, accompanied by his pal Skeets, tries his best to be a suave, irresistible man-about-town, but after a few abortive attempts he finally realizes that he isn't cut out to be a lothario. Ellen, on the other hand, attracts handsome, debonair David Mackenzie, who tries to persuade her to leave her former life behind. Somewhat tempted by the offer, she decides against it at the last minute and returns to her suburban home, her comfortable life, and her adoring (and chastened) Henry.

REVIEWS

"As a legit play, *By Your Leave* impressed as a might-have-been last season. Improved as a film, but it's still short of its possibilities. Once the customers are in they'll get some laughs and entertainment, but they're not going to be easy to entice because of lack of marquee weight

With Frank Morgan in *By Your Leave*.

. . . . .It's the direction that hurts, being slow-paced and timid. Acting by both of the principals is to the hilt." (*Variety*)

PRODUCTION NOTES AND COMMENTS

A humble little programmer that failed to make money for RKO despite its meager $176,000 cost, *By Your Leave* suffered principally from restraints on it imposed by the Production Code. Henry Smith's vacation encounters with the opposite sex, somewhat bawdier on stage, were toned down in Allan Scott's script. The charming star turns by Morgan and Tobin accounted for most of the pleasure moviegoers gleaned from the picture. Betty Grable had a minor role as one of the sweet young things pursued by Morgan.

THE NITWITS
(RKO Radio, 1935)

Credits: Producer, Lee Marcus; director, George Stevens; screenplay, Fred Guiol and Al Boasberg, based on the story by Stuart Palmer; songs, L. Wolfe Gilbert and Felix Bernard, Dorothy Fields and Jimmy McHugh; camera, Edward Cronjager; editor, John Lockert.

Cast: Bert Wheeler (Johnnie); Robert Woolsey (Newton); Fred Keating (Darrell); Betty Grable (Mary); Evelyn Brent (Mrs. Lake); Erik Rhodes (Clark); Hale Hamilton (Mr. Lake); Charles Wilson (Captain Jennings); Arthur Aylesworth (Lurch); Willie Best (Sleepy); Lew Kelly (J. Gabriel Hazel); Dorothy Granger (Phyllis).

Songs: "Music in My Heart" (Fields-McHugh), "The Black Widow Will Get You if You Don't Watch Out," "You Opened My Eyes" (Gilbert-Bernard).

Release Date: June 7, 1935. *Running Time:* 81 minutes.

SYNOPSIS

Under the name of "The Black Widow," a blackmailer is terrorizing the city. Among his victims is Winfield Lake, head of a song publishing company, who engages Darrell, a private detective. In the Lake Building is a cigar counter operated by Johnnie and Newton. Newton has invented an electrical apparatus intended to shock the truth out of any liar. Johnnie's avocation is song writing, inspired by his romance with Mary Roberts, Lake's pretty secretary. Together, they play a punchboard for a wedding-ring prize, but to Mary's disappointment only win a revolver.

When Mary learns that Lake needs a murder theme song, she informs Johnnie. Lake now takes advantage of his position and forces his attentions on Mary—when Johnnie interrupts the scene, knocks out Lake and orders Mary to quit her job. Soon after, Lake is found murdered. Suspicion points to Mary because her punchboard gun is found on Lake's desk, where Johnnie inadvertently left it. Johnnie "confesses" to save Mary, and Newton "confesses" to save Johnnie. But the police arrest Mary, refusing even to admit the boys to jail.

Any one of the dead man's many enemies may have committed the crime: Mrs. Lake, who was jealous of Mary; Lurch, Lake's head auditor who was falsifying accounts; Clark, a disgruntled song writer who quarreled with Lake.

Johnnie and Newton, turning amateur sleuths, install the truth detector in the death chair, expecting that the murderer will return to the scene of the crime. When Darrell falls into the trap, he shouts, "I am The Black Widow!" But the two goofs conclude that the invention is just another one of Newton's failures.

Darrell now marks Newton and Johnnie for death in the same manner Lake was killed, but Lurch accidentally gets the fatal bullet fired from Darrell's gun poised in an aperture in the ceiling. Later, Johnnie and Newton overcome Darrell, in disguise, at the appointed place where Black Widow victims were ordered to leave the extorted money. Again, they fail to realize the truth. They are about to free him when Captain Jennings enters and arrests Darrell as The Black Widow and the murderer of Lake and Lurch. He reveals that the private detective, while delivering Mary to the police as the killer, switched his murder gun with her punchboard gun, which never contained any bullets. Further, Darrell "advised" Black Widow victims to deliver the money to the extortioner—himself.

All ends happily. Newton, having won the punchboard wedding ring, presents it to Johnnie and Mary.

With Charles Wilson and Fred Keating in *The Nitwits*.

With Hale Hamilton in *The Nitwits*.

REVIEWS

"Old-fashioned nonsensical foolishness . . . . There are a couple of songs and one dance duet in it [but] a murder mystery, full of threat, menace and dire things, motivates the real comedy . . . . Anything that even closely resembles unity, coherence or the logical following-up of a plot is unceremoniously tossed out a window." (*Motion Picture Herald*)

"[A] full-grown whodunit, with the director sticking to the plot and weaving the comedy into the fabric. Not a bad job, but the combination runs too long for best results in spite of some undeniably funny business and a finish that moves with the speed of the oldtime pantomime slapstick . . . . Comedy pair give their standard performances with Miss Grable a trifle too mechanical . . . . Nicely directed, but script would have profited by editing before production." (*Variety*)

PRODUCTION NOTES AND COMMENTS

The declining grosses of Wheeler and Woolsey vehicles forced RKO to cut budgets on their mid-'30s pictures, and *The Nitwits*, at a negative cost of $239,000, was brought in for little more than half the money spent on *Hold 'Em Jail*, Betty Grable's previous outing with the team. Having already spoofed costume dramas, war films, prison pictures, gangster tales, and Westerns, it was only natural that the team should take on murder mysteries, in 1935 at the height of their screen popularity.

Woolsey, Keating, and Wheeler in *The Nitwits*.

The storyline was contributed by whodunit specialist Stuart Palmer, who created the spinster sleuth Hildegarde Withers (herself the protagonist of an RKO series) and subsequently wrote many movie mysteries in the '30s and '40s. Unfortunately, his plot suffered in translation from script to screen; *The Nitwits* seems padded in spots, with the comedy interpolations forced and sometimes unfunny. But Grable, in her second ingenue role, at least got plenty of footage and warbled winningly (especially "You Opened My Eyes") with Bert Wheeler. Although she performed competently, RKO didn't see fit to promote her to full-fledged stardom, and she had minor supporting roles in her remaining three films for the studio.

OLD MAN RHYTHM

(RKO Radio, 1935)

Credits: Associate producer, Zion Myers; director, Edward Ludwig; screenplay, Sig Herzig and Ernest Pagano, based on the story by Lewis Gensler, Herzig, and Don Hartman; additional dialogue, H. W. Henemann; choreography, Hermes Pan; art director, Van Nest Polglase; songs, Gensler, Johnny Mercer; music director, Roy Webb; camera, Nick Musuraca; editor, George Crone.

Cast: Charles "Buddy" Rogers (Johnny Roberts); George Barbier (John Roberts, Sr.); Barbara Kent (Edith Warren); Grace Bradley (Marian Beecher); Betty Grable (Sylvia); Eric Blore (Phillips); Erik Rhodes (Frank Rochet); John Arledge (Pinky Parker); Johnny Mercer (Colonel); Donald Meek (Paul Parker); Dave Chasen (Andy); Joy Hodges (Lois); Douglas Fowley (Oyster); Evelyn Poe (Honey); Margaret Nearing (Margaret); Ronald Graham (Ronald); Sonny Lamont (Blimp); William Carey (Bill); Lucille Ball, Marian Darling, Jane Hamilton, Maxine Jennings, Kay Sutton (College Girls); Jack Thomas, Erich Von Stroheim, Jr., Carlyle Blackwell, Jr., Bryant Washburn, Jr., Claude Gillingwater, Jr. (College Boys).

Songs: "Old Man Rhythm," "I Never Saw a Better Night," "There's Nothing Like a College Education," "Boys Will Be Boys," "When You Are in My Arms," "Come the Revolution Baby" (Mercer-Gensler).

Release Date: August 2, 1935. *Running Time:* 75 minutes.

SYNOPSIS

Johnny Roberts hasn't been taking his college chores very seriously. The son of a wealthy businessman, he's more interested in making time with cute co-eds than in making good grades, and his constant philandering threatens to get him expelled. John Sr. decides that the one way to keep his boy in line is to enroll in the college

himself. Campus life appeals to the older man, who quickly dopes out the situation: gold-digging vamp Marion Beecher has got her sights set on Johnny, but his dad thinks that demure Edith Warren would be a much better match for the young man.

REVIEWS

"Lilting music and Charles 'Buddy' Rogers—there's the combination of this song picture of the campus . . . . No effort is made to emphasize realism, yet that is no obstacle to movement of the picture." (*Motion Picture Herald*)

"Aside from some well-staged tunes and a few juicy comedy moments, *Old Man Rhythm* stacks up as inconsequential fare. [T]he frail story [is] counteracted by the smooth pacing and breeziness of the direction. In those nabes where they take their illusions less critically this hodge-podge of co-ed romancing and katzenjammer may prove diverting, but left to stand on its own it won't pull 'em through the stiles . . . . Cast is topheavy with lookers, while the dancing interludes leave little wanting." (*Variety*)

PRODUCTION NOTES AND COMMENTS

Old Man Rhythm wasn't intended to be anything more than program filler—as its negative cost of $243,000 would indicate—and as such didn't raise any eyebrows. But it seems somewhat more entertaining today than it might have in 1935, when the screen was fairly cluttered with breezy musical comedies, many of them major-studio A pictures. That's chiefly due to the clever songs written by Johnny Mercer, whose subsequent cinematic offerings would be included in more prestigious produc-

Buddy Rogers, Barbara Kent and George Barbier in *Old Man Rhythm*.

tions. Buddy Rogers was obviously too old to be the brash college kid he played, but his obvious exuberance and ingratitating charm naturally forced viewers to suspend their disbelief. Barbara Kent, a rising star of the late silent era whose sound vehicles failed to sustain her ascent, made a pallid ingenue; Grace Bradley, on the other hand, was dynamic as the campus flirt. Veteran character actor George Barbier won most of the laughs as Rogers' dad, and Betty Grable was prominent throughout the proceedings.

COLLEGIATE
(Paramount, 1936)

Credits: Producer, Louis D. Lighton; director, Ralph Murphy; screenplay, Walter DeLeon and Francis Martin, based on the story *Charm School* by Alice Duer Miller; choreography, LeRoy Prinz; songs, Mack Gordon and Harry Revel; music director, Georgie Stoll; camera, William Mellon; editor, Doane Harrison.

Cast: Joe Penner (Joe); Jack Oakie (Jerry Craig); Ned Sparks (Scoop Oakland); Frances Langford (Juliet Hay); Betty Grable (Dorothy); Lynne Overman (Sour Puss); Betty Jane Cooper (Dance Instructress); Mack Gordon, Harry Revel (Themselves); Henry Kolker (Mr. MacGregor); Donald Gallagher (Thomas J. Bloodgood); Albert Conti (Headwaiter); Helen Brown (Dance Teacher); Johnny Wrey, Ted Shea, Bob Goodstein, Ruby Shaeffer, Jimmy Dime, Jack and Bob Crosby (Chorus Boys); Dorothy Jarvis, Katherine Hankin, Nancy Emery, Irene Bennett, Martha O'Driscoll (Chorus Girls); Edgar Dearing (State Trooper); Guy Usher (Lawyer); Marjorie Reynolds (Girl).

Songs: "I Feel Like a Feather in the Breeze," "You Hit the Spot," "Rhythmatic," "My Grandfather's Clock in the Hallway" (Gordon-Revel).
Release Date: December 27, 1935. *Running Time:* 81 minutes.

SYNOPSIS

Broadway playboy Jerry Craig learns that a clause in the will of his recently deceased aunt makes him the dean of a girl's college. At first he tries to avoid the assignation, but with the help of addle-brained Joe, an amnesiac with a bulging bankroll, he eventually decides to take over the school. But Jerry's not much interested in academics; instead, he decides that college girls don't need reading and writing as much as they need rhythm. To that end he hires famous songwriters Mack Gordon and Harry Revel to head up the school's music department, and former George White's Scandals star Betty Jane Cooper as dance instructor. Aided by Joe, Joe's valet Sour-Puss, and Scoop

Jack Oakie, Frances Langford, and Joe Penner in *Collegiate*.

Oakland, Jerry turns the inherited institution into the swingin-est campus in the country, initially to the chagrin of Miss Hay, one of the teachers, whom he eventually wins over. Even Joe gets a girl—a cuddly co-ed named Dorothy—before the final fadeout.

REVIEWS

"When *Collegiate* opened at the Paramount Theatre, mobs crashed windows and doors, so I hear, in their impatience to see Joe Penner. At the moment, Mr. Penner's exact power escapes me, and I think that I shall wait until he appears in a Shakespearean role, doubtless inevitable, before I attempt any analysis. The absence of his duck is a radical departure in the eyes of his public. Not alone a Penner vehicle, *Collegiate* turns out to be this year's adaptation of Alice Duer Miller's 'Charm School.' Jack Oakie inherits the girls' seminary in this case, and the songs he teaches his pupils are by Gordon and Revel, and humor is instilled by the acrid Ned Sparks. The whole affair is inconsequential, except to the Penner public." (*The New Yorker*)

"Fun in a girl's school is the tune to which this adaptation of Alice Duer Miller's 'Charm School' spins. Always light and gay, breaking up its straight story continuity with cleverly interpolated gags, it bubbles and froths merrily . . . . Fast moving, peppy with music and dancing providing appeal for those who like their entertainment amusing." (*Motion Picture Herald*)

"Light, diverting, no sock, but no bore. It'll probably be an in-and-outer, big where they're strong for Joe Penner and Jack Oakie, and indifferent in other spots . . . it's an engaging enough filmusical . . . . Betty Grable [is an] attractive vis-a-vis to Penner." (*Variety*)

In *Collegiate*.

PRODUCTION NOTES AND COMMENTS

By the time Paramount's scriptwriters and tunesmiths got done "adapting" Alice Duer Miller's *Charm School* for this Jack Oakie-Joe Penner musical comedy, very little other than the basic premise remained. Previously filmed under its original title as a 1921 Wallace Reid silent, Miller's popular story was updated to incorporate peppy musical numbers and provide a vehicle for radio comic Penner, in 1935 at the peak of his popularity. Winsome Frances Langford—who had appeared in the studio's *Every Night at Eight* (introducing the song "I'm in the Mood for Love") earlier that year—still wasn't entirely at ease in front of the camera, and she seemed poorly matched with the effusive Oakie. Betty Grable, playing a comely co-ed who falls for Joe Penner, fared considerably better with her supporting role, doing some fancy stepping with the comedian in a musical number and holding her own among the notorious group of veteran scene-stealers. The songs by Gordon and Revel, while not up to their best, were certainly pleasant and winningly performed.

With Joe Penner in *Collegiate.*

FOLLOW THE FLEET
(RKO Radio, 1936)

Credits: Producer, Pandro S. Berman; director, Mark Sandrich; screenplay, Dwight Taylor, based on the play *Shore Leave* by Hubert Osborne and Allan Scott; music director, Max Steiner; choreography, Hermes Pan; songs, Irving Berlin; camera, David Abel; editor, Henry Berman.

Cast: Fred Astaire (Baker); Ginger Rogers (Sherry Martin); Randolph Scott (Bilge Smith); Harriet Hilliard (Connie Martin); Astrid Allwyn (Iris Manning); Ray Mayer (Dopey); Harry Beresford (Captain Hickey); Addison [Jack] Randall (Lt. Williams); Russell Hicks (Jim Nolan); Brooks Benedict (Sullivan); Lucille Ball (Kitty Collins); Betty Grable, Joy Hodges, Jennie Gray (Trio); Tony Martin (Sailor); Maxine Jennings (Hostess); Frank Jenks, Frank Mills, Edward Burns (Sailors); Herbert Rawlinson (Webber); Jane Hamilton (Waitress).

Songs: "Let's Face the Music and Dance," "Let Yourself Go," "I'm Putting All My Eggs in One Basket," "Get Thee Behind Me, Satan," "But Where Are You," "We Saw the Sea," "I'd Rather Lead a Band" (Berlin).

Release Date: February 21, 1936. *Running Time:* 110 minutes.

SYNOPSIS

While on shore leave in San Francisco, sailors Bat Baker and Bilge Smith head for the nearest dance hall in search of feminine companionship. Bat is surprised to see his former vaudeville partner, Sherry Martin, singing in the waterfront joint. Their reunion is bittersweet: Bat joined the Navy after proposing to and being turned down by Sherry. Bilge is introduced to Sherry's sister Connie, who's also a talented singer; they are initially attracted to each other, but Bilge later falls under the spell of a glamorous blonde society girl named Iris. Meanwhile, Sherry convinces Bat to dance with her at a fund-raiser aimed at saving and restoring an old schooner Connie bought for Bilge. Back on board, Bat learns he can't get leave to dance in the benefit—but he jumps ship just before showtime and swims to shore, hotly pursued by Bilge—his superior officer—who's been ordered to arrest him. At the show, Bilge reunites with Connie, and allows Bat to dance with Sherry.

REVIEWS

"This picture differs [from previous Astaire-Rogers vehicles] in the character of the story, an additional factor in the exhibitors' favor. . . . While the love interest is well taken care of with a proper balance of light drama and

With Rogers, Jennie Gray, and Joy Hodges in *Follow the Fleet*.

With Lucille Ball and Harriet Hilliard in *Follow the Fleet.*

suspense . . . the comedy content is given a broader swing in dialogue, action and situations, and the substantiating chorus singing-dancing effects." (*Motion Picture Herald*)

"One of the comforts of the cinema season . . . . Some of the best Berlin music and the most delectable Astaire-Rogers dancing . . . . The score and the dancing are at least up to the enchantments in this field supplied by *Top Hat*." (*New York Herald Tribune*)

"As for Fred Astaire and Ginger Rogers, I like them as well as anybody does, but wish that someone would write a tolerable story for them . . . . Such charming persons deserve at least a vehicle that will hold together past the first dance—as *Roberta* did, I seem to remember, until the very end." (*The Nation*)

PRODUCTION NOTES AND COMMENTS

Based on a Broadway play produced by legendary showman David Belasco, *Follow the Fleet* had two cinematic precedents: a 1925 silent starring Richard Barthelmess titled *Shore Leave*, and RKO's 1930 musicalized version, *Hit the Deck* (later remade by MGM). Although it sported some of the most memorable Astaire-Rogers numbers, *Follow the Fleet* fell somewhat short of the duo's earlier efforts. Many reviewers complained that the slender storyline didn't adequately support the film's nearly two-hour running time, for example, and some noted that the Scott-Hilliard segment of the story diluted audience interest which otherwise would have been focused 100 percent on Fred and Ginger.

Betty Grable, who appeared briefly as a member of the backup trio supporting Ginger Rogers in the "Let Yourself Go" number, apparently shot additional scenes that were subsequently cut from the already-overlong film. She was certainly under-utilized, especially inasmuch as she'd appeared to better advantage in recent RKO films such as *The Nitwits* and *Old Man Rhythm*. The brevity of her role was commented upon by some reviewers, including *Variety*'s "Bige," who noted: "Betty Grable is on and off so quickly it's hardly a screen test."

DON'T TURN 'EM LOOSE
(RKO Radio, 1936)

Credits: Producer, Robert Sisk; director, Ben Stoloff; screenplay, Harry Segall, based on the story by Ferdinand Reyher; camera, Jack MacKenzie; editor, William Morgan.

Cast: Lewis Stone (Mr. Webster); James Gleason (Daniels); Bruce Cabot (Bat Roberts); Betty Grable (Mildred); Nella Walker (Mrs. Webster); Louise Latimer (Letty); Grace Bradley (Grace); Frank M. Thomas (Attorney Pierce); Maxine Jennings (Mary); Frank Jenks (Pete); Harry Jans (Vic); John Arledge (Walter); Addison [Jack] Randall (Al); Fern Emmett (Hattie); Arthur Hoyt (Judge Bass); Frenchy Durelle (Deputy Warden); Phillip Morris (Guard); Tommy Graham (Secretary); Gordon Jones (Joe); John Ince (Parole Board Member).

Release Date: Sept. 18, 1936. *Running Time:* 65 minutes.

SYNOPSIS

Small-town high school principal John Webster secures a berth on the state parole board, where one of his "applicants" is the notorious gangster Bat Roberts. Webster is startled by Roberts' appearance, for reasons known only to himself: Bat is his own renegade son, long ago banished from the family for his lawless ways. Roberts secretly gives his father an ultimatum—unless Webster recommends parole for him, Bat will reveal his true identity and thereby disgrace the family name. Webster reluctantly complies, but upon being released from prison Bat resumes his criminal career with a vengeance. By now a notorious killer, he spares no one who gets in his way. Finally, a heartsick but determined Webster, seeing his outlaw son about to kill a detective, shoots Bat himself; the paroled criminal's death ends a reign of terror.

REVIEWS

"This picture is strong, dramatic entertainment . . . certain improbabilities of the story are successfully overcome by direction and characterization which mould the tale into a compact and highly dramatic chronicle of present-day life. Performances of the principals are highly commendable." (*Motion Picture Herald*)

With Lewis Stone in *Don't Turn 'Em Loose*.

"It is to be doubted if, for sheer slam-bang heart-trapping, the Hollywood cinema has filmed a more thumping scene than that in which the college executive, newly elected to the Parole Board, confronts his notorious, murderous son . . . . It is straining things a little to believe the ending . . . scenarists Harry Segall and Ferdinand Reyher, the bit in their teeth, raced to this conclusion about two paces in advance of credibility." (*Literary Digest*)

"By any other name [the picture] would be one of those tough, blustering, high-mortality-rate gangster melodramas which were to have been swept out of Hollywood by the freshening breeze of the new screen morality. Now we find them under a veneer of investigation, reform and expose . . . . For the record, it may be listed as a fast-moving, easily told piece of crime fiction, but it leaves the parole system, as such, pretty much as it found it." (*New York Times*)

PRODUCTION NOTES AND COMMENTS

A fast-moving, action-packed melodrama with no extraneous scenes or elements, *Don't Turn 'Em Loose* evenly split its reviewers: Half of them felt it to be a strong, moralistic plea to keep hardened criminals behind bars, the other half saw it as a crassly exploitative, violent, unbelievable gangster film cloaked in reformist garb. The public was more noncommittal, apparently; while economically made (at a negative cost of $127,000, it was the most inexpensive major-studio film in which Grable appeared), and turned only a modest profit for RKO.

Acting honors, such as they were, went to Stone and Cabot. Grable played Stone's daughter, her wholesomeness sharply contrasting with Cabot's amoral viciousness.

PIGSKIN PARADE
(20th Century-Fox, 1936)

Credits: Producer, Darryl F. Zanuck; associate producer, Bogart Rogers; director, David Butler; screenplay, Harry Tugend, Jack Yellen, and William Conselman, based on the story by Arthur Sheekman, Nat Perrin, and Mark Kelly; music director, David Buttolph; songs, Sidney Mitchell and Lew Pollack; camera, Arthur Miller; editor, Irene Morra.

Cast: Stuart Erwin (Amos Dodd); Patsy Kelly (Bessie Winters); Jack Haley (Slug Winters); Johnny Downs (Chip Carson); Betty Grable (Laura Watson); Arline Judge (Sally Saxon); Dixie Dunbar (Ginger Jones); Judy Garland (Sairy Dodd); Tony Martin (Tommy Baker); Fred Kohler, Jr. (Biff Bentley); Elisha Cook, Jr. (Herbert Terwilliger Van Dyck); Pat Flaherty (Referee); Jack Murphy (Usher); Dave Sharpe (Messenger Boy); Si Jenks (Baggage Master); Jack Stoney

(Policeman); John Dilson (Doctor); Ben Hall (Boy in Stadium); Lynn Bari (Girl in Stadium); Charles Wilson (Yale Coach); Alan Ladd (Student); Edward Le Saint (Judge).

Songs: "It's Love I'm After," "Texas Tornado," "The Balboa," "You Do the Darndest Things, Baby," "T.S.U. Alma Mater," "Hold That Bulldog," "You're Slightly Terrific" (Mitchell-Pollack), "Woo Woo," "We'd Rather Be in College," "Down With Everything" (Yacht Club Boys)

Release Date: October 23, 1936. *Running Time:* 93 minutes.

SYNOPSIS

While lining up football games for the upcoming season, a publicity-hungry Yale staffer mistakenly invites tiny Texas State University (rather than the University of Texas) to gridiron competition. The gaffe is exposed promptly, but Yale's board decides to go ahead with the game rather than risk embarassment by canceling. The students of Texas State, thrilled with the invitation but ill-equipped to play such a formidable team, recruit a new football coach: Flushing, New York's own Slug Winters, who eagerly accepts the assignment and travels west with his tart-tongued wife Bessie. They're met at the ramshackle train station by a delegation of T.S.U. students including Chip Carson, the team's chief booster, and his girl friend Laura Watson. Slug is welcomed with open arms, and vows to lead T.S.U. to victory.

One critical shortcoming soon becomes apparent: the team lacks a capable quarterback. The students scour the countryside for a likely candidate, and find one in bashful farm boy Amos Dodd, who pitches watermelons with lightning speed and unerring accuracy. Amos isn't keen on attending college, but he's convinced to try it by his

With Johnny Downs in *Pigskin Parade*.

Left to right: Jack Haley, Patsy Kelly, Stu Erwin, Judy Garland, Johnny Downs, and Grable in *Pigskin Parade*.

younger sister Sairy. Although Amos' "technique" is somewhat eccentric—he can throw only when he's barefoot—he eventually masters the game's strategy and ultimately leads the team in a triumphant rout of Yale.

REVIEWS

"It's funny in a goofy, catch-as-catch-can sort of way. The songs, dances and even the Yacht Club Boys are also up to standard. The authors . . . seemed to have started the writing of their script with little except the notion that football could be a laughable subject. With plenty of gags, with Patsy Kelly hurling wisecracks at Jack Haley, with Judy Garland's songs and Dixie Dunbar's dancing, the film gets along very nicely indeed . . . . Judy Garland, a tiny newcomer, with a piquant face and surprising voice, is one of the film's biggest assets." (*New York Sun*)

"[M]oves down the entertainment field with gusto and eclat emerging as a genuinely funny burlesque of football and its musical comedy concomitants. With such people as the Yacht Club Boys, Patsy Kelly, Jack Haley and Stuart Erwin jiggling on the gridiron, it may be endorsed whole-heartedly as one of the season's most entertaining contributions . . . . We don't say that *Pigskin Parade* deserves a Nobel prize or anything so solid, but it is good fun and almost every one but the Yales should like it." (*New York Times*)

"This is grand fun that should score heavily in every theater. It touches a high mark in film foolery and has been skillfully directed by David Butler. Six writers share in the credits—and there is credit enough for all." (*Film Daily*)

PRODUCTION NOTES AND COMMENTS

Pigskin Parade, one of the least-seen and most underappreciated musicals of the '30s, brought Betty Grable back to Fox (now 20th Century-Fox, and headed by Darryl F. Zanuck) after a six-year absence. Unfortunately, though, she didn't get much chance to strut her stuff. Cast as the bubbly blonde girl friend of Johnny Downs, she figured prominently in several scenes—including the film's big dance number, "The Balboa"—but was overshadowed by other cast members' musical con-

With Elisha Cook, Jr. and Johnny Downs in *Pigskin Parade*.

tributions. Judy Garland, making her feature-film debut, snagged most of the critics' kudos for her vocalizing, and whatever songs she didn't get were effectively crooned by Tony Martin or dizzily delivered by the wacky Yacht Club Boys. And pert, petite Dixie Dunbar won the movie's terpsichorean honors with her rat-a-tat tapping. In fact, given the impressive array of musical talent in the picture, Grable was probably lucky to make as favorable an impression as she did. More than anything else, however, her turn in *Pigskin Parade* reinforced her status as one of moviedom's comeliest coeds.

THIS WAY PLEASE
(Paramount, 1937)

Credits: Producer, Mel Shauer; director, Robert Florey; screenplay, Grant Garrett, Seena Owen, and Howard J. Green, based on the story by Maxwell Shane and Bill Thomas; songs, Sam Coslow, Frederick Hollander, Al Siegel, Jock and George Gray; choreography, LeRoy Prinz; music director, Boris Morros; camera, Harry Fischbeck; editor, Anne Bauchens.

Cast: Charles "Buddy" Rogers (Brad Morgan); Mary Livingstone (Maxine Barry); Betty Grable (Jane Morrow); Ned Sparks (Inky Wells); Jim and Marian Jordan (Fibber McGee and Molly); Porter Hall (S. J. Crawford); Lee Bowman (Stu Randall); Cecil Cunningham (Miss Eberhardt); Wally Vernon (Bumps); Romo Vincent (Trumps); Jerry Bergen (Mumps); Rufe Davis (Sound Effects Man).

Songs: "Is It Love or Is It Infatuation?" (Coslow-Hollander), "This Way Please," "Delighted to Meet You," "What This Country Needs Is Voom Voom" (Siegel-Coslow), "I'm the Sound Effects Man" (Gray).

Release Date: September 15, 1937. *Running Time:* 73 minutes.

SYNOPSIS

Although Jane Morrow, a pretty usherette, falls for Brad Morgan, popular and dynamic orchestra leader, her case looks hopeless. But while rehearsing with chorus girls on the theater's rooftop he meets her and is strongly attracted. A romance starts, much to the dismay of Jane's friends. Maxine, head usherette, Inky, publicity man of the theater where Jane works, and Stu Randall, house manager, all try to break it up without success.

Morgan tries to get Jane a job in the show, but only gets her fired for his pains. They quarrel and Morgan quits the show. When he leaves, Jane takes his place on the stage. He is furious at what he considers a deliberate frame-up.

In a pretended reconciliation, he asks her to marry him in a ceremony to be performed on the theater stage. To get even with her he plans not to show up at the ceremony, but later changes his mind. When he sees Stu about to take his place at the ceremony, he makes a quick dash to the stage and marries the girl himself.

REVIEWS

"Musical comedy with theatre setting and a slight story which concerns a love affair between headliner at theatre, Buddy Rogers, and a girl, Betty Grable, who takes a job as an usher thinking she is being engaged as a singer and dancer. Significant, because it introduces to the screen, Mary Livingston of radio fame. Fibber McGee and Molly also appear briefly. A better than average program picture." (*California Congress of Parents and Teachers*)

"A routine romance with music, built around a talented theatre usherette and popular leader of a featured band. Story idea as a whole is an amusing hodge-podge lacking both rhyme and reason. Several radio personalities are

With Buddy Rogers in *This Way Please*.

With Buddy Rogers in *This Way Please*.

introduced, but the production as entertainment is below standard." (*East Coast Preview Committee*)

"Nothing in this slowly paced comedy with music to get excited about. It is neither comic nor melodious. It's a . . . glimpse into the working of a metropolitan first run theatre which puts on presentations. Betty Grable, whose looks are on the plus side, applies for a dancing job and is showed onto aisle 3 with a flashlight. All of it has been done before, usually under more entertaining circumstances. There are a couple of songs which don't get much chance. [The title] *This Way Please* suggests its own wisecrack." (*Variety*)

PRODUCTION NOTES AND COMMENTS

The first of Grable's films under her term contract to Paramount, *This Way Please* offered her second billing, a solo dance number (simply staged but nicely executed), and more dialogue than she was used to getting. Normally that would have been enough to guarantee a favorable impression, but Betty's career hardly benefitted from her participation in this slapdash melange. The film's substandard quality—in itself surprising, inasmuch as director Robert Florey had previously helmed several successful Paramount programmers—drew plenty of critical brickbats, and much attention was lavished on debuting radio personalities Mary Livingstone (Mrs. Jack Benny) and Jim and Marian Jordan (Fibber McGee and Molly). Even more embarassingly, many reviewers waxed enthusastic over the cornpone comedy of animal imitator Rufe Davis at Betty's expense; seldom has any film's female lead gotten less attention from the press. Sadly, *This Way Please* was just the first of several mediocre Paramount productions in which Grable appeared.

With Virginia Dabney (standing, center) and Mary Livingstone (seated right) in *This Way Please.*

THRILL OF A LIFETIME
(Paramount, 1937)

Credits: Producer, Fanchon; director, George Archainbaud; story and screenplay, Seena Owen, Grant Garrett, and Paul Gerard Smith; art directors, Hans Dreier, Franz Bachelin, and Russell Patterson; music director, Boris Morros; songs, Yacht Club Boys, Sam Coslow and Frederick Hollander; camera, William Mellor.

Cast: Judy Canova (Judy Lovelee); Betty Grable (Gwen); Buster Crabbe (Don Lansing); Dorothy Lamour (Herself); Johnny Downs (Stanley Jackson); Ben Blue (Skipper); Eleanore Whitney (Betty Jane); Leif Erickson (Howard "Howdy" Nelson); Zeke and Anne Canova (Themselves); Fanchonettes (Specialties); Howard M. Mitchell (Businessman); Franklin Pangborn (Sam Wattle); Tommy Wonder (Billy); Marie Burton, Paula DeCardo, Norah Gale, Harriette Haddon, Lola Jensen, Gwen Kenyon, Joyce Matthews (The Girls); Billy Daniels, Bill Roberts, Frank Abel, Lee Bennett, Carlyle Blackwell, Jr., Bob Parrish (The Boys).

Songs: "Keeno, Screeno and You," "I'll Follow My Baby," "Thrill of a Lifetime," "Paris in Swing," "Sweetheart Time" (Coslow-Hollander), "It's Been a Whole Year," "If We Could Run the Country for a Day" (Yacht Club Boys).

Release Date: November 10, 1937. *Running Time:* 76 minutes.

With Buster Crabbe in *Thrill of a Lifetime.*

With Johnny Downs (second from left), Eleanore Whitney, The Yacht Club Boys, Leif Erickson, Buster Crabbe (back row), and Ben Blue and Judy Canova (foreground) in *Thrill of a Lifetime*.

SYNOPSIS

Howdy Nelson, playwright, runs a camp where Love is always in bloom. To it he invites the Yacht Club Boys, thinking they are theatrical producers interested in a play he has written. Dancers Stanley and Betty Jane bring their partner, Judy, to the camp to find a husband for her, since they can't marry until she is settled. When she falls in love with Skipper, Betty Jane and Stanley are jubilant.

Nelson's secretary, Gwen, is vainly in love with him, and the romantic setting finally get him down. In spite of all the romantic entanglements, Nelson puts on his show. A real producer sees it, is impressed, and signs up everyone from the Yacht Clubbers to Judy and Skipper for a Broadway show.

REVIEWS

"Ben Blue and Judy Canova . . . are out in front on this one. Paramount has plans to shove this duo right along and *Thrill of a Lifetime* gives them ample opportunity for their eccentric dancing and singing . . . . Fact that the whole thing is slightly naive is in its favor, because not too much is promised. Therefore, the clowning by Blue and Miss Canova, the singing by the Yacht Club Boys of their number, 'If We Could Run the Country for a Day,' and the dancing by Downs and Misses Whitney and Grable supply sufficient reason for audience satisfaction." (*Variety*)

"Ridiculous, second-rate entertainment. Incoordinated [*sic*], shallow slapstick, with comedy verging on vulgarity. Good cast wasted." (*National Society of New England Women*)

"A musical farce wherein a loosely woven story furnished a background for some pleasing dance numbers, lovely music and an exceptional chorus . . . more amusing and better numbers than some recent musicals." (*California Congress of Parents and Teachers*)

PRODUCTION NOTES AND COMMENTS

Thrill of a Lifetime was such a mixed-up mess that even Paramount's publicity wizards seemed at a loss to promote it effectively. To begin with, the Yacht Club Boys—an amiable, talented and experienced group heretofore confined to supporting roles and specialty

With Leif Erickson in *Thrill of a Lifetime.*

numbers—got star billing; the notion that these veteran film funsters could be expected to carry the picture was, at best, ill-advised. Doubly so, when one finally saw the film, which clearly seemed intended to launch hillbilly hoyden Judy Canova, lately of Warner Bros. (where, in the 1935 musical *In Caliente*, she had registered strongly with a comedic rendition of "The Lady in Red")

Grable, the nominal female lead, played one of those insufferably efficient movie secretaries who, upon removing her spectacles and letting her hair down, becomes a ravishing creature hotly pursued by her erstwhile employer—in this case, Leif Erickson. But she wasn't spotlighted by anything in the script, and merely got lost in the morass of footage devoted to Canova and the Yacht Clubbers. While some reviewers were perceptive enough to see in Canova an emerging talent, others dismissed the picture out of hand, and it limped through theatrical release without distinction.

COLLEGE SWING
(Paramount, 1938)

Credits: Producer, Lewis Gensler, director, Raoul Walsh; screenplay, Walter DeLeon and Francis Martin (uncredited: Preston Sturges), based on the story by Ted Lesser, adapted by Frederick Hazlitt Brennan; choreography, LeRoy Prinz; music director, Boris Morros; songs, Frank Loesser, Manning Sherwin, Burton Lane, and Hoagy Carmichael; camera, Victor Milner; editor, LeRoy Stone.

Cast: George Burns (George Jonas); Gracie Allen (Gracie Alden); Martha Raye (Mabel); Bob Hope (Bud Brady); Edward Everett Horton (Hubert Dash); Florence George (Ginna Ashburn); Ben Blue (Ben Volt); Betty Grable (Betty); Jackie Coogan (Jackie); John Payne (Martin Bates); Cecil Cunningham (Dean Sleets); Robert Cummings (Radio Announcer); Skinnay Ennis (Skinnay); The Slate Brothers (Themselves).

Songs: "I Fall in Love With You Every Day," "What a Rumba Does to Romance," "You're a Natural," "The Old School Bell" (Loesser-Sherwin), "Moments Like This," "How 'Dja Like to Love Me?," "What Did Romeo Say to Juliet?" (Loesser-Lane), "College Swing" (Loesser-Carmichael).

Release Date: April 28, 1938. *Running Time:* 86 minutes.

SYNOPSIS

Gracie Alden may be the dumbest student in Alden College, but all she has to do is pass an examination and she can run the place to suit herself. According to the will of the college's founder, a remote ancestor of Gracie's who lived two centuries ago, the first female member of the Alden family to pass an examination inherits the property.

A clever young student, Bud Brady, who sees a chance to start an educational revolution and make himself a fortune at the same time, sets out to help Gracie prepare for the fateful test. Through the simple device of stealing the questions beforehand, he prepares his backward student perfectly. At the examination, Gracie hits every question right on the nose, astonishing the entire faculty, and especially the leader of the trustees, Hubert Dash, a woman-hating millionaire. Although it means havoc, the terms of the will must be fulfilled, and the university is handed over to Gracie.

With Jackie Coogan (left) and Skinnay Ennis in *College Swing.*

With Skinnay Ennis (reading paper), Florence George, and John Payne in *College Swing*.

Under Gracie's administration, "liberal education" is so liberalized that even Bud is surprised. The new owner takes upon herself the coveted post of Dean of Men, assembles a faculty of madcap clowns, appoints Bud "Professor of Applied Romance," and makes his a required course.

Meanwhile, Dash becomes suspicious and attempts to uncover the trickery used by Gracie and Bud to attain power. While Dash applies himself to solving the mystery, Gracie applies herself to Dash, and, after a gay excursion through the local night clubs and countryside, teaches the woman-hater something about romance. But he goes ahead with his plans to oust her, and forces her to take the examination for the second time. Although Bud tries to fix things again by broadcasting the answers to her, the machinery breaks down and Gracie is left stranded in front of her examiners. Faced with the loss of the college, Gracie announces that she has something to make up for it—a husband! When Dash anxiously asks her to name her spouse to the examiners, she replies that it is the trustee himself, who eloped with her during one of their wild parties. The educational revolution comes to a halt while Gracie surrenders the college to Dash and he surrenders himself to Gracie.

REVIEWS

"A musical extravaganza which, in spite of a varied cast of talented actors, falls below the standard of present-day motion pictures. A clever beginning is soon lost in a maze of jerky and disconnected scenes, with a definite tendency to vulgarity. If you like Martha Raye and night club entertainment, you will enjoy; otherwise, stay away." (*American Legion Auxiliary*)

"Elaborately staged, farcical melange of music, both tuneful and swing, lovely settings, some graceful dancing, all interspersed with raucous slapstick comedy and burlesque. The story . . . is a mere thread which is soon lost in the maze of events that follow." (*General Federation of Women's Clubs*)

"[P]oor musical. Only the youthful tempo of the sum total and the marquee values of Burns and Allen, Martha Raye, Edward Everett Horton, Jackie Coogan, et al, will get it attention. It's a medley of vaude specialties, bits and numbers strung together in not too happy a manner. Blend of the campus with the 52nd street idiom makes for weird plot results. Betty Grable does her usual soubret; Jackie Coogan's contribution is more or less a bit . . . . Of

A *College Swing* group shot. Standing (from left): Bob Hope, Ben Blue, John Payne. Seated (from left): Gracie Allen, Martha Raye, George Burns, Grable, and Florence George.

With Skinnay Ennis and Florence George, shooting a scene for *College Swing*.

the comedy, it's a pot pourri of everything from the hokum multiplication and subdivision business to a reprise of the English-inflected 'thenk-ya!' type of running gag. In between, Gracie Allen rings in an Irish reel, which about tops everything." (*Variety*)

PRODUCTION NOTES AND COMMENTARY

Back on campus once again, Grable did her level best to make it appear as though she was thrilled to be part of this plotless, witless musicomedy—in retrospect, making her a much better actress than anyone suspected at the time. Although she did some fancy stepping in the "College Swing" production number (in which she appeared with then-husband Jackie Coogan), Betty was overshadowed, as in *Pigskin Parade*, by an all-star lineup that included Burns and Allen, Bob Hope, and Martha Raye.

Despite the efforts of a handful of writers (including an uncredited Preston Sturges), *College Swing* was even lighter in the plot department than the studio's previous campus capers, and placed the full burden of success on the shoulders of its accomplished cast—which, as it developed, weren't up to carrying the load. Feeble scripting and hamfisted direction (the latter contributed by Raoul Walsh, whose heart clearly wasn't in his work) obviously hampered the players, and the songs by Frank Loesser, Burton Lane, and Hoagy Carmichael, while pleasant enough, lacked the "oomph" needed to make them memorable.

GIVE ME A SAILOR
(Paramount, 1938)

Credits: Producer, Jeff Lazarus; associate producer, Paul Jones; director, Elliott Nugent; screenplay, Doris Anderson and Frank Butler, based on the play by Anne Nichols; songs, Ralph Rainger and Leo Robin; choreography, LeRoy Prinz; music director, Boris Morros; art directors, Hans Dreier and Earl Hedrick; camera, Victor Milner, William Shea.

Cast: Martha Raye (Letty Larkin); Bob Hope (Jim Brewster);

With Bob Hope, Jack Whiting (front), J.C. Nugent, Nana Bryant, and Clarence Kolb (rear) in *Give Me a Sailor.*

Betty Grable (Nancy Larkin); J. C. Nugent (Mr. Larkin); Jack Whiting (Walter Brewster); Clarence Kolb (Captain Tallant); Nana Bryant (Mrs. Brewster); Emerson Treacy (Meryl); Bonnie Jean Churchill (Ethel May Brewster); Kathleen Lockhart (Mrs. Hawks); Ralph Sanford (Ice Man); Edward Earle (First Businessman); Eddie Kane (Second Businessman).

Songs: "What Goes On Here in My Heart?," "The US and You," "A Litle Kiss at Twilight," "It Don't Make Sense" (Rainger-Robin).

Release Date: August 19, 1938. *Running Time:* 80 minutes.

SYNOPSIS

Ensign Jim Brewster and Lt. Walt Brewster are brothers, as well as rivals for Nancy Larkin from San Francisco. Jim's ace-in-the-hole is the compact he made with Nancy's ugly duckling sister Letty, by which she promised to help him win Nancy if he helps her win Walter. Hearing that Walt plans to drive to the remote fishing camp of Captain Tallant, Letty stows away in the rumble seat. She arrives in camp only to find Jim has been presuaded by Nan to take Walt's place in the errand. Caught in a downpour, they seek refuge in a country inn, are caught there, and are forced into an unwelcome engagement.

Letty wins a "Most Beautiful Legs" contest the day before the wedding; it turns out that the picture was submitted by a friend without her knowledge. Overnight she becomes a celebrity. Jim breaks the engagement, and announces that Walter is Letty's real fiance. Their wedding is to be the crowning event of San Francisco's "Navy Day," but Letty leaves Walt and breaks up Jim and Nan, who are about to elope. The pairings are reversed.

REVIEWS

"Farce co-starring Martha Raye and Bob Hope will probably do fair at the wicket, but will do no great shaking of laughs out of 'em. Best bet for draw will be the stars' pull at the b.o. Business and lines meted out to both Miss Raye and Hope are mediocre, and what scoring is done and laughs levied are occasioned by her bag of trouping tricks and his facility at handling light lines and situations . . . . Miss Grable has an unsympathetic role . . . . " (*Variety*)

"In this comedy of love in the navy, the ugly duckling becomes a Cinderella through the accidental photograph of her yum-yum legs instead of her yum-yum cake. Having won the legs contest, Letty gets her choice of radio and motion picture contracts and of lovers. After testing the kissing ability of a naval officer, she prefers a sailor. Many comic situations will make this entertaining for adults." (*California Congress of Parents and Teachers*)

With Martha Raye in *Give Me a Sailor.*

"Fairly amusing farce of Cinderella theme wherein a conniving girl ensnares her generous sister's affinity until the latter enters a beauty contest. Martha Raye's best picture." (*Daughters of the American Revolution*)

PRODUCTION NOTES AND COMMENTS

Playing second fiddle to Bob Hope and Martha Raye for the second picture in a row, Grable here drew one of the most disagreeable assignments of her Paramount tenure. To begin with, her character as scripted was clearly unsympathetic, and Elliott Nugent's direction amplified the role's negative aspects while accomplishing the amazing feat of portraying the brassy, big-mouthed Raye as a Cinderella type. Even more incredibly, the plot demanded that audiences believe Raye's legs to be prettier than Grable's, a suspension of disbelief that must have taxed even the most open-minded moviegoers. Ralph Rainger and Leo Robin, who contributed many of Grable's best-remembered screen songs, were at a loss to produce any hit tunes for this routine programmer, which got by solely on the box-office strength of its leads.

CAMPUS CONFESSIONS
(Paramount, 1938)

Credits: Associate producer, William Thomas; director, George Archainbaud; screenplay, Lloyd Corrigan and Erwin Gelsey; art directors, Hans Dreier and William Flannery; music director, Boris Morros; camera, Henry Sharp; editor, Stuart Gilmore.

Cast: Betty Grable (Joyce Gilmore); Eleanore Whitney (Susie Quinn); William Henry (Wayne Atterbury, Jr.); Fritz Feld ("Lady Macbeth"); John Arledge (Freddy Fry); Thurston Hall (Deal Wilton); Roy Gordon (Coach Parker);

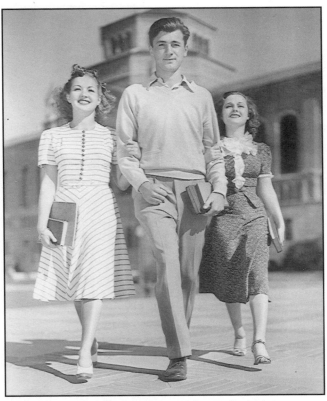

With Hank Luisetti and Eleanore Whitney in *Campus Confessions*.

Sunbathing between takes on *Campus Confessions*.

Lane Chandler (Buck Hogan); Matty Kemp (Ed Riggs); Sumner Gitchell ("Blimp" Garrett); Hank Luisetti (Himself).

Release Date: September 19, 1938. *Running Time:* 67 minutes.

SYNOPSIS

Due to the theory of Wayne Atterbury Sr. that college should concentrate on training the mind, Middleton College, which his millions are supporting, has never won a single athletic victory. When Atterbury's son, Wayne Jr., enters Middleton, his agreement with his father's views immediately gets him in wrong with the rest of the students, notably Joyce Gilmore, beautiful reporter for the school paper. Atterbury decides to remove his son from Middleton, but Wayne, stung by Joyce's taunts, insists on remaining and fighting it through. Wayne tries to ingratiate himself with his fellow frosh by tossing a swank party for them, but come party-time he finds himself alone, while the rest of the gang is down on the creek having a weenie roast.

Hank Luisetti, Middleton's basketball star, is Wayne's only friend, and Wayne invites him and the rest of the squad to practice at the family estate during the summer while his father is away. They discover that Wayne is a natural-born basketball player and he makes the team, working out a Atterbury-Luisetti combination that's an unbeatable scoring setup. The team sweeps through its schedule victoriously up to the eve of the final "big" game with State. Old Man Atterbury returns home, furious that Wayne has grown interested in athletics. He demands that the State game be cancelled, but the Dean suggests that he'll give Luisetti a special math quiz and flunk him to make him ineligible, which will undoubtedly cost Middleton the game and cool its athletic fever. Wayne refuses to speak to his father, who follows the team to the gym. During the game, Atterbury gets excited, starts rooting for Middleton, and learns from Joyce that the breakup of the Wayne-Hank combination is responsible for the team's poor showing. Atterbury orders an impromptu quiz for the bench-warming Luisetti, who passes, goes back into the lineup, and spurs the team to victory.

REVIEWS

"Hank Luisetti, while not the hero, is the chief asset of this picture. A novice in acting, he is the world's best performer on the basketball floor, and when he raises the score 21 points in six minutes to win the game for the home team, there is little or no exaggeration of his amazing skill. The college atmosphere is not authentic but is no worse than that of the usual campus comedy." (*Women's University Club*)

With Hank Luisetti in *Campus Confessions.*

"[F]ast-paced and sparkling collegiate comedy. It's a programmer which, in spots where basketball is popular, should draw substantially, especially in college and high-school circles. Prowess of Luisetti with the casaba is neatly displayed. A well-chosen cast is lacking in marquee names, but it performs adequately with William Henry, outstander, showing possbilities of developing strongly. [It] has refreshing twists and gags new to rah-rah films, plus a fast clip maintained after initial reel. This overcomes story weaknesses." (*Variety*)

PRODUCTION NOTES AND COMMENTS

Grable's musical talents were completely overlooked in this modest but surprisingly entertaining low-budget offering, the first film in which she had top billing. Once again cast in the Betty Co-Ed mold, she supplied a peppy portrayal of the perky collegiate journalist who taunts smug rich kid William Henry. Contemporary reviewers

With William Henry in *Campus Confessions.*

were, for the most part, favorably impressed with Henry's own performance; he had been similarly cast before and, by the time of *Campus Confessions*, was already well practiced in such priggish characterizations. Other reviews doted on another kind of performance, that of basketball whiz Hank Luisetti, who dazzled moviegoers with his court proficiency if not his histrionic ability. In fact, Paramount slanted most of the picture's written publicity around Luisetti, while making sure that Grable's bathing-suited form adorned most of the stills, posters, and ad mats. *Campus Confessions* was reasonably well received but, conceived and marketed as the bottom half of a double bill, didn't break out of B-picture class.

MAN ABOUT TOWN
(Paramount, 1939)

Credits: Producer, Arthur Hornblow, Jr.; director, Mark Sandrich; screenplay, Morrie Ryskind, based on the story by Ryskind, Allan Scott, and Zion Meyers; music director, Victor Young; art directors, Hans Dreier, Robert Usher; songs, Frank Loesser and Frederick Hollander, Leo Robin and Ralph Rainger, Loesser and Matt Malneck; camera, Ted Tetzlaff; editor, LeRoy Stone.

Cast: Jack Benny (Bob Temple); Dorothy Lamour (Diana Wilson); Edward Arnold (Sir John Arlington); Binnie Barns (Lady Arlington); Phil Harris (Ted Nash); Eddie Anderson (Rochester); Monty Woolley (M. Dubois); Isabel Jeans (Mme. Dubois); Betty Grable (Susan); E. E. Clive (Hotchkiss); Leonard Mudie (Gibson); Pina Troupe (Themselves): Peggy Stewart (Mary); Patti Sacks (Jane); Matty Maineck Orchestra and the Merrill Abbott Dancers (Themselves).

Songs: "Fidgety Joe" (Loesser-Malneck), "Strange Enchantment," "That Sentimental Sandwich" (Loesser-Hollander), "Bluebirds in the Moonlight" (Rainger-Robin).

Release Date: July 7, 1939. *Running Time:* 85 minutes.

SYNOPSIS

Theatrical producer Bob Temple, who has preceded his troupe to London in order to make plans for presenting a show, has been tagged by the showgirls as a kind, respectable bore. He privately yearns to be known as a ladykiller, a secret shared by his valet Rochester. In love with his singing star, Diana Wilson, Bob is depressed when she comes to town with handsome, outgoing Ted Nash in tow. Rochester suggests Bob make Diana jealous by

From left: Binnie Barnes, Isabel Jeans, Jack Benny, Dorothy Lamour, Edward Arnold, and Monty Woolley in *Man About Town*.

seeing other women. His mild flirtations with Lady Arlington and Madamoiselle Dubois yield him a black eye, but also prompts the women to use his attentions to make their husbands jealous. Diana and Ted are skeptical when Lady Arlington invites Bob to her country place for the weekend, little realizing her true intent. Bob's plans backfire, leaving an outraged Sir John Arlington ready to make mincemeat of him before Rochester cleverly intervenes. Once a worried Diana learns that Bob has only been trying to impress her, she realizes that she really does love him, and all ends happily.

REVIEWS

"*Man About Town* has its entertaining and laugh moments, but is burdened with several production numbers and three songs that slow things down considerably. Given hypo of Benny's radio plugs, picture will get by for nominal biz in the keys, and give a good account of itself in the subsequent runs. Good and substantial family fare with easily understandable comedy lines and situations. Despite an episodic script, which uses blackout situations in numerous spots, director Mark Sandrich keeps the pace moving along steadily . . . . Betty Grable is decorative in [a] brief appearance." (*Variety*)

"Morrie Ryskind and Allan Scott have turned out a script steeped in the heady lunacies of farce and laced with a bumper of wit. Mark Sandrich, who became a national institution when he made Astaire and Rogers one, has directed it skillfully, weaving in his song, dance and spectacle numbers without suggesting that the story has taken the afternoon off . . . . It is, in sum, a happy occasion for all concerned, including the audience." (*New York Times*)

PRODUCTION NOTES AND COMMENTS

Fate played a cruel trick on Grable who, after toiling diligently in undistinguished programmers for Paramount, finally won the female lead in a prestige picture for the studio, only to surrender it to Dorothy Lamour after being stricken suddenly with appendicitis. Her one completed number, the energetic "Fidgety Joe," was left in the final film, making some reviewers puzzled by the inclusion of her character, which seemed extraneous to the plot.

Airwaves star Benny was accompanied by radio regulars Phil Harris and Rochester, and while they all appeared to better advantage as themselves—or, rather, in their radio personas—in *Buck Benny Rides Again* (1940), they certainly made favorable impressions with moviegoers in *Man About Town*. (Benny had actually made his starring screen debut in 1929's *Medicine Man*,

Publicity shot for *Man About Town*.

and Harris made his in 1933's *Melody Cruise*, which featured Grable in a small role.) Not quite a runaway hit, it established Benny as a formidable draw and paved the way for future screen successes. For Grable, though, it represented a lost opportunity and even spelled the beginning of the end for her at Paramount; after one more minor film, she left the studio, never to return.

In *Man About Town* with chorus girls.

From left: Richard Denning, John Hartley, Jackie Coogan, and Buster Crabbe with Grable in *Million Dollar Legs*.

MILLION DOLLAR LEGS

(Paramount, 1939)

Credits: Director, Nick Grinde; screenplay, Lewis Foster and Richard English, from a story by Foster; camera, Harry Fischbeck; editor, Stuart Gilmore.

Cast: Betty Grable (Carol Parker); John Hartley (Greg Melton); Donald O'Connor (Sticky Boone); Jackie Coogan (Russ Simpson); Buster Crabbe (Coach Baxter); Peter Hayes (Freddie Fry); Dorothea Kent (Susie Quinn); Thurston Hall (Gregory Melton, Sr.); Roy Gordon (Deal Wixby); Matty Kemp (Ed Riggs); William Tracy (Egghead Jackson); Joyce Matthews (Bunny); Russ Clark (Referee); Wallace Rairden (Crandall); John Hart (Haldeman); Anthony March (MacDonald); Rob Ireland (Hall); Roger Laswell (Alden); Si Jenks (Bus Driver); Bill Conselman, Jr. (Husky Student); Byron Foulger (Mr. Daly); Billy Gilbert (Schultz); Tom Dugan (Man); George Anderson (President Greene).

Release Date: July 14, 1939. *Running Time:* 65 minutes.

SYNOPSIS

College student Greg Melton, Jr. is a first-rate athlete, but his wealthy, overly enthusiastic father believes that a wise investiture of money is needed to cinch his son's place on the struggling crew team. The elder Melton lavishes funds upon the campus, much to Greg's chagrin: He doesn't want to be pegged as a spoiled rich kid getting by on his family's money. His sweetheart, campus heart-throb Carol Parker, shares Greg's sentiments. Meanwhile, fellow student and genial con-man Freddie Fry—who collects 10 percent graft on the campus hot-dog concession—comes up with a brainstorm to finance the purchase of new boat shells. He gets a hot tip on a horse race and pools student money for a bet. The long shot pays off handsomely, enabling Freddie and his pals to buy the needed equipment. With the help of Coach Baxter—and despite some romantic complications with Carol—Greg leads the team to a dramatic victory over its traditional rival.

REVIEWS

"A trim little affair which moves along at a merry clip tossing off nifties in the vernacular of the current collegiate generation. There is room to doubt that it will wholly please the palates of elders, but it will unquestionably tickle the younger majorities, to whose taste it is patterned, and will capably augment a bill needing balancing lightness and speed.

"The film practices a mild deceit in title, unless it is so justified by one longshot of Betty Grable's sightly under-

With John Hartley in *Million Dollar Legs.*

pinnings. However, said title would seem to be all to the good on the marquee. With Miss Grable is combined the talents of a personable and fairly capable roomful of collegians who manage to make the half-mad sequence of co-educational antics jell with satisfying comedy effect. It is fresh stuff [and] has more than the usual quota of bright quips and surprising twists." (*Hollywood Reporter*)

"Latest collegiate comedy by Paramount is light and fluffy fare for youthful audiences of high school and college age. Devoid of marquee strength, picture will slip in as lower bracketer in the subsequent duals . . . . Major fault of the picture is title misnomer. Tab indicates to audiences it's a girly leg show—instead, it parades the hefty gams of college athletes with crew aspirations. The underpinning display is more sturdy than shapely . . . . Betty Grable and John Hartley provide mild romantic interest, with Dorothea Kent seen briefly in some flapper comedy episodes." (*Variety*)

PRODUCTION NOTES AND COMMENTS

Million Dollar Legs, Betty Grable's last Paramount film, was yet another collegiate comedy geared for undiscriminating B-picture audiences, and while it outstripped some of its predecessors in entertainment value, it also hastened the departure of Grable from Hollywood. Interestingly enough, although the film's publicity

A Paramount publicity portrait.

capitalized on the already-celebrated Grable gams, the title referred to the legs of the racehorse on which the college kids bet all their money. In fact, while Betty had done more posing for leg-art photos than anything else during her stay at Paramount, she didn't acquire the "gal with the million-dollar legs" nickname until she went to Fox. Like her previous campus comedy, *Million Dollar Legs* made no demands on Grable's terpsichorean talents, although a reasonably bright script and winning performances by the cast (especially Peter Lind Hayes, singled out by most critics for his supercharged trouping) punched up the comedy enough to render musical interpolations unnecessary.

THE DAY THE BOOKIES WEPT

(RKO Radio, 1939)

Credits: Producer, Robert Sisk; director, Leslie Goodwin; screenplay, Bert Granet and George Jeske, based on the story *Crazy over Pigeons* by Daniel Fuchs; art director, Van Nest Polglase; music director, Arthur Horton; special effects, Vernon L. Walker; camera, Jack MacKenzie; editor, Desmond Marquette.

Cast: Joe Penner (Ernest Ambrose); Betty Grable (Ina Firpo); Richard Lane (Ramsey Firpo); Tom Kennedy (Pinky Brophy); Thurston Hall (Colonel March); Bernadene Hayes

(Margie); Carol Hughes (Patsy March); William Wright (Harry); Prince Albert (The Horse).

Release Date: September 15, 1939. *Running Time:* 64 minutes.

SYNOPSIS

A group of taxi drivers, who are perpetually broke owing to their propensity for playing the ponies, are crying the blues one day when they hit upon an idea: Why not pool their money, buy their own racehorse, and have someone train it to be a winner? The job falls to an eccentric but astute pidgeon-fancier named Ernest, who is at first reluctant to accept the responsibility. He's finally persuaded to take on the job, buying a horse named Hiccup (out of Bourbon, by Distillery). Ernest does his best to groom Hiccup for stardom, but the horse loses every race. Moreover, the nag has a peculiar hereditary trait: He prefers booze to water. A blustery old Kentuckian, the Colonel, remembers this quirk, and just before a big race, Hiccup is treated to a keg of beer left in the stable. He wins the race in a walk—or, that is, a stagger—bringing tears to the eyes of the bookies who felt themselves safe in accepting bets on a sure loser. Ernest and his vis-a-vis Ina, along with the cab drivers, win a bundle on the event.

REVIEWS

"Being a sucker for a long shot, nothing delights us more than seeing . . . a Joe Penner comedy being rated in these columns as one of the funniest shows of the season. Until today, the best we've ever said about Mr. Penner's comic talents was that they came to the square root of zero . . . now we take it back. Every time he opens his mouth the script-writers put a good line into it . . . . It's all

With Carol Hughes and Thurston Hall in *The Day the Bookies Wept.*

With Edward Earle (left), Joe Penner, and Richard Lane in *The Day the Bookies Wept*.

very silly, but heaps of fun, and it has been capitally played . . . ." (*New York Times*)

"This is a very entertaining little comedy . . . it will afford more than considerable support as the No. 2 feature and, being a laugh-getter, is ideal where the other picture is drama or spectacle. Producer [Robert] Sisk has paced *Bookies* briskly, dotting the action carefully with the laughs, never letting the romantic element get too serious or too far away from the basic purpose of the picture, which is comedy. Penner is excellent and times his laughs well, while for able support he has Betty Grable . . . plus others. Not much was spent on this picture, but it points to making a good profit." (*Variety*)

PRODUCTION NOTES AND COMMENTS

Nobody expected very much of *The Day the Bookies Wept*. To begin with, it was just a B picture brought in for

$162,000, and clearly aimed at the bottom half of the double bill. (In fact, it was the cheapest picture Grable had made since *Don't Turn 'Em Loose*, her previous RKO release.) More importantly—or *un*importantly, depending on how one felt—it was the next-to-last starring vehicle of radio favorite Joe Penner, whose film following had eroded steadily since his promising debut at Paramount just five years earlier. The rather obnoxious comedian had worn out his welcome at the nation's ticket windows . . . or so it seemed.

The RKO Bs ramrodded by producer Robert Sisk were an uneven lot at best, but occasionally a first-rate little picture stood out in bold relief. Thanks to a clever script by Bert Granet and George Jeske, brisk direction by prolific megger Leslie Goodwins, and engaging performances from the cast, *Bookies* was one such programmer, bringing RKO some $263,000 in film rental for a profit of about $100,000. Amazingly, the film elicited complementary reviews from most reviewers, even those big-city sophisticates to whom Penner had always been anathema. Betty Grable didn't have very much to do opposite the scene-stealing Penner, but she looked pert and pretty and gave a good accounting of herself. This was, however, the last film she made before leaving Hollywood for Broadway, where she scored a personal triumph in *DuBarry Was a Lady*.

DOWN ARGENTINE WAY
(20th Century-Fox, 1940)

Credits: Producer, Darryl F. Zanuck; associate producer, Harry Joe Brown; director, Irving Cummings; screenplay, Darrell Ware and Karl Tunberg, based on the story by Rian James and Ralph Spence; music director, Emil Newman; songs, Mack Gordon and Harry Warren; choreography, Nick Castle and Geneva Sawyer; art directors, Richard Day and Joseph C. Wright; camera, Leon Shamroy and Ray Rennahan; editor, Barbara McLean.

In *Down Argentine Way.*

Cast: Don Ameche (Richard Quintana); Betty Grable (Glenda Crawford); Carmen Miranda (Herself); Charlotte Greenwood (Binnie Crawford); J. Carroll Naish (Casiano); Henry Stephenson (Don Diego Quintana); Kay Aldridge (Helen Carson); Leonid Kinskey (Tito Acuna); Chris-Pin Martin (Esteban); Robert Conway (Jimmy Blake); Bobby Stone (Panchito); Charles Judels (Ambassador); Edward Fielding (Crawford); Edward Conrad (Anastasio); Frank Puglia (Montero); Nicholas Brothers (Themselves); Thomas and Catherine Dowling (Themselves); Six Hits and A Miss (Themselves); Flores Brothers (Themselves); Bando de Luna (Themselves).

Songs: "Down Argentine Way," "Sing to Your Senorita," "Two Dreams Met," "Nenita" (Gordon-Warren), "South American Way" (Dubin-McHugh), "Doin' the Conga" (Gene Rose).

Release Date: Oct. 11, 1940. *Running Time:* 90 minutes.

SYNOPSIS

Argentinian horse breeder Don Diego Quintana, whose thoroughbreds are internationally renowned, sends his handsome son Ricardo to the United States to broker a deal with a wealthy New York heiress who "collects" blue-ribbon jumpers. Ricardo arrives in the States with a consignment, but when his father learns that the girl is Glenda Crawford, he refuses to honor the deal. Glenda's father likewise voices his disapproval. It develops that there is a long-standing feud between the Quintanas and the Crawfords. This baffles the young people, bound by family traditions but undeniably attracted to each other. When Ricardo returns home, Glenda elects to follow him to Argentina on a "vacation," enlisting her aunt Binnie as a chaperone. She attempts, with Ricardo's help, to win over the elder Quintana and end the feud, which is discovered to have been foolish and unnecessary. While pursuing this goal, Glenda falls in love with the colorful and romantic South American lifestyle, and is treated to the exotic rhythms of the conga and rumba, courtesy of popular nightclub entertainer Carmen Miranda. Glenda finally charms Don Diego, and also convinces him that his prize jumper is also a first-rate flat racer.

REVIEWS

"Gay, colorful, exciting and tuneful, this musical comedy is gilt-edged entertainment that can be sold to heavy returns in any type theater . . . easily ranks way up front in the long parade of musicomedies the screen has known. The shapely Betty Grable [makes] a triumphant return to the screen as love interest opposite Don Ameche." (*Film Daily*)

In *Down Argentine Way,* her first starring vehicle.

With Don Ameche (left) and J. Carrol Naish in *Down Argentine Way.*

"Lavish, gay, brilliantly colorful . . . so rich in entertainment values that it has all the earmarks of an unqualified box-office winner. Betty Grable, more attractive than ever, her talents enhanced by experience, in her most important role to date gives the best performance of her career and never was so beautifully photographed." (*Hollywood Reporter*)

"Don Ameche, ranking personality in the cast, is seen as an Argentine who sings now and again between horse trades to an American heiress portrayed by Betty Grable, recipient of much mention by the columnists for her showing in this attraction . . . . This is an item for the rhumba and conga trade, a study in Technicolor of the Latin rhythms which have come into popularity . . . ." (*Motion Picture Herald*)

"Should click in a big way in the southern hemisphere, and will probably inspire a new cycle of pictures laid in the Amazon, pampas and Andes regions. Carmen Miranda['s] showmanship, presentation and delivery are topnotch.

Showstoppers are uncovered in the dance team of the Nicholas Bros., who provide a routine of acrobatic taps that shines as one of the best specialties in the picture. Miss Grable is light on vocal abilities, which, however, are overcome by her dances and beauty under the cameras." (*Variety*)

PRODUCTION NOTES AND COMMENTS

Originally announced to the trade press in the fall of 1939 as *Down Rio Way,* a vehicle for top Fox star Alice Faye, *Down Argentine Way* marked a turning point in Grable's career. In 1940 she had been signed to a Fox contract by Darryl Zanuck but allowed to appear in the Broadway production of *Du Barry Was a Lady,* in which she won surprisingly good reviews. When Faye was stricken with appendicitis just days before production was to have begun, Zanuck summoned Grable back to Hollywood at once to replace her.

It was something of a gamble, as Zanuck was banking

With Naish, Henry Stephenson, and Ameche in *Down Argentine Way.*

With Ameche in *Down Argentine Way.*

on the picture to open up for Fox the lucrative Latin American markets—which took on additional importance as World War II closed off European markets. Even though Grable was a hit on Broadway, featuring her in an expensive Technicolor musical represented a major move for the studio.

Fortunately, she rose to the challenge. With little time to prepare before the commencement of shooting, she worked 14-hour days for a week, learning her lines, rehearsing her numbers, and enduring seemingly endless costume fittings. The production itself was an arduous one. It took nearly ten months for two units to shoot the picture, making it the company's longest shooting schedule up to that time. The second unit shot over 20,000 feet of film (more than three hours' worth) during its month-long stay in South America, and although most of it never saw use in the picture, it provided invaluable coverage for studio scenes involving rear-screen projection. Hollywood artifice took care of the rest: three-fourths of the film was shot outdoors on 32 different locations in Southern California.

There was another problem: Miranda's unbreakable contract with a New York night club forced the studio to send the second unit back east to shoot her numbers there for later interpolation into the finished film. This extra expense pushed its negative cost to nearly $800,000.

Down Argentine Way was an unqualified success, not only scoring high with American audiences, but accomplishing its mission as a breakthrough film to the Latin American market, thanks largely to the participation of Carmen Miranda. Most importantly, though, it launched Grable as a Fox star; she won rave reviews from critics both in the trade and the major consumer media, with only *Variety* (notoriously conservative in its appraisal of new talent) tempering its praise of her.

In *Tin Pan Alley*.

TIN PAN ALLEY
(20th Century-Fox, 1940)

Credits: Producer, Darryl F. Zanuck; associate producer, Kenneth Macgowan; director, Walter Lang; screenplay, Robert Ellis and Helen Logan, based on the story by Pamela Harris; song (new), Mack Gordon and Harry Warren; music director, Alfred Newman; choreography; Seymour Felix; camera, Leon Shamroy; editor, Walter Thompson.

Cast: Alice Faye (Katie Blane); Betty Grable (Lily Blane); Jack Oakie (Harry Calhoun); John Payne (Skeets Harrigan); Allen Jenkins (Sgt. Casey); Esther Ralston (Nora Bayes); Harold and Fayard Nicholas (Dance Specialty); Ben Carter (Boy); John Loder (Reggie Carstair); Elisha Cook, Jr. (Joe Codd); Fred Keating (Harvey Raymond); Billy Gilbert (Sheik); Lillian Porter (Telephone Operator); Brian Sisters (Specialty); Robert Brothers (Specialty); Princess Vanessa Ammon (Specialty); Tyler Brooke (Bert Melville); Hal K. Dawson (Hotel Clerk); William B. Davidson (Hotel Manager); Lionel Pape (Lord Stanley); Billy Bevan (Doorman); Dewey Robinson (Dumb Guy); Robert Emmett Keane (Manager); John Sheehan (Announcer); George Watts (Mike Buckner); Jack Roper (Nick Palerno): James Flavin (Sergeant); Franklin Farnum (Man in Audience); Harry Strang (Doughboy).

Songs: "You Say the Sweetest Things, Baby" (Gordon-Warren), "K-K-K-Katy" (Geoffrey O'Hara), "America, I Love You" (Edgar Leslie, Archie Gottler), "Goodbye, Broadway, Hello, France" (Francis Riesner, Benny Davis, Billy Baskette), "Moonlight Bay" (Edward Madden, Percy Wenrich), "Honeysuckle Rose" (Andy Razaf, Fats Waller), "Moonlight and Roses" (Ben Black, Neil Moret, Edwin H. Lemare), "The Sheik of Araby" (Harry B. Smith, Francis Wheeler, Ted Snyder).

Release Date: November 1, 1940. *Running Time:* 94 minutes.

SYNOPSIS

Fledgling songwriters Skeets Harrigan and Harry Calhoun are broke and about to be evicted from their Tin Pan Alley office when Harry persuades his old friends and fellow vaudeville troupers, Katie and Lily Blane, to introduce one of his songs in their act. The tune flops again, but the tryout serves to introduce the girls to Skeets, and Katie takes a shine to him immediately. She even fronts him money to buy a song she plugs around town, making it a big success and launching the boys' song-publishing company.

Although Katie and Skeets have a rocky relationship, she sticks with the boys while Lily goes to London, where she becomes a solo star for impresario Harvey Raymond.

With Jack Oakie, Alice Faye, and John Payne in *Tin Pan Alley*.

In the turbulent days just before America's entry into World War I, Skeets promises Katie she can introduce his new patriotic song at a prestigious benefit, but renegs on the deal when famous stage star Nora Bayes requests the tune for the same benefit. Heartbroken, Katie leaves Skeets for good and joins Lily in London.

Without Katie, Skeets loses his drive and the business gradually declines. When war is declared, Skeets and Harry join the army and are sent overseas. By this time Katie and Lily are performing together again, and they encounter the boys in London after a show. Skeets and Katie reaffirm their love for each other just before the boys leave for the front and, happily, are reunited back in New York after the war.

REVIEWS

"*Tin Pan Alley* has . . . a timeliness in its revival of such songs as 'America, I Love You' and 'Goodbye, Broadway, Hello, France,' which proved its effectiveness by producing waves of applause on the occasion of its preview in Hollywood. Alice Faye . . . adds to the singing of songs a bit of dancing thereto, sharing two numbers with Betty Grable, the songs being Hawaiian and Turkish, the costumes and execution to match." (*Motion Picture Herald*)

"The teaming of Alice Faye and Betty Grable was a dangerous piece of casting in that one might be reckoned to spoil the show for the other, but this was not the case. There was perfect balance to their assignments, each doing her top work in individual scenes . . . . Alice sang beautifully and little Grable grabbed sustained looks in her song numbers and particularly in those cute little wiggles she put into most of her dances." (*Hollywood Reporter*)

"If *Tin Pan Alley* is inevitably episodic and doesn't strain any of the conventions set by such precursors as *Alexander's Ragtime Band* it still is full-bodied popular entertainment because it is directed with verve and deftly

In a cut number from *Tin Pan Alley.*

With Jack Oakie in *Tin Pan Alley.*

With Alice Faye in *Tin Pan Alley.*

assembled. [T]he Misses Faye and Grable [have] a chance for some fettlesome wriggling through several big numbers—an occupation in which they are more adept than in acting." (*New York Times*)

PRODUCTION NOTES AND COMMENTS

Originally intended as a followup to Fox's enormously successful *Alexander's Ragtime Band, Tin Pan Alley* was to have reunited that film's stars, Faye, Tyrone Power and Don Ameche; scheduling conflicts found the male leads committed to other productions, so John Payne and Jack Oakie took their places. A million-dollar production that spared no expense in recreating pre-World War I New York City, it more than recouped Fox's investment.

Even Hollywood insiders and columnists were surprised by Darryl Zanuck's casting of Grable, who had won stardom after the success of *Down Argentine Way*, with Faye, the undisputed queen of the Fox lot. But a much-anticipated feud between the stars never materialized, and the always gracious Faye actually presented Grable with several gifts—including a portable radio—during shooting.

Although Betty's chores were not as arduous as her co-star's, she labored under considerable stress. For one thing, her divorce from Jackie Coogan was underway (she won her freedom during the picture's last weeks of shooting). More importantly, under an agreement that pre-dated her Fox contract, she was committed to a two-week engagement at a Chicago theater that loomed prominently as shooting progressed. The unit worked late several nights and on two Sundays to complete her scenes, and although Betty caught a bad cold during the closing days of principal photography, she pushed herself to finish on time.

Tin Pan Alley gave Alice Faye most of the best songs—and the romantic interest as well—but Grable fared extremely well as the youthful, flirtatious trouper who earned solo stardom after leaving the sister act. She more than held her own with Faye in their numbers together, revealing a trimmer figure in grass skirt and harem costume, and really shined in her big production number, "Honeysuckle Rose." Reviewers took especial notice of the balance between the two distaff stars: They appreciated Faye's dreamy vocalizing of the romantic songs (and her spirited rendition of "America, I Love You"), but were equally taken with Grable's youthful exuberance and lively hoofing.

MOON OVER MIAMI
(20th Century-Fox, 1941)

Credits: Producer, Harry Joe Brown; director, Walter Lang;

screenplay, Vincent Lawrence and Brown Holmes, based on the story by Stephen Powys, adapted by George Seaton; music director, Alfred Newman; songs, Leo Robin and Ralph Rainger; art directors, Richard Day and Ward B. Inhen; camera, Peverell Marley, Leon Shamroy, and Allen M. Davey; editor, Walter Thompson.

Cast: Don Ameche (Phil McNeil); Betty Grable (Kay); Robert Cummings (Jeff Bolton); Charlotte Greenwood (Aunt Susie); Jack Haley (Mike, the Bartender); Carole Landis (Barbara); Cobina Wright, Jr. (Connie); George Lessey (William Bolton); Robert Conway (Lester); Condos Brothers (Themselves); Robert Greig (Brearly); Minor Watson (Reynolds); Fortunio Bonanova (Mr. Pretto); George Humbert (Boss of Drive-In); Spencer Charters (Postman); Lynn Roberts (Jennie May); Larry McGrath (Bartender).

Songs: "What Can I Do for You?", "You Started Something," "Kindergarten Conga," "Oh Me Oh Mi-a-mi," "Is That Good," "Solitary Seminole," "Loveliness and Love," "I've Got You All to Myself" (Rainger-Robin).

Release Date: July 4, 1941. *Running Time:* 91 minutes.

SYNOPSIS

Texas carhops Kay and Barbara Latimer and their aunt Susan receive a letter from Iowa informing them that a deceased relative left them with $4000 to be divided equally. They agree to use the money to finance a trip to Miami where Kay will pose as an heiress and, once ensconced at a posh resort, attempt to snag a millionaire for a husband, putting them all on easy street. Barbara goes along as Kay's secretary, and Susan poses as her maid.

While attending a party at the hotel, Kay meets millionaire playboy Jeff Bolton and his friend, Phil McNeil. The childhood friends vie for Kay's favors almost immediately, each trying to outdo the other. Meanwhile, Susan fends off one of the bellboys, Jack, who gets fat tips by keeping fortune hunters away from the vacationing millionaires. Barbara, tired of playing the Plain Jane, accompanies Kay one night when both Phil and Jeff are around. She takes a fancy to Jeff, who reciprocates. Kay, for her part, prefers Phil and is happy to wind up with him. Ashamed of what she's been doing, she confesses the hoax to Phil, who in turn reveals that he, too, is penniless and has been playing the same game. Outraged, Kay leaves him flat. She again turns her attentions to Jeff, who proposes. But before the wedding can take place, Phil demands she abandon her plan, and she melts into his arms. This leaves Jeff free to marry Barbara, and even Aunt Susan winds up in a clinch—with Jack.

With Carole Landis, Robert Cummings, Jack Haley, and Don Ameche in *Moon Over Miami.*

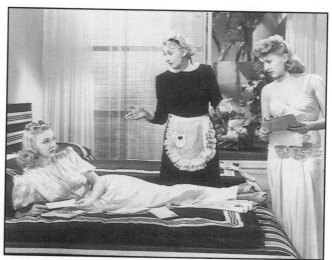

With Landis and Charlotte Greenwood in *Moon Over Miami.*

With Landis, Cummings, and Ameche in *Moon Over Miami.*

Dancing the "Conga to a Nursery Rhyme" with choreographer Hermes Pan in *Moon Over Miami.*

Dancing the "Conga to a Nursery Rhyme" with choreographer Hermes Pan in *Moon Over Miami.*

REVIEWS

"If you are content—and we were very content—to be dazzled by Betty Grable and Carole Landis in color, to listen to some saucy tunes warbled with a lilt and to beat time in a couple of swirling production numbers, well, one can think of less pleasant ways of spending a hot summer's eve. [*Moon Over Miami*] rarely lets you remember it's old hat [and shows] Miss Grable in a range of pretty and petulant moods. How her moods photograph!" (*New York Times*)

"This glittering song-and-dance show demonstrates the advantages of giving its singer something to sing, its dancers rhythms that set an audience to beating in time with the danceable music. All do their singing chores effectively, and Miss Grable's dancing is something to write home about." (*Hollywood Reporter*)

"Offers a sparkling collection of numbers by Leo Robin and Ralph Rainger, sung and danced ably by the principals, sometimes with chorus, in the course of the proceedings. . . . It is a letdown . . . in point of story, which limps badly, and humor, neither plot nor dialogue measuring up. The story . . . is worked out much as usual." (*Motion Picture Herald*)

PRODUCTION NOTES AND COMMENTS

Originally announced as *Miami*, this musical remake of *Three Blind Mice*, a 1937 production that starred Loretta Young, Pauline Moore and Marjorie Weaver as the three millionaire-hunters, reportedly cost more than any other Fox musical to date. (Negative cost, however, was listed at $950,000, which would make it less expensive than Alice Faye's *Alexander's Ragtime Band*.) Nearly a year in preparation, it took a full four months to shoot, including six weeks in Florida for second-unit director Otto Brower and his crew. As was the case with *Down Argentine Way* (and, for that matter, all the Fox musicals set in exotic, picturesque locations), most of the location work—which took the crew to Winterhaven, Silver Springs, Ocala, and Rainbow Springs in addition to Miami—wound up being used for montages and rear-projection scenes featuring the principals.

Reflecting Grable's newly won prominence, the script was revamped to feature her in nearly every scene. In fact, her character appeared in all but six of the script's 100-plus pages, and she worked on every single day the first unit was in production. This rigorous schedule took its toll on the star, who collapsed from exhaustion while performing the "Conga to a Nursery Rhyme" number with Hermes Pan.

A YANK IN THE R.A.F.
(20th Century-Fox, 1941)

Credits: Producer, Darryl F. Zanuck; associate producer, Lou Edelman; director, Henry King; screenplay, Darrell Ware and Karl Tunberg, based on a story by Melville Crossman [Zanuck]; songs, Leo Robin and Ralph Rainger; musical director, Alfred Newman; photography, Leon Shamroy; editor, Barbara McLean.

Cast: Tyrone Power (Tim Blake); Betty Grable (Carol Brown); John Sutton (Wing Commander Morley); Reginald

With Tyrone Power in *A Yank in the R.A.F.*

In uniform for *A Yank in the R.A.F.*

Gardiner (Roger Pillby); Donald Stuart (Harry Baker); Morton Lowry (Squadron Leader); Ralph Byrd (Al); Richard Fraser (Thorndyke); Denis Green (Redmond); Bruce Lester (Richardson); Gilchrist Stuart (Wales); Lester Matthews (Group Captain); Frederick Worlock (Canadian Major); Ethel Griffies (Mrs. Fitzhugh).

Songs: "Hi-Ya, Love," "Another Little Dream Won't Do Us Any Harm" (Robin-Rainger).

Release Date: October 3, 1941. *Running Time:* 97 minutes.

SYNOPSIS

During the early days of World War II, before America is drawn into the conflict, brash, reckless pilot Tim Blake ferries bombers from Canada to Britain. Caught in London during an air raid by Nazi bombers, Tim takes refuge in a shelter and runs smack into another American: his former fiancee Carol Brown, who broke off their engagement when she became disgusted with his irresponsibility. Tim learns that Carol is working as a volunteer nurse during the day and dancing at night in a night club frequented by British servicemen. The impulsive American decides to join the Royal Air Force so he can be near Carol and possibly win her back.

Tim's competitors for Carol's attentions are Wing Commander Morley and Flying Officer Roger Pillby. He is assigned to Morley's plane, which exacerbates tensions between the two men. Carol is beginning to soften toward Tim when he stands her up on a date. Morley takes that opportunity to propose to Carol, who subsequently tells Tim she's through with him for good. Later, during a bombing raid off the coast of Holland, Pillby loses his life and Morley's plane is shot down. Tim helps his badly wounded rival escape in a fishing boat. While Morley recovers, a sober, impassioned Tim realizes the war is serious business. He fights valiantly in the battle of Dunkirk, shooting down three German planes. Moreover, he wins his own personal battle: Carol sees that he is a changed man and marries him.

With Power and John Sutton in *A Yank in the R.A.F.*

PRODUCTION NOTES AND COMMENTS

Darryl Zanuck, keenly aware that the conflict in Europe had touched the lives of many Americans (and, incidentally, had cost his studio considerable revenue from the loss of lucrative foreign markets), drew upon newspaper headlines for his inspiration for *A Yank in the R.A.F.*. Once again adopting his old pen name, Melville Crossman (originally coined during his tenure at Warner Bros.), Zanuck wrote an original story called "The Eagle Flies Again," which was adapted into scenario form by Darrell Ware and Karl Tunberg.

Some columnists, upon learning that Betty Grable had been cast as the American nurse, were openly skeptical about Zanuck's decision to spotlight her in a dramatic film. She surprised them all by turning in a perfectly competent if not particularly brilliant performance, and her chemistry with Tyrone Power (whom she briefly dated) was unmistakable. While the film turned on the actions of Power's character, Betty's histrionic contribution further endeared her to movie audiences.

Henry King's smooth direction guided the generally predictable plot over its few rough spots, and editor Barbara McLean skillfully juxtaposed actual combat footage filmed at Dunkirk with studio-shot battle scenes. Initially, Power's character was shot down and killed in the battle of Dunkirk, paving the way for Betty to marry John Sutton. Preview audiences, however, reacted negatively to this development, and the picture's finale was reshot to provide a happy ending.

I WAKE UP SCREAMING
(20th Century-Fox, 1941)

Credits: Producer, Milton Sperling; director, H. Bruce Humberstone; screenplay, Dwight Taylor, based on the novel by Steve Fisher; music, Cyril J. Mockridge; camera, Edward Cronjager; editor, Robert Simpson.

Cast: Betty Grable (Jill Lynn); Victor Mature (Frankie Christopher); Carole Landis (Vicky Lynn); Laird Cregar (Ed Cornell); William Gargan (Jerry McDonald); Alan Mowbray (Robin Ray); Allyn Joslyn (Larry Evans); Elisha Cook, Jr. (Harry Williams); Chick Chandler (Reporter); Morris Ankrum (Assistant District Attorney); Wade Boteler, Ralph Dunn (Detectives); Brooks Benedict (Man); Forbes Murray (Mr. Handel).

Release Date: November 14, 1941. *Running Time:* 82 minutes.

SYNOPSIS

Promoter Frankie Christopher is accused of the murder of Vicki Lynn, a young actress he "discovered" as a waitress and subsequently promoted with the aid of ex-actor Robin Ray and gossip columnist Larry Evans. Frankie hides out with Vicky's sister Jill, with whom he has fallen in love, but is captured anyway. The relentless and obsessive investigating officer, Ed Cornell, admits that he knows Frankie is innocent but, because evidence is completely incriminating, says, "That won't prevent you from going to the hot chair." Frankie realizes he must find Vicky's murderer himself, so he escapes and looks for some clues. Ultimately, he traps Vicky's neighbor, Harry Williams, in his room, which is decorated with photographs of the dead woman, and the pimply faced elevator operator confesses that he murdered Vicky. Harry also relates that he confessed to Cornell but was told to keep silent because both men were jealous of Frankie and planned to see him executed for the murder. Frankie exposes Cornell's complicity, and the brutish detective acknowledges his own obsession with Vicky. Cleared of the murder rap, Frankie picks up his romance with Jill.

Poster design for *I Wake Up Screaming* carrying the movies original title.

With Carole Landis and Laird Cregar in I Wake Up Screaming.

With Victor Mature in I Wake Up Screaming.

With Mature and Landis in I Wake Up Screaming.

REVIEWS

"There are a few melodramas a season that demand to be seen. This is one of them. The elements of romance, mystery, suspense and an ending, as unpredictable as the number of people in the audience, have been woven into a dramatic pattern of fascinating melodrama. The trade press coterie . . . were individually and collectively impressed to the extent of arguing over the eventful outcome." (*Motion Picture Herald*)

"It is a whodunit with distinction. Twentieth Century-Fox carefully cast the picture with its best name talent. The writing was put into the hands of top scriveners and the direction in the hands of an experienced megaphoner. The result is a polished and intelligent job all down the line . . . . There are probably no two worse actors in all California than Betty Grable and Victor Mature, but you don't even object to them here." (*Chicago Sun*)

"The terrific suspense of this picture makes it the most exciting film fare to reach the screen since *The Maltese Falcon* was shown hereabouts and one of the few murder mysteries to justify the grade A treatment it received in production. The entire cast turn in excellent performances. Betty Grable, who grows more confident with each appearance on the screen, is fine in a sympathetic role and Carole Landis is properly hard and brittle as the victim." (*New York Daily News*)

PRODUCTION NOTES AND COMMENTS

This early exercise in what would be later dubbed "film noir," taken from a hard-boiled mystery novel by veteran pulpster (and, later, screenwriter) Steve Fisher, was initially called *Hot Spot* and was actually previewed under that title. Cooler heads prevailed, however, and the title of Fisher's book was affixed to the film when it went into wide distribution. In the earliest press releases Grable got a left-handed compliment from Fox publicist Harry Brand, who wrote: "Betty Grable finally overcomes the handicap of possessing one of the finest figures in the nation: the blonde beauty has completed the transition from dancing star to dramatic actress in *Hot Spot*."

For the second picture in a row Grable and Landis played sisters, and while Betty won star billing, it was Carole who got the more interesting role, as the ambitious, opportunistic waitress who used the men in her life while climbing the ladder of stardom. Nonetheless, Betty provided an appealing, all-American girl type and a moral center in a story peopled largely by amoral characters. (She also played a brief scene fetchingly clad in bathing suit, which delighted male viewers.) Some reviewers pointed out that she was ill-equipped for such a role but, in truth, it's difficult to imagine that a more

experienced dramatic actress could have brought much more to such a clearly and simply limned character. On the whole, *I Wake Up Screaming* holds up extremely well—which is more than can be said for its 1953 remake, *Vicki*.

SONG OF THE ISLANDS
(20th Century-Fox, 1942)

Credits: Producer, William LeBaron; director, Walter Lang; screenplay, Joseph Schrank, Robert Pirosh, Robert Ellis, and Helen Logan; music director, Alfred Newman; choreography, Hermes Pan; songs, Mack Gordon, Harry Owens, R. Alex Anderson, and Al Stillman; camera, Ernest Palmer; editor, Robert Simpson.

Cast: Betty Grable (Eileen O'Brien); Victor Mature (Jefferson Harper); Jack Oakie (Rusty); Thomas Mitchell (O'Brien); George Barbier (Harper); Billy Gilbert (Palpla's Father); Hilo Hattie (Palpla); Lillian Porter (Palpla's Cousin); Hal K. Dawson (John Rodney); Harry Owens and His Royal Hawaiians (Themselves); Amy Cordone (Specialty); Bruce Wong (House Boy); Alex Pollard (Valet); Harold Lishman (Old Native).

Songs: "Blue Shadows and White Gardenias," "O'Brien Has Gone Hawaiian," "Sing Me a Song of the Islands," "Down on Ami Ami Oni Oni Isle," "Maluna Malolo Mawaena," "What's Buzzin' Cousin" (Gordon-Owens), "Cockeyed Mayor of Kaunakakai" (Anderson-Stillman), "Hawaiian War Chant," "Home on the Range."

Release Date: March 13, 1942. *Running Time:* 75 minutes.

With Victor Mature in *Song of the Islands*.

With Mature and Jack Oakie *In Song of the Islands.*

SYNOPSIS

On a cattle ranch on Ami Ami, one of the smaller Hawaiian Islands, a great luau is prepared for Eileen O'Brien, who is returning to her father's ranch after three years of school on the mainland. She reaches their little beach in an out-rigger rowed over from the larger island, and there is feasting until dawn.

A few days later, Jeff Harper and Rusty Smith land on the O'Brien beach. The son of an American cattle king who owns the adjoining ranch, Jeff and his pal Rusty have come to Hawaii to inspect Jeff's father's property. Eileen meets them on the beach and, supposing that she is some kind of blonde native, they make several rather cavalier remarks about her, to learn later to their discomfiture that her English is as good as Jeff's and far better than Rusty's.

Jeff and Rusty find that Rodney, the Harper foreman, runs the vast ranch with irritating efficiency, forbidding the native laborers to attend neighborhood feasts and insisting upon a grim attention to work, in contrast to

O'Brien, who runs his ranch by good-natured hit or miss, refusing to allow any modern "improvements" that would spoil the islanders' paradise. Rodney explains to Jeff that if the Harper ranch could buy or lease deep-water dockage from O'Brien the Harper cattle could be dock-loaded instead of being made to swim out of lighters to be lifted onto cattle boats in the roadstead by cranes. Jeff says he will try to arrange the lease.

This mission requires that Jeff and Rusty spend a good deal of time on the O'Brien ranch, and they are soon caught up in the lazy spell of the islands, Jeff in love with Eileen and Rusty in "love" with a cute little Hawaiian girl but constantly pursued by stout Palola, who wants him for her husband.

When Jeff tells Rodney that he may stay in Hawaii "forever," Rodney gets visions of being shifted to another part of the Harper empire and, not wishing to leave Hawaii, he telephones Harper Sr. on the mainland, warning him that Jeff intends to marry and settle there. Harper Sr., a choleric, humorless money-grubber, hops a clipper and comes to see for himself. Jeff warns him that O'Brien

In *Song of the Islands.*

With Oakie and Mature in *Song of the Islands*.

may give Jeff the wharfage but is not a man to be bullied. The two older men tangle, and negotiations are broken off. Jeff goes back to his father and convinces him that the O'Briens live better than the Harpers, which he proves by curing the elder Harper's dyspepsia with a diet of native fruits. The old man finally comes around, makes the peace with O'Brien, and stays on the island long enough to attend the wedding feast for Eileen and Jeff.

REVIEWS

"The story would have been silly at any time [but] the film is entertaining because of its brilliant Technicolor, the musical numbers, and the skirt-swishing. Betty Grable is the chief skirt-swisher. She also sings most of the songs. Since she is easy to look at and color becomes her no end, she's a honey of a heroine." (*Liberty*)

"Miss Grable . . . is the most likely to instill an air of good nature, with her undeniable youth, blondeness, and health. Just when the pretty heroine might be expected to feel the first pangs of ennui, a strange skiff appears on the horizon, drifts up to the beach, and out of it steps Victor Mature. Probably the whole film is of the sort to be shown at a camp to men who have just come back from a 30-mile hike." (*The New Yorker*)

"It never stops entertaining. When Betty Grable and her little brown friends are not shaking, waving or tossing the hula, somebody off in a corner or up a palm tree is plinking out some music and the show rides along." (*St. Louis Post-Dispatch*)

"This confection in Technicolor contains just about everything in the cookbook. It offers Betty Grable in Hawaii, in song, in several varieties of hula, in ample display of both talents and charms and in and out of love . . . ." (*Motion Picture Herald*)

PRODUCTION NOTES AND COMMENTS

As was typical of most big-budget Hollywood musicals, *Song of the Islands* found studio technicians laboring mightily to simulate a locale unreachable by cast or crew—in this case an island in the South Seas, which at that time were swarming with Japanese submarines and battleships. The whole two acres of Fox's Stage 14 became a Hawaiian landscape, covered with imported palm trees and tropical shubbery. Set designers constructed a 30-foot waterfall for the stage, and painted a huge mural of the Pacific horizon on 10,000 square feet of canvas. More than 300 Polynesian extras were used in the filming.

FOOTLIGHT SERENADE
(20th Century-Fox, 1942)

Credits: Producer, William LeBaron; director, Gregory Ratoff; screenplay, Robert Ellis, Helen Logan, and Lynn Starling, based on the story *Dynamite* by Fidel LaBarba and Kenneth Earl; art directors, Richard Day and Roger Hemen; music director, Charles Henderson; songs, Leo Robin, Ralph Rainger, Herb Magidson, Allie Wrubel; choreography, Hermes Pan; camera, Lee Garmes; editor, Robert Simpson.

Cast: John Payne (Bill Smith); Betty Grable (Pat Lambert); Victor Mature (Tommy Lundy); Jane Wyman (Flo LaVerne); James Gleason (Bruce McCay); Phil Silvers (Slap); Cobina Wright, Jr. (Estelle Evans); June Lang (June); Frank Orth (Doorman); Mantan Moreland (Dresser); Irving Bacon (Porter); Charles Tannen (Stage Director); George Dobbs (Dance Director); Sheila Ryan (Girl); Frank Coghlan, Jr. (Usher); Harry Barris (Composer); Trudy Marshall (Secretary); Don Wilson (Announcer); John Dilson (Clerk).

Songs: "Are You Kidding?", "I'm Still Crazy for You," "I Heard the Birdies Sing," "Living High," "I'll Be Marching to a Love Song," "Land on Your Feet" (Rainger-Robin), "I'm Stepping Out With a Memory Tonight" (Magidson-Wrubel).

Release Date: August 1, 1942. *Running Time:* 80 minutes.

Publicity pose for *Footlight Serenade*.

SYNOPSIS

Extroverted champion prizefighter Tommy Lundy decides to test his mettle behind the footlights for awhile, so theatrical producer Bruce McKay fashions a Broadway show with a boxing background for the champ. Chorus girls Pat Lambert and Flo La Verne land jobs in the new production, thanks to their friendship with Slap, the stage manager. Getting a spot in the show is a morale booster for Pat, whose fiance, Bill Smith, has just postponed their wedding because he doesn't have a job.

During rehearsals, the irrepressible Tommy takes a shine to Pat, who casually detests the swell-headed fighter. He repeatedly vies for her attentions, insisting on private rehearsals with her—much to the chagrin of leading lady Estelle Evans. Bill, who resents Tommy's designs on his fiancee, gets a job with a show as one of the boxers who will spar on stage with the champ. Although he's no professional boxer, Bill is good enough with his dukes to give Tommy a run for his money, which exacerbates tensions between them. By the time the show has opened, Pat has married Bill and snagged the female lead (because Estelle has fought with Tommy and left in a huff). Learning that Pat is married, the good-natured if rough-edged champ backs off and wishes them well. The show is a hit, but Tommy decides that show business isn't for him.

REVIEWS

"Gay, bright and engaging song-and-dance show is certain to register a hit. Miss Grable's dance routines are all standouts, yet special mention must be made of the novel shadow dance she pertly performs in a boxing match with herself, and the grand stepping she does in rehearsal with Hermes Pan as her partner." (*Film Daily*)

"This is one of those strikes across the heart of the plate that not even the bleacherites find fault with . . . it's got a pace that never slackens for as much as the drawing of a long breath . . . five musical numbers by Leo Robin and Ralph Rainger amply display the abilities of Miss Grable and others in that field . . . . " (*Motion Picture Herald*)

"Victor Mature has been cast rather ingeniously [as] a world's champion prizefighter, a Max Baer-like figure who lands himself a part in a Broadway musical comedy on the strength of his title and his lively personality. You just assume that he has submerged his own talent altogether, and any time he yawns or whistles or otherwise registers emotion, it's so much gravy." (*The New Yorker*)

"[F]ilmusical of modest proportions that will roll through the summer bookings for par biz. 20th-Fox apparently is attempting to swing Betty Grable into the

With Victor Mature and John Payne in *Footlight Serenade*.

With Jane Wyman (third from right) and chorus girls in *Footlight Serenade*.

song-and-dance headline spot, and although picture is a typical backstage number, it gives her several chances to click in both the vocal and terp departments." (*Variety*)

PRODUCTION NOTES AND COMMENTS

The starring trio of Grable, Payne and Mature were originally slated to appear in a lighthearted drama titled *White Collar Girl*, but persistent script problems derailed that opus in February of 1942. With time, resources, and money already alloted, studio brass rushed the cast and crew into production on *Strictly Dynamite*, a backstage story about a boxer-turned-performer (based on real-life pugilist Fidel La Barba, but thought by many critics and moviegoers to resemble former champ Max Baer).

For his role as the wise-cracking, egotistical fighter, Mature was trained by former contender Jack Roper, who even appeared on screen sparring with the actor. Payne's background included some amateur boxing, a skill he'd previously displayed on screen in *Tin Pan Alley* (1940). The film's three fight sequences cost a reported $40,000 to stage and shoot, and nervous Fox executives had Lloyd's of London write $50,000 insurance policies on both Mature and Payne.

Grable's turn in *Footlight Serenade* (as it was rechristened during production) was similarly arduous. She picked up a bad cold while shooting her first scene with Payne, who was just recovering from the flu. Working for several days with a fever, she was briefly sidelined after the shooting of an adagio dance with Mature. Roughly hoisted into the air by Mature, Grable was to plunge from shoulder height and be caught around the waist by him before she could hit the floor. Mature caught her inexpertly, though, and the resulting bruising tore her

Teaching Mature how to dance in *Footlight Serenade*.

abdomenal muscles. Her other dance scenes had to be postponed to allow her time to heal, and when she returned her abdomen was heavily and securely taped beneath her tight-fitting costumes.

One of Grable's production numbers, "I'll Be Marching to a Love Song," was shot in two versions, one of which wound up in the 1945 *All-Star Bond Rally* short as a self-contained sequence.

During production, Fox's publicity department announced that Grable had just broken the studio's fan-mail record, previously held by Shirley Temple, by receiving 14,800 letters—many from servicemen—in one month.

SPRINGTIME IN THE ROCKIES
(20th Century-Fox, 1942)

Credits: Producer, Darryl F. Zanuck; director, Irving Cummings; screenplay, Walter Bullock and Ken Englund, based on the story by Philip Wylie, adapted by Jacques Thery; songs, Mack Gordon and Harry Warren; music director Alfred Newman; choreography, Hermes Pan; art directors, Richard Day, Joseph C. Wright; camera, Ernest Palmer; editor, Robert Simpson.

Cast: Betty Grable (Vicky); John Payne (Dan); Carmen Miranda (Rosita); Cesar Romero (Victor); Harry James and His Music Makers (Themselves); Bando De Luna (Themselves); Charlotte Greenwood (Phoebe Gray); Edward Everett Horton (McTavish); Frank Orth and Harry Hayden (Bickle and Brown); Jackie Gleason (Commissioner); Trudy Marshall (Marilyn); Chick Chandler (Stage Manager); Iron Eyes Cody (Indian); Bess Flowers (Mrs. Jeepers).

Songs: "I Had the Craziest Dream," "Run Little Raindrop Run," "A Poem Set to Music," "Pan-Americana Jubilee," "Chattanooga Choo Choo" (Gordon-Warren).

Release Date: November 6, 1942. *Running Time:* 91 minutes.

SYNOPSIS

Broadway stars Vicky and Dan, a team on stage and off, find their relationship jeopardized by his wandering eye. In fact, his weakness for pretty girls keeps them battling on a continual basis, so when their current show closes, Vicki decides to split up for good and get out of town. She joins her former dancing partner, Victor, for a tour of the northwest. After going on a bender, a distressed Dan decides to follow Vicky, beg her forgiveness, and woo her back to Broadway for a new show. He is accompanied to Lake Louise—where Vicky and Victor are dancing at a resort hotel where Harry James and his band are playing—by two people he engaged while inebriated:

With John Payne in *Springtime in the Rockies*.

With Payne, Carmen Miranda, Cesar Romero, and Charlotte Greenwood in *Springtime in the Rockies*.

prissy valet McTavish and fiery Latin American secretary Rosita.

Dan has a difficult time convincing Vicky that he's sincere, and the presence of McTavish and Rosita—along with stiff competition from Victor, who doesn't want to lose Vicky again—doesn't make his task any easier. But after several misunderstandings and misadventures, the two lovers are reunited, and Dan brings the whole kit and kaboodle back to Broadway to appear in their new production.

REVIEWS

"Enhanced by Technicolor mounting, and boasting a topline group of major league performers, picture is a breezy and tuneful bundle of entertainment geared for present audience requirements. Betty Grable, in addition to providing eye appeal as the femme lead, steps out with several song and dance numbers of showmanship calibre. Carmen Miranda develops as a comedienne to add to her effervescing deliveries of South American songs. Director Cummings scores every opportunity to click with comedy situations and lines, keeps tempo at a steady pace." (*Variety*)

"In a form neither has ever surpassed, Betty Grable and John Payne are on hand to dance, sing and take care of the light romantic interest that hold proceedings together. The spritely dancing of Betty Grable is matched by the personable performance she gives. [A]n hour-and-a-half of sparkling diversion." (*Hollywood Reporter*)

"Miss Miranda's singing of 'Chattanooga Choo Choo' in Portugese is the high spot of the show, which doesn't put it at any dizzy altitude." (*The New Yorker*)

"Cesar Romero and Betty Grable . . . give two exibitions of ballroom dancing with smooth grace. Some effort might have been made, however, to support the title and do justice to the beauty spot of Canada which it ignores." (*Motion Picture Herald*)

With Payne in *Springtime in the Rockies.*

With Payne in *Springtime in the Rockies.*

With Edward Everett Horton, Greenwood, Dick Elliott, Bess Flowers, Romero, and Miranda in *Springtime in the Rockies.*

Payne and Jackie Gleason in *Springtime in the Rockies.*

PRODUCTION NOTES AND COMMENTS

Canada's beautiful Lake Louise, sublimely captured by Fox's second-unit crew, provided yet another colorful backdrop for a Grable musical. Bolstered by Grable's meteoric rise to stardom—and her concomitant strength at the nation's box-offices—Fox continued to lavish money on her films, making them irresistable escapist entertainments during the World War II years.

Springtime utilized three choruses of 150 dancers in its elaborate production numbers. The "Poem Set to Music" number featuring Betty and Cesar Romero was claimed by Fox publicity to be the first ballroom adagio employed in a "narrative dance," telling a story in keeping with the lyric of the piece. She performed the dance in a 25-pound costume beaded with lead, necessitating multiple takes and frequent rest periods.

Nor was Betty the only principal taxed to the limit by a dance routine. The script called for comic relief supporting player Edward Everett Horton to perform a dance routine with Carmen Miranda; despite his relative inexperience in screen hoofing, however, Horton zipped through the complicated, five-minute-long sequence in just one take.

Springtime was the second film of Harry James (Universal's *Private Buckaroo*, released earlier in the year, was his first), who was shoehorned into the story after

Fox executives noted the success of bandleader Glenn Miller in a similar assignment in the studio's *Orchestra Wives* earlier that year. James, who was color-blind, also had an anomaly of the optic nerve that caused him to get dizzy under the intense, bright lights needed for Technicolor photography. He resorted to wearing dark glasses on the set both during rehearsals and in shots where he couldn't be clearly seen.

CONEY ISLAND

(20th Century-Fox, 1943)

Credits: Producer, William Perlberg; director, Walter Lang; screenplay, George Seaton; art director, Richard Day; music director, Alfred Newman; songs (new), Leo Robin and Ralph Rainger; choreography, Hermes Pan; camera, Ernest Palmer; editor, Robert Simpson.

Cast: Betty Grable (Kate Farley); George Montgomery (Eddie Johnson); Cesar Romero (Joe Rocco); Charles Winninger (Finnegan); Phil Silvers (Frankie); Matt Briggs (Hammerstein); Paul Hurst (Louie); Frank Orth (Bartender); Phyllis Kennedy (Dolly); Carmen D'Antonio (Dancer); Andrew Tombes (Carter); Harry Seymour (Piano Player); Hal K. Dawson (Cashier); Bud Williams (Singing Waiter); Alec Craig (Man); Herbert Ashley, James Lucas, Francis Sayles (Hecklers); Tom Dugan (Fitch); Trudy Marshall, Claire James (Girlfriends); Tene Ramey, Gus Reed, Delos Jewkos, George Grumlick (Singing Waiters); Delos Jowkes, Harry Masters, Frank Orth, Joe Niemoyer (Quartette).

Songs: "Take It From There," "Lulu From Louisville," "Get the Money," "There's Danger in a Dance," "Old Demon Rum," "Beautiful Coney Island" (Rainger-Robin), "Cuddle Up a Little Closer" (Karl Hoschna-Otto Harbach), "Pretty Baby" (Gus Kahn, Tony Jackson, Egbert Van Alstyne), "Put Your Arms Around Me, Honey" (Albert von Tilzer, Junie McCree), "Who Threw the Overalls in Mrs. Murphy's Chowder?" (George L. Giefer), "Darktown Strutters Ball" (Shelton Brooks), "Deep River" (traditional), "Oh Susanna," "The Old Folks at Home" (Stephen Foster), "Let Me Call You Sweetheart" (Beth Slater Whitson).

Release Date: June 18, 1943. *Running Time:* 96 minutes.

With Matt Briggs and Cesar Romero in *Coney Islands.*

A costume test shot for *Coney Island*.

With George Montgomery in *Coney Island*.

In costume as seen in the finished film.

SYNOPSIS

Bright lights and bawdy beer joints draw New Yorkers to Coney Island near the turn of the century. One of the most prosperous Islanders is smooth-talking Joe Rocco, whose honky tonk features brassy blonde singer Kate Farley, a big favorite with Coney customers. One night Joe is unpleasantly surprised by the arrival of handsome con man Eddie Johnson, with whom he once worked in a carnival. Eddie, citing an old double-cross that Joe once pulled, expects to be taken in as a full partner. Rocco balks at this, but Eddie and his perpetually drunken pal Finnegan stage a con of their own, bamboozling Joe into hiring him.

Eddie becomes the producer of the joint's lavish floor shows, gradually softening Kate's rough edges to make her a much more effective performer—while also making a play for her, much to Joe's consternation. She is offered a starring role by Willie Hammerstein, the well-known producer, in a big musical show at Broadway's Victoria Theatre. Rocco attempts to spike the romance between his unwelcome partner and his former headliner, but his efforts fail and Kate eventually finds happiness with Eddie.

REVIEWS

"There's not much about Coney Island in the film *Coney Island*, at least not much in the way of scholarly documentation. [I]t doesn't tell you anything about the period except some of the current songs. These are sung by Betty Grable, when she is not mixed up in some fruitless goings-on with George Montgomery, Cesar Romero, and Charles Winninger." (*New Yorker*)

"Loosely historical Bowery-Barbary Coast sort of thing

In *Coney Island*.

In *Coney Island*.

in old tunes, quaint costumes and some of the prettiest Technicolor. Betty Grable . . . dances, sings, pouts and talks incessantly for most of the footage and, so well does she do them, you keep liking her. Maybe her generously displayed chassis enhances the values of her histrionism." (*Dallas Morning News*)

"Very likely to out-gross its equally vividly Technicolored predecessors . . . its similar story is even more smoothly presented. As a showcase for the captivating talents of Betty Grable . . . picture is smartly tailored and will send Miss Grable's already substantial stock soaring higher at the box office." (*Hollywood Reporter*)

"Showmen who have done business with Fox musicals can stop remembering them fondly now and start selling the topper of them all . . . it sparkles, crackles, sizzles in spots and entertains all over." (*Motion Picture Herald*)

PRODUCTION NOTES AND COMMENTS

Coney Island was the picture that finally saw Betty Grable boosted to top stardom. A colorful, sumptuous production that cost Fox $1,620,000, it earned the studio nearly $3,500,000 in domestic film rental—some $1,500,000 more than her previous release, *Springtime in the Rockies*.

By this time critics were accustomed to Grable's trade-

In *Coney Island.*

mark brand of Technicolored escapism, so the carping was kept to a minimum. Astute New York critics with extensive backgrounds in local show-biz history were, however, compelled to comment on the film's historical inaccuracies and anachronisms. Legendary producer Willie Hammerstein, for example, never made musicals, and the venerable Victoria Theatre was strictly a vaudeville house. These reservations aside, though, *Coney Island* was judged to be effective entertainment for wartime audiences.

The romantic triangle utilized by *Coney Island*'s scripters was already old hat, but it didn't stop Fox from remaking the film with Grable in 1950: *Wabash Avenue* switched locale from New York to Chicago, but in most other respects was a virtual carbon copy of the earlier picture.

SWEET ROSIE O'GRADY

(20th Century-Fox, 1943)

Credits: Producer, William Perlberg; director, Irving Cummings; screenplay, Ken Englund, based on the story by Frederick Stephani, Walter R. Lipmen, and Edward Van Every; art directors, James Basevi and Joseph C. Wright; songs (new), Mack Gordon and Harry Warren; music direc-

As *Sweet Rosie O'Grady.*

tors, Alfred Newman and Charles Henderson; choreography, Hermes Pan; camera, Ernest Palmer; editor, Robert Simpson.

Cast: Betty Grable (Madeleine Marlowe); Robert Young (Sam McGee); Adolphe Menjou (Thomas Moran); Reginald Gardiner (Duke Charles); Virginia Grey (Edna Van Dyck); Phil Regan (Composer); Sig Rumann (Joe Flugelman); Alan Dinehart (Arthur Skinner); Hobart Cavanaugh (Clark); Frank Orth (Cabby); Jonathan Hale (Mr. Fox); Stanley Clements (Danny); Byron Foulger (Rimplemayer); Lilyan Irene (Gracie); St. Brendan's Choir (Themselves); Leo Diamond and His Solidaires (Themselves); Oliver Balke (Editor—Rogers); Edward Earle, James Metcalfe, Bruce Warren, John Dilson, Paul Maxey, Sam Wren, Hooper Atchley (Salesmen); Joe King (Burl Ship Official); Dorothy Granger (Singer).

Songs: "My Heart Tells Me," "Get Your Police Gazette," "The Wishing Waltz," "Going to the County Fair," "My Sam," "Oh, Where Is the Groom?" (Gordon-Warren), "Waiting at the Church" (Fred W. Leigh, Henry E. Pether), "Sweet Rosie O'Grady" (Maude Nugent), "Two Little Girls in Blue" (Charles Graham), "Heaven Will Protect the Working Girl" (Edgar Smith-A. Baldwin Sloane).

Release Date: October 1, 1943. *Running Time:* 74 minutes.

SYNOPSIS

During the 1880s, most red-blooded American males are avid perusers of The Police Gazette, and they get plenty of good reading in articles exposing famed musical-comedy star Madeleine Marlowe as former Brooklyn burlesque queen Rosie O'Grady. Although Gazette reporter Sam McGee, author of the stories, is a constant thorn in the side of his editor, Thomas Moran, he retains his job thanks to the circulation-boosting scoops he frequently delivers.

Over in London, Madeleine and her wealthy actress friend Edna Van Dyck wind up a successful run in the Trafalgar Square Theater and make plans for a triumphant return to New York. Madeleine, ardently pursued by the Duke of Trippingham, is infuriated when she sees copies of the Gazette and vows to "fix" McGee. Upon arriving in New York, she encounters McGee—whom she's never met—disguised as a steamship official, and tells him the details of her romance with the Duke. When she learns how he's tricked her into giving an exclusive interview, the fuming Madeleine takes her first step against him by telling reporters gathered at her hotel that Sam's expose of her was planned as a publicity buildup, and that they plan to announce their engagement shortly.

Madeleine's phony story breaks in the other papers just as Sam is putting his own article to bed. An outraged

Shooting a musical number for *Sweet Rosie O'Grady*; note the lights placed around her.

Director Irving Cummings (in light suit) watches Grable rehearse a scene from *Sweet Rosie O'Grady* with Alan Dinehart.

With chorus in a number from *Sweet Rosie O'Grady*.

Moran fires his erstwhile star reporter, who then concentrates his energies on forcing the actress to confess that she framed him. After a series of mind-boggling complications—which include the publishing of a trumped-up "diary" supposedly written by Rosie O'Grady and the arrival of the Duke to claim his fiancee—Madeleine and Sam fall in love. The Duke, good sport that he is, releases Madeleine from her promise to marry him and takes up with Edna. Sam regains his job and proposes to Madeleine.

REVIEWS

"[I]f this be a somewhat slowed-down and covered-up Grable, it is nevertheless a Grable surrounded by all the glitter and sparkle at her studio's command . . . . Production by William Perlberg simulates the place and period of setting with the proficiency which the studio has established as a high par for its ventures in nostalgia . . . . The picture is at its best in the production numbers . . . . " (*Motion Picture Herald*)

"Betty Grable in one of her most beguiling roles . . . uses the nostalgic song eloquently to weave a sentimental tale [that] will refresh audiences with buoyant entertainment and garner its full share of coin amongst 20th-Fox important money makers of the year. Only in its adapted costumes of the period is it old-fashioned. Otherwise, in tempo, temper and speech *Sweet Rosie* is of the present, after the growing fashion in film musicals to ignore the 'quaint' reminders of another era." (*Variety*)

"Nothing more entertaining . . . has ever emerged from the long line of filmusical productions in Technicolor from 20th Century-Fox. The answer seems to be that here, for the first time, the vitality of Betty Grable is matched by a story that does her as proud as she does it. The yarn is legitimately funny, adroitly guided by the polished hand of Irving Cummings, and produced on a lavish scale by William Perlberg. Miss Grable gives a joyous performance of Rosie, and her dancing is tops." (*Hollywood Reporter*)

PRODUCTION NOTES AND COMMENTS

Sweet Rosie O'Grady, as contemporary reviews indicated, is indeed one of Grable's very best films, owing mostly to a bright script with amusing, well-developed situations, the skillful direction by Irving Cummings, and an evocative albeit glamorized depiction of the period. Although the score lacked the hit songs that enlivened the star's previous Fox vehicles ("My Heart Tells Me" being best among them), Betty made the best of her musical opportunities, particularly in dance sequences that paired her with choreographer Hermes Pan.

The title tune was performed by Grable and the Robert

With Robert Young and Adolphe Menjou in *Sweet Rosie O'Grady.*

Mitchell "Boychoir," a group of 20 boys between the ages of eight and 14, which was founded in 1934 for Los Angeles' St. Brendan's Church. The well-known singers at that time were also performing in a weekly radio program and numerous benefit broadcasts for charitable organizations.

The extravagant production, which racked up a $1,185,000 negative cost, was shut down for seven weeks when the star took a tumble during rehearsal of one of her dance numbers, pulling a knee tendon and taking her off her fabled underpinnings. Even so, it was brought in for nearly a half-million dollars less than its predecessor, and accounted for approximately $5,900,000 in worldwide film rental.

FOUR JILLS IN A JEEP
(20th Century-Fox, 1944)

Credits: Producer, Irving Starr; director, William A. Seiter; screenplay, Robert Ellis, Helen Logan, and Snag Werris, based on the story by Froma Sand and Fred Niblo, Jr.; choreography, Don Loper; music directors, Emil Newman, Charles Henderson; songs, Harold Adamson, Jimmy McHugh, Mack Gordon, Harry Warren, Karl Hoschna, Otto Harbach, Sam Coslow, Leo Robin, George M. Cohan, and Edmund L. Gruber; special effects, Fred Sersen; art directors, James Basevi, Albert Hogsett; camera, Peverell Marley; editor, Ray Curtiss.

Cast: Kay Francis (Herself); Carole Landis (Herself); Martha Raye (Herself); Mitzi Mayfair (Herself); Jimmy Dorsey and Band (Themselves); John Harvey (Ted Warren); Phil Silvers (Eddie); Dick Haymes (Lt. Dick Ryan); George Jessel (Mas-

ter of Ceremonies); Glenn Langan (Capt. Stewart); Lester Matthews (Capt. Lloyd); Ralph Byrd (Sergeant); Miles Mander (Col. Hartley); Kirk Alyn (Pilot); Lester Dorr (Soldier); Eddie Acuff (Sentry); Paul Harvey (General); Guest Stars: Alice Faye, Betty Grable, Carmen Miranda.

Songs: "Crazy Me," "You Send Me," "How Blue the Night," "How Many Times Do I Have to Tell You?" (Adamson-McHugh), "Cuddle Up a Little Closer" (Hoschna-Harbach), "You'll Never Know" (Gordon-Warren), "Mr. Paganini" (Coslow), "No Love, No Nothing" (Robin-Warren), "Over There" (Cohan), "When the Caissons Go Rolling Along" (Gruber).

Release Date: March 17, 1944. *Running Time:* 89 minutes.

SYNOPSIS

The story opens in a radio station where entertainers Kay Francis, Carole Landis, Martha Raye, and Mitzi Mayfair are participating in a "Command Performance" show being broadcast to U.S. troops overseas. When they learn that Jimmy Dorsey and his orchestra are England-bound for a tour of army camps, the girls express their excitement, and a British Foreign Office colonel arranges for them to accompany the band.

Overseas, they are met by Sergeant Eddie Hart, assigned as liaison man to accompany them on their tour. Carole is rescued from a muddy mishap by Captain Ted Warren, an American pilot to whom she is immediately attracted. Mitzi encounters Lieutenant Dick Ryan, her former singing partner, who doubles as a cronner for Jimmy Dorsey in a London Red Cross show. Following a whirlwind courtship, Carole marries Ted at Christmas time, but their honeymoon is abruptly terminated when the girls leave for a tour of North African installations.

The *Four Jills in a Jeep:* Carole Landis (left front), Martha Raye (behind wheel), Mitzi Mayfair (left rear), and Kay Francis.

With Francis in *Four Jills in a Jeep*.

The actresses arrive in Africa to find themselves needed more as nurses than as entertainers, and they are put to work in a makeshift hospital between shows. Later, after surviving a Nazi bombardment, the girls are shuttled out of the war zone. They wish their men good luck, and return to entertaining in other locales.

REVIEWS

"In spite of the efforts of five writers, the narrative thread of four courageous girls and three incidental, low-keyed romances is hardly sufficient . . . However, it is still highly exploitable entertainment . . . Betty Grable, the blonde beauty who took first place as a money-making star in the *Motion Picture Herald-Fame* poll, goes back to an earlier success for the tune 'Cuddle Up a Little Closer.'" (*Motion Picture Herald*)

"Something went wrong in the writing of *Four Jills in*

a Jeep. Direction and acting are no better. The production looks thrown together, as though it had been written on the set and photographed in a few days. For good measure it throws in some shots of Alice Faye, Betty Grable and Carmen Miranda singing songs they made popular in other movies." (*New York Sun*)

"It has to be stated bluntly that the film . . . made about that star-spangled journey is something less than okay. [It] is just a new piece of capitalization upon a widely publicized affair. It gives the painful impression of having been tossed together in a couple of hours." (*New York Times*)

"Its self-praise, its recurrent theme of 'look what we girls did for our country' is almost sickening. Undoubtedly the studio couldn't resist making capital on its girls' U.S.O. tour, but it has done so in the worst possible taste." (*New York Herald Tribune*)

PRODUCTION NOTES AND COMMENTS

Based on the real-life adventures of its four female protagonists, *Four Jills in a Jeep* (originally announced as *Command Performance, U.S.A.* but retitled after Carole Landis' successful book version of the stars' trip) succeeded in making banal a quite remarkable overseas excursion that encompassed 37,000 miles over four continents. The entertainers made over 300 appearances overseas, and even dove into foxholes during an air raid while trouping in North Africa.

Originally intended to be a movie version of the *Command Performance* radio show aimed exclusively at American soldiers, the film featured top Fox stars Grable (who cooed "Cuddle Up a Little Closer" from *Coney Island*), Alice Faye, and Carmen Miranda, who were announced in October of 1943 as being slated to appear. New York nightclub favorite Dick Haymes, who had recently sold a million records of "You'll Never Know" (which Faye had introduced in *Hello, Frisco, Hello*), joined the cast after being signed by Fox to a seven-year contract.

Following the film's release—and its well-deserved drubbing at critics' hands—Landis admitted that any resemblance between the real trip and its filmic representation was purely accidental, but she also maintained that the studio exercised "good judgment" in whitewashing the decidedly non-glamorous, often dangerous ordeal. Sadly, her real-life marriage to soldier Tom Wallace, dramatized in the film, ended in divorce just two years later.

PIN-UP GIRL

(20th Century-Fox, 1944)

Credits: Producer, William LeBaron; director, H. Bruce Humberstone; screenplay, Robert Ellis, Helen Logan, and Earl Baldwin, based on the story by Libbie Block; music supervisor, Fanchon; choreography, Hermes Pan; songs, Mack Gordon and Jimmy Monaco; music directors, Emil Newman and Charles Henderson; art directors, James Basevi and Joseph C. Wright; camera, Ernest Palmer.

Cast: Betty Grable (Lorry Jones); John Harvey (Tommy Dooley); Martha Raye (Molly); Joe E. Brown (Eddie); Eugene Pallette (Barney Briggs); Roller Follies, Inc. (Skating Varieties); Dave Willock (Dud Miller); Condos Brothers (Themselves); Charles Spivak and His Orchestra (Themselves); Dorothea Kent (Kay); Marcel Dalio (Headwaiter); Roger Clark (George); Gloria Nord (Roller-Skating Headliner); Irving Bacon (Window Cleaner); Mantan Moreland (Red Cap); Hermes Pan and Angela Blue (Specialty Number); J. Farrell MacDonald (Trainman); Lillian Porter (Cigarette Girl); Max Wilenz (Waiter).

With Charlie Spivak in *Pin-Up Girl.*

Songs: "You're My Little Pin-Up Girl," "Time Alone Will Tell," "Don't Carry Tales Out of School," "Story of the Very Merry Widow," "Red Robins, Bob Whites and Blue Birds," "Once Too Often," "Yankee Doodle Hayride" (Gordon-Monaco).

Release Date: May 1, 1944. *Running Time:* 83 minutes.

SYNOPSIS

Lorry Jones is the toast of Misoula, Missouri's U.S.O. club. She's also an inveterate fibber who tells admiring soldiers—to whom she autographs scads of pin-up pictures—that she's heading for Washington, D.C. to begin a U.S.O. camp tour. In reality, she's going there to work as a Civil Service stenographer, as her practical girl friend Kay points out. But the overly imaginative Lorry covets a more glamorous life and doesn't see any harm in pretending to be a star.

While stopping off in New York en route to Washington, Lorry and Kay visit the Club Chartreuse, a fashionable night spot run by veteran entertainer Eddie Hall and featuring brash singer Molly McKay. The girls crash a private party for Eddie's old pal Tommy Dooley, a recently returned hero who distinguished himself at Guadalcanal. Lorry pretends to be a Broadway star named Laura Lorraine and, after an impromptu performance with Charlie Spivak's band, charms the handsome young soldier—much to the dismay of Molly, who's got her own sights set on Tommy.

Adjusting her makeup between takes on *Pin-Up Girl* while dance director Kenny Williams looks on.

The starry-eyed Lorry, infatuated with Tommy but realizing she can't further the deception, leaves with Kay and goes on to Washington. Weeks later, while working in the Bureau of Aeronautics building, the girls spot Tommy and run for cover. Appalled at the thought of being exposed as a stenographer, Lorry hastily disguises herself with Kay's glasses and frumpy clothes, and slicks down her hair. Tommy, sent to the Bureau to report on Japanese fighting tactics, doesn't recognize Lorry but raves about the Broadway star he met in New York.

Lorry maintains her "secret identity" even after meeting Tommy as Laura Lorraine. She even lands a singing job at Club Diplomacy, Eddie Hall's new Washington nightclub. The unexpected arrival of one of Lorry's servicemen heartthrobs from Missouri exposes the girl, and Tommy slinks away, believing that he's only one of many soldiers to whom Lorry has been "professionally" friendly. But Lorry, by now billed as "the nation's number one pin-up girl," takes the novel method of apologizing to him by song, after which they are happily reunited.

REVIEWS

"*Pin-Up Girl* . . . is not an exceptional musical comedy, yet it is handsomely produced, light and lively and

With Dorothea Kent in *Pin-Up Girl*.

tuneful. The popularity of its star ensures its success. The picture shows the luscious Grable girl as the boys want to see her, in revealing costumes . . . . " (*New York Daily News*)

"Tasteful color photography and catchy songs are the chief assets of *Pin-Up Girl* . . . . Even the pin-up charms of Betty Grable and the big mouths of Martha Raye and Joe E. Brown fail to add much dramatic quality to an extended and rather tedious cabaret show." (*New York Herald Tribune*)

"Its assets are the socko title, Betty in Technicolor, Joe E. Brown in a role too small, two unusual and original musical numbers and the spirited direction of H. Bruce Humberstone in the face of obvious difficulties. Where the movie becomes unraveled at the seams and almost falls apart is the plot department." (*Los Angeles Examiner*)

"Betty Grable, exhibiting her form, charm and voice, is here supported by very tuneful music, exquisite color, a capable cast and settings of real extravagance . . . . It is the kind of entertainment calculated to take the chill out of the war and to give the boys overseas a not impercept-

ible vision of what they are fighting for." (*Motion Picture Herald*)

PRODUCTION NOTES AND COMMENTS

It's a tribute to Betty Grable's endearing, effusive screen personality that she could make attractive a basically unappealing character: *Pin-Up Girl*'s Lorry Jones is, basically, a pathological liar whose elaborate fictions and manipulative conduct nearly cost her the man she loves. Of course, it's probably churlish to engage in such armchair analysis; we are, after all, talking about World War II musical-comedy escapism here.

The real reason for *Pin-Up Girl* was, obviously, to capitalize on Grable's fame as the darling of millions of servicemen all over the world, and in that it was wildly successful. Producer William LeBaron invested the film with the glossy production values customarily expected of the star's immensely popular movies, as reflected in its $1,615,000 negative cost. He even signed Alice Sullivan, the wizard who designed the lavish stage productions at New York's famous Roxy Theatre, to help direct *Pin-Up Girl*'s musical numbers, since H. Bruce Humberstone wasn't particularly skilled in that area. Sullivan worked with choreographer Hermes Pan and the legendary showman Fanchon to achieve eye-popping results.

If one could quibble at all with *Pin-Up Girl*, it would be with the underuse of veteran troupers Joe E. Brown and Martha Raye, whose considerable talents didn't get the exposure they deserved.

BILLY ROSE'S DIAMOND HORSESHOE
(20th Century-Fox, 1945)

Credits: Producer, William Perlberg; writer-director, George Seaton; based on the play *The Barker* by Kenyon Nicholson; music directors, Alfred Newman and Charles Henderson; choreography, Hermes Pan; songs, Mack Gordon and Harry Warren; art directors, Lyle Wheeler and Joseph C. Wright; camera, Ernest Palmer; editor, Robert Simpson.

Cast: Betty Grable (Bonnie Collins); Richard Haymes (Joe Davis, Jr.); Phil Silvers (Blinky Walker); William Gaxton (Joe Davis, Sr.); Beatrice Kay (Claire Williams); Carmen Cavallaro (Himself); Willie Solar (Himself); Margaret Dumont (Mrs. Standish); Roy Benson (Harper); George Melford (Stage Doorman); Hal K. Dawson (Carter); Kenny Williams (Dance Director); Reed Hadley (Intern); Eddie Acuff (Clarinet Player); Edward Gargan (Stagehand); Ruth Rickaby (Wardrobe Woman); Dorothy Day (Dorothy); Julie London (Girl); Cyril Ring (Man); Milton Kibbee (Prop Man); Lee Phelps (Bartender); Virginia Walker (Girl); Bess Flowers (Duchess of Duke); Charles Coleman (Major Domo); Paul Bakanas (King Otto IV); Eric Wilton (Sir How Dare You).

Songs: "The More I See You," "I Wish I Knew," "Cooking Up a Show," "Welcome to the Diamond Horseshoe," "In Acapulco," "You'll Never Know," "Play Me an Old-Fashioned Melody," "A Nickel's Worth of Jive" (Gordon-Warren), "Car-

With Dick Haymes in *Billy Rose's Diamond Horseshoe.*

rie Marry Harry" (Junie McCree, Albert von Tilzer), "Let Me Call You Sweetheart" (Beth Slater Whitson-Leo Friedman), "Sleep Baby Sleep" (S.A. Emery), "Shoo Shoo Baby" (Phil Moore), "Aba Daba Honeymoon" (Arthur Fields-Walter Donovan), "I'd Climb the Highest Mountain" (Lew Brown-Sidney Clare), "My Melancholy Baby" (George A. Norton-Ernie Burnett).

Release Date: May 1, 1945. *Running Time:* 104 minutes.

SYNOPSIS

The crowd-pleasing floor shows at Billy Rose's Diamond Horseshoe are headlined by veterans Joe Davis and Claire Williams and relative newcomer Bonnie Collins. Joe, an old song-and-dance man, is constantly grumbling about being upstaged by the young, vivacious and beautiful Bonnie, who dislikes him just as heartily. Claire, Joe's girl friend, tries to keep the peace. The aging entertainer is also bothered by the decision of his son, Joe Jr., to quit medical school (with only six months to go) to become a performer. He begins neglecting Claire, who offers Bonnie a mink coat if she'll get rid of the kid. The plan is simple: When the younger Davis arrives, Bonnie is to make a play for him, let him fall for her, then brush him off. That, the girls reason, should send the young man packing.

As it develops, though, Bonnie falls in love with Joe Jr. (who has joined the show as an assistant stage manager) and plans to elope with him. A furious Joe Sr., having warned his son against taking up with showgirls, gets Bonnie fired. She persuades Joe Jr. to return to medical school, and even takes a singing job in a cheap night club to support them. When the elder Davis learns of Bonnie's loyalty and sacrifice, he tries to get her back into the Diamond Horseshoe. Upon hearing that she'll never work there while he does, Joe Sr. quits abruptly, paving the way for her return. Later, with Bonnie back on top and his son now an intern, Joe Sr. encounters Bonnie and apologizes to her. Father and son are reunited happily.

REVIEWS

"[T]ip-top film entertainment . . . Production heads at Fox have made so many big, Technicolor musical pictures that they have the formula down pat . . . . The fact that they have used it time and again doesn't mean that the latest musical from Fox lacks spontaneity, speed and good clean fun." (*New York Daily News*)

"Seldom have business and pleasure been conjoined to such a notable degree . . . a snappy entertainment in the strictly gala musical-spectacle line. Betty Grable plays the glamorous cutie with considerable down-to-earthiness." (*New York Times*)

With Haymes (kneeling), William Gaxton, Beatrice Kay, Phil Silvers (in hat) and company in *Billy Rose's Diamond Horseshoe*.

"Fox signalizes the return of Betty Grable with appropriate fanfare, luxurious costumes and trappings, an elaborate production in Technicolor and a flock of good, new tunes. The bright vivacity of Miss Grable herself makes it a happy occasion all around. She is much in evidence and up to her previous best form, singing, dancing and even acting a little . . . . " (*Motion Picture Herald*)

"Betty Grable is back in box-office stride with her new Technicolor musical. Its familiar backstage story of professional rivalry and amorous intrigue serves as a framework for lively singing and dancing and several lavish production numbers. In his first directing job, screenwriter George Seaton has turned out a Grable grosser." (*Look*)

PRODUCTION NOTES AND COMMENTS

Billy Rose's Diamond Horseshoe was a long time in the making. Producer William Perlberg initially contacted

impresario Rose in the fall of 1943 about securing rights to film a story based on his famous New York night spot; after lengthy negotiations, Fox paid Rose a whopping $76,000 for the privilege. Trade-paper accounts of the transaction indicated that Rose himself was expected to appear in the film, but the closest he got to the final product was off-screen phone conversations with the character played by Phil Silvers. Lavish settings—including a faithful recreation of Rose's well-known night club—and elaborate production numbers pushed production cost to a staggering $2,500,000, making *Diamond Horseshoe* the most expensive Grable starrer to date by nearly a million dollars.

Virtually none of the contemporary reviewers picked up on the fact that *Diamond Horseshoe*'s plot was revamped from a 1917 John Kenyon Nicholson play, *The Barker*, that had been filmed by Fox in 1933 as *Hoopla*, with Clara Bow in the Grable part, Richard Cromwell in the Haymes role, and Preston Foster essaying the father role played here by William Gaxton. (It had previously

With showgirls in *Billy Rose's Diamond Horseshoe*.

In the "Cooking Up a Show" number in *Billy Rose's Diamond Horseshoe*.

been filmed under its original title, as a 1928 silent starring Milton Sills and Dorothy Mackaill.) The studio's willingness to rely on such a hoary old plot underscored the one persistent weakness of all Grable's handsomely produced vehicles: the scripts.

THE DOLLY SISTERS
(20th Century-Fox, 1945)

Credits: Producer, George Jessel; director, Irving Cummings; screenplay, John Larkin and Marian Spitzer; art directors, Lyle Wheeler and Leland Fuller; music directors, Alfred Newman and Charles Henderson; songs, Mack Gordon, Jimmy Monaco, Lew Brown, Albert von Tilzer, Gus Kahn, Walter Donaldson, Charles Henderson, Harry Revel, Shelton Brooks, Lee Roberts, Joe Young, Sam Lewis, Bert Grant, Sam Ehrlich, Con Conrad, Joseph McCarthy, Harry Carroll, Ballard Macdonald, and Buddy Fields; camera, Ernest Palmer; editor, Barbara McLean.

Cast: Betty Grable (Jenny); John Payne (Harry Fox); June Haver (Rosie); S. Z. Sakall (Uncle Latsie); Reginald Gardiner (Duke); Frank Latimore (Irving Netcher); Gene Sheldon (Professor Winnup); Sig Rumann (Talmmis); Trudy Marshall (Lenore); Collette Lyons (Flo Daly); Evon Thomas (Jenny as a child); Donna Joe Gribble (Rosie as a child); Robert Middlemass (Hammerstein); Paul Hurst (Dowling); Lester Allen (Morrie Keno); Frank Orth (Stage Manager); William Nye (Bartender); Herbert Ashley (Fields); Trudy Berliner (German Actress); Eugene Borden (Chauffeur); Claire Richards (Operator); Andre Charlot (Phillipe); Mae Marsh (Flower Lady); Virginia Brissac (Nun); Frank Ferguson (Reporter); Crauford Kent (Man); J. Farrell MacDonald (Doorman); Albert Petit (Croupier).

Songs: "I Can't Begin to Tell You" (Gordon-Monaco), "I'm Always Chasing Rainbows" (McCarthy-Carroll), "Powder, Lipstick and Rouge" (Gordon-Revel), "Give Me the Moonlight" (Brown-von Tilzer), "On the Mississippi" (MacDonald-Fields-Carroll), "We Have Been Around" (Gordon-Henderson), "Carolina in the Morning" (Kahn-Donaldson), "Arrah Go On, I'm Gonna Go Back to Oregon" (Young-Lewis-Grant), "Darktown Strutters Ball" (Brooks), "The Vamp" (Byron Gay), "Smiles" (Callahan-Roberts), "Oh Frenchie" (Ehrlich-Conrad), "Pack Up Your Troubles" (Powell-Asaf), "The Sidewalks of New York (James Blake-Charles B. Lawlor).

Release Date: November 5, 1945. *Running Time:* 114 minutes.

SYNOPSIS

By 1912, the 18-year-old Dolly Sisters, Jenny and Rosie, have been a sister act for eight years, performing in the New York restaurant of the amiable uncle who has raised them. In an attempt to make money that will pay off the uncle's gambling debts, the girls take an engagement at the Bijou Theater in Elmira, New York, where they

With John Payne, Trudy Marshall and Gene Sheldon in *The Dolly Sisters*.

With Haver in *The Dolly Sisters*.

meet Harry Fox, a vaudevillain with big ideas. Jenny falls in love with Harry, disregarding the scorn of her more "practical" sister. Back in New York City, Harry gets the sisters their first big break by convincing them to pose as foreign stage stars: Producer Oscar Hammerstein, it turns out, is looking for Continental performers. The ruse works, and the girls become overnight sensations. Jenny wants to marry Harry, but he hesitates because he has yet to achieve show-biz success comparable to hers. She then takes one of the songs he's written and makes it a hit, giving him the self-confidence to marry her.

Rosie disapproves of the union, especially when it prompts Jenny to turn down a potentially lucrative engagement in Paris' Folies Bergere during 1917. But the sudden entry of America into World War I stirs Harry's patriotism, and after he enlists in the service Jenny agrees to appear with Rosie. The girls become the toast of Paris, and are wooed by wealthy Europeans; one of them, the fabulously wealthy Duke of Breck, takes a particular shine to Jenny, who gently rebuffs him. Harry is mustered out of the service and, finding Jenny in Paris, suggests they go home. Rosie, however, insists that she remain to finish their latest engagement; loyalty to her sister—

With John Payne, Haver, and Frank Orth in *The Dolly Sisters*.

The company of *The Dolly Sisters* poses; director Cummings sits between Grable and Haver.

along with the lure of their extravagant Parisian lifestyle—convinces Jenny to stay. A bitter, disgruntled Harry leaves, muttering about divorce.

Jenny takes Harry seriously, divorcing him to marry the Duke but finding it difficult to forget him. Badly injured when her car plunges over a cliff, Jenny is cabled a tender message by Harry and decides to break off her engagement to the Duke and leave Europe. Rosie marries a handsome young man named Irving Netcher and continues to work solo. Back in the States, she asks Jenny to appear with her in a benefit performance, where they are reunited with Harry, to whom Jenny joyously returns.

REVIEWS

"[P]ractically indistinguishable from all the rest of these gaudy, lavish spectacles. Perhaps this one will be remembered mainly for the sight of Betty Grable and June Haver as sisters, looking startlingly alike . . . . A good, if commonplace, show of the sort that seems particularly to appeal about holiday time." (*New York Sun*)

"*The Dolly Sisters* is a preposterously garish and unutterably banal pseudo-biography, two dreary hours long, about as nostalgic as a jukebox and redeemed only (for my fleshly tastes) by its frank and frequent feasting, in flesh-tone Technicolor, on two of the most hubba-hubba anatomies in the business." (*PM*)

"Dramatic license, a very convenient device to have able and willing in a nearby typewriter, is drawn upon often. *The Dolly Sisters* won't stand up under onslaught aimed at wholesale fidelity to facts, but it will stand up as a highly commercial musical. Miss Haver, on whom 20th Century-Fox pins starry hopes these days, needs seasoning, and emerges second best to Miss Grable, who undoubtedly is Hollywood's unchallenged leadoff in soubrettes." (*Motion Picture Herald*)

With Haver and showgirl in *The Dolly Sisters*.

With Haver and Payne in *The Dolly Sisters.*

PRODUCTION NOTES AND COMMENTS

The script for *The Dolly Sisters*, ostensibly based on the lives of the famous entertainers, showed remarkable similarity in character relationships and story structure to *Tin Pan Alley*, the 1940 Fox musical that starred Alice Faye and Grable as a sister act. John Payne played the same type in both pictures; interestingly, in *Dolly Sisters* Grable took the part of the serious, romantically inclined sister, whereas in *Tin Pan Alley* she'd played the more fun-loving, pragmatic sibling, a characterization adopted by June Haver for *Dolly*. Zanuck frequently teamed younger, up-and-coming stars with established favorites, and in 1945 Haver was getting the same buildup Grable

had received in 1940. Unlike Alice Faye, who got along with her younger, less experienced *Tin Pan Alley* co-star, Grable despised Haver, according to Betty's biographer.

Fortunately, the tension didn't show on screen. *The Dolly Sisters* sported some of the most opulent and memorable production numbers of any Grable film; especially notable were the "Darktown Strutters Ball" number (with Grable and Haver in blackface) and Betty's rendition of "I'm Always Chasing Rainbows," which introduced that venerable standard to a new generation.

Turned out for $2,510,000, *The Dolly Sisters* was a smash, returning to Fox some $4,000,000 in domestic film rental—making it Grable's biggest success to date.

Harry James in *Do You Love Me?*

DO YOU LOVE ME?

(20th Century-Fox, 1946)

Credits: Producer, George Jessel; director, Gregory Ratoff; screenplay, Robert Ellis and Helen Logan, based on the story by Bert Granet; art directors, Lyle Wheeler and Joseph C. Wright; music directors, Emil Newman and Charles Henderson; choreography, Seymour Felix; songs, Harold Adamson, Jimmy McHugh, Charles Henderson, Lionel Newman, Harry James, Harry Ruby, Herb Magidson, and Matt Malneck; camera, Edward Cronjager; editor, Robert Simpson.

Cast: Maureen O'Hara (Katherine Hilliard); Dick Haymes (Jimmy Hale); Harry James (Barry Clayton); Reginald Gardiner (Herbert Benham); Richard Gaines (Ralph Wainwright); Stanley Prager (Dilly); Harry James Music Makers (Themselves); B. S. Pulley (Taxi Driver); Chick Chandler (Earl Williams); Alma Kruger (Mrs. Crackleton); Almira Sessions (Miss Wayburn); Douglas Wood (Mr. Dunfee); Harlan Briggs (Mr. Higbee); Julia Dean (Mrs. Allen); Harry Hayes Morgan (Professor Allen); Eugene Borden (Headwaiter); Lex Barker (Guest); Betty Grable (Clayton's Admirer).

Songs: "As if I Didn't Have Enough on My Mind" (Henderson-Newman-James), "I Didn't Mean a Word I Said" (Adamson-McHugh), "Moonlight Propaganda" (Magidson-Malneck), "Do You Love Me?" (Ruby).

Release Date: May 1, 1946. *Running Time:* 91 minutes.

SYNOPSIS

Prim, young Katherine Hilliard is dean of the Hilliard Foundation, a strictly classical Philadelphia music school founded by her ancestors. Brought up in a rarified atmosphere, Katherine has an aversion to popular music, especially jazz, and is outraged when one of her students professes an admiration for bandleader and hot trumpet player Barry Clayton. While taking a train to New York, where she plans to hire famous conductor Herbert Benham to participate in the school's classical music festival, she encounters Clayton and his band rehearsing in a private compartment. Clayton invites Katherine in, but it doesn't take long for him to size her up as dull, cold, and unattractive.

Stirred by Clayton's appraisal of her, Katherine gets a total makeover upon reaching New York; not surprisingly, she is a beautiful woman who has been smothered in unappealing clothes and hidden behind glasses and unbecoming hairdos. She plans to shock Clayton by showing up at the night club where he's appearing. Needing a male escort, she hires Jimmy Hale, a seemingly bankrupt young man but in actuality a very talented crooner who's invited to sing with Barry's band. Clayton realizes he's misjudged Katherine, but faces stiff competition from Jimmy for her attentions.

Brief romantic complications arise when Ralph Wainwright, Katherine's stuffy suitor from Philadelphia, arrives in New York and is shocked to see the "new" Miss Hilliard. Meanwhile, conductor Benham, who sees merit in all music, persuades Barry and Jimmy to join him at the Hilliard Foundation's music festival, where they mix jazz with classical music. The concert is a huge success, and jazz is added to the curriculum. Jimmy wins Katherine's heart, while Barry is comforted by the affection of a leggy blonde fan.

REVIEWS

"In weaning the heroine from her addiction to classical music, Mr. James is aided by Dick Haymes, who periodically moos a tune equipped with lyrics that are, in their small way, a triumph of economy in songwriting. 'Do you love me?' the ballad begins, and then goes on, 'Do you love me, do you love me, do you love me, tell me, do you?' Although the question is indubitably an important one, its incessant reiteration eventually becomes as maddening as the Pepsi-Cola jingle, and just about as difficult to dismiss from the mind. The plot . . . requires Marueen O'Hara, the heroine, to try to look homely for a while, an obviously impossible feat." (*The New Yorker*)

"A trifle flimsier in plot than most recent musicals, *Do You Love Me?* is nonetheless solid film fare that will delight the fans and music lovers to whom it has been directed." (*Los Angeles Examiner*)

"[A] tuneful, lushly colored, handsomely dressed, unusually foolish musical. Shot most likely to fascinate cinemaddicts: a mere glimpse of the famed face and legs of Betty Grable (Mrs. Harry James in real life) . . . ." (*Time*)

Reginald Gardiner and Maureen O'Hara in *Do You Love Me?*

With Dick Haymes in *The Shocking Miss Pilgrim.*

"Somewhere along the production line this musical lost speed, spontaneity and spang. Some of it is fun, but most of it is jumpy, uncertain and unexciting. . . ." (*Cue*)

PRODUCTION NOTES AND COMMENTS

Do You Love Me? provided an amiable but patently ridiculous showcase for Fox's newest singing star, Dick Haymes, and bandleader Harry James (married to Grable, whose brief but delightful cameo was mentioned in most reviews). Although produced on an unnecessarily lavish scale—with a negative cost of $2,245,000—the picture managed to turn a fair profit, racking up some $3,000,000 in domestic film rental alone. And while it certainly drew more than its fair share of critical brickbats upon initial release, *Do You Love Me?* has withstood the test of time reasonably well, seeming not much sillier than many of the era's other musical movies. Moreover, it offers the incomparable image of a youthful, gorgeous, Technicolored Maureen O'Hara—an image that graced (and redeemed) even lesser films.

THE SHOCKING MISS PILGRIM
(20th Century-Fox, 1947)

Credits: Producer, William Perlberg; director-screenplay, George Seaton, based on the story by Ernest and Frederica Maas; songs, George and Ira Gershwin; music director, Alfred Newman; art directors, James Basevi, Boris Leven; camera, Leon Shamroy; editor, Robert Simpson.

Cast: Betty Grable (Cynthia Pilgrim); Dick Haymes (John Pritchard); Anne Revere (Alice Pritchard); Allyn Joslyn (Neander Woolsey); Gene Lockhart (Saxon); Elizabeth Patterson (Catherine Dennison); Arthur Shields (Michael Mich-

ael); Elisabeth Risdon (Mrs. Prichard); Charles Kamper (Herbert Jothan); Roy Roberts (Mr. Foster); Stanley Prager (Lookout in Office); Edward Laughton (Quincy); Hal K. Dawson (Peabody); Lillian Bronson (Viola Simmons); Pierre Watkin (Wendell Paige); Mary Field, Kay Riley (Teachers); John Sheehan (Vendor); Vic Potel (Speaker); Frank Dawson (Waiter).

Songs: "For You, For Me, For Evermore," "Aren't You Kinda Glad We Did?", "Changing My Tune," "Back Bay Polka," "One Two Three," "But Not in Boston," "Sweet Packard," "Stand Up and Fight," "Waltzing Is Better Sitting Down," "Waltz Me No Waltzes," "Demon Rum" (The Gershwins).

Release Date: January 31, 1947. *Running Time:* 85 minutes.

SYNOPSIS

In 1874, New York's Packard Business School graduates its first class of female "typewriters" (stenographers who craft letters on new-fangled machines). Among the eight brave girls who hope to break into the male-controlled business world, ardent and outspoken Cynthia Pilgrim expects to achieve great success. She lands a position in Boston's Pritchard Shipping Company. Old man Pritchard's son John, the firm's office manager, is shocked that a woman expects to work for a living. His Aunt Alice, a militant suffragette, is sympathetic to Cynthia and demands she be given a fair opportunity to succeed.

Although initially a social outcast in stuffy Boston, Cynthia proves herself to be highly efficient. Even John—who doesn't agree with all her progressive ideas—softens his original harsh appraisal, eventually falls in love and proposes to Cynthia. But when she announces her intention to speak at a meeting of Prohibitionists, he raises

With Anne Revere and Haymes in *The Shocking Miss Pilgrim*.

With Lillian Bronson and Elizabeth Patterson in *The Shocking Miss Pilgrim*.

With Haymes in *The Shocking Miss Pilgrim*.

strenuous objection. Rather than back down, Cynthia allows the relationship to dissolve and, although she later suspects she's made the wrong decision, finds contentment in the pursuit of her career. She proudly returns to New York to address the Packard School's latest graduating class, where she is found by John, who sweeps her away—with her own blessing.

REVIEWS

"A picture that has many assets—assets which exhibitors will have little trouble selling to the public. There is Betty Grable, to whom Technicolor again does full justice [and] Dick Haymes, the company's new singing discovery . . . but primarily it is a vehicle for presenting 11 unpublished compositions from the prolific pen of the late George Gershwin and for which Ira Gershwin has written the lyrics." (*Motion Picture Herald*)

"The most momentious thing to be said [about the film] is that it tries to present Betty Grable in something other than spangles and black silk hose. The humor (if that's what you'd call it) derives from loud and repeated references to Miss Grable as a 'typewriter' and from endless jibes at Boston stuffiness. As comedy, *Miss Pilgrim* is much flatter than Miss Grable's bodice. Hollywood will have to do much better if it means to hide the lady's legs." (*New York Times*)

"Some unpublished George Gershwin tunes have been dug out of his trunk for *The Shocking Miss Pilgrim*, bit I don't think they're quite up to his standard. This is just as well, for it would be an awful shame to waste good music on a lethargic script about a suffragette in Boston back in the days when it was scandalous for any lady to go to work in an office. As Miss Pilgrim, Betty Grable is unlikely to the point of caricature." (*New Yorker*)

PRODUCTION NOTES AND COMMENTS

Betty Grable's first attempt to escape the somewhat rigid confines of her admittedly simple but successful formula yielded a poor picture. Most reviews commented on the 11 unpublished George Gershwin tunes—freshly outfitted with lyrics by his brother Ira, who found the songs tucked away in his late brother's effects—that made up the score, noting that even they couldn't save the enterprise. The Grable name was enough to ensure reasonable box-office success, but after seeing the picture many of her fans were disappointed. Betty herself, who had fought for at least one scene in one of her trademark revealing costumes, remembered *Miss Pilgrim* with considerable bitterness. Justifiably so, too, because it doesn't hold up nearly as well as her formulaic wartime exercises. The attempt to mold Grable into a character comedienne, which would include the later *That Lady in Ermine* and *The Beautiful Blonde From Bashful Bend*, was laudable in intent but woefully inadequate in execution.

Director George Seaton, in trying to recreate an authentic turn-of-the-century atmosphere, went to some extraordinary lengths to secure vintage props. One of these was an 1874 Remington typewriter, one of the company's first, which was the object of a comparison drawn between the machine and the Grable character, who was also referred to as a "typewriter."

The Shocking Miss Pilgrim, with a negative cost of $2,595,000, earned $2,734,000 in domestic film rental, making it Grable's least successful since 1942's *Springtime in the Rockies*.

MOTHER WORE TIGHTS
(20th Century-Fox, 1947)

Credits: Writer-producer, Lamar Trotti; director, Walter Lang; based on the book by Miriam Young; music directors, Alfred Newman and Charles Henderson; art directors, Richard Day and Joseph C. Wright; choreography, Seymour Felix and Kenny Williams; songs, Mack Gordon, Josef Myrow, Harry Warren, Gus Kahn, Isham Jones, L. Wolfe Gilbert, Anatole Friedland, Albert von Tilzer, Junie McCree, and Fred Fisher; camera, Harry Jackson; editor, J. Watson Webb, Jr.

Cast: Betty Grable (Myrtle McKinley Burt); Dan Dailey (Frank Burt); Mona Freeman (Iris Burt); Connie Marshall (Mikie Burt); Vanessa Brown (Bessie); Robert Arthur (Bob Clarkman); Sara Allgood (Grandmother McKinley); William Frawley (Mr. Schneider); Ruth Nelson (Miss Ridgeway); Anabel Shaw (Alice Flemmerhammer); Michael Dunne (Roy Bivens); George Cleveland (Grandfather McKinley); Veda Ann Borg (Rosemary Olcott); Sig Rumann (Papa); Lee Patrick (Lil); Señor Wences (Specialty); Maude Eburne (Mrs. Muggins); William Forrest (Mr. Clarkman); Kathleen Lockhart (Mrs. Clarkman); Chick Chandler (Ed); Will Wright (Withers); Frank Orth (Stage Doorman); Harry Chesire (Minister); Billy Greene (First Policeman); David Thursby (Second Policeman); Tom Stevenson (Hotel Clerk); Ann Gowland (Mikie—Age 3); Karolyn Grimes (Iris—Age 16); Joan Gerians (Baby—One Month Old); Anne Baxter (Narrator).

Songs: "You Do," "Kokomo, Indiana," "There's Nothing Like a Song," "Rolling Down to Bowling Green," "This Is My Favorite City," "Fare Thee Well Dear Alma Mater" (Gordon-Myrow), "Tra-la-la-la-la" (Gordon-Warren), "Swingin' Down the Lane" (Kahn-Jones), "Stumbling" (Confrey), "Lily of the Valley" (Gilbert-Friedland), "Put Your Arms Around me, Honey" (von Tilzer-McCree), "Daddy, You've Been a Mother to Me" (Fisher).

With Dan Dailey in *Mother Wore Tights*.

Release Date: August 20, 1947. *Running Time:* 107 minutes.

SYNOPSIS

At the turn of the century, high-school graduate Myrtle McKinley plays a highly "visible" role in her class's commencement exercises—much to the annoyance of her grandma, who voices her disapproval of the girl's unseemly display of legs. Myrtle proclaims then and there that she's determined to go into show business. She gets a spot in a burlesque chorus line in San Francisco, where the featured comic is charismatic Frank Burt, who takes a shine to Myrtle—personally *and* professionally—teaching her some dance routines in their spare time. Myrtle is flattered when Frank asks her to be his partner, but she knows enough about show people to be a little skeptical. Frank's intentions are honorable, though, and he also proposes to Myrtle. After their marriage, they tour the country on the vaudeville circuit.

Myrtle leaves the act when she has her daughters, Iris and Mikie. She is a devoted mother for several years, but finally succumbs to the lure of the greasepaint and, leaving the girls with her grandparents, rejoins Frank on the road. In 1915 the family goes on summer holiday to the Berkshire Hills, where most vacationers are society types, many of them more than a little stuffy. But the happy-go-lucky, irrepressible Burts gradually win them over, and the summer is a big success—especially for 13-year-old Iris, who develops a crush on young Bob Clarkman.

Years pass, and the girls are sent to exclusive boarding schools in hopes they'll get every advantage. As a high-school senior, Iris dates Bob Clarkman, by now a Harvard man. Exposed to a different class of people, she shuns her family background and is appalled and humiliated when

her parents play a theater near the school. Frank and Myrtle are stunned and hurt by their daughter's harsh words and bitter feelings toward them, but Iris eventually realizes that she's been a snob. As a way of saying she's sorry, the girl sings a Burt family favorite at her graduation ceremony. Over the following years Iris herself becomes a star, and when Frank and Myrtle finally retire they take comfort in the fact that one of their own is carrying on the family tradition.

REVIEWS

"She's had a lot of good ones, but this is one of Betty Grable's best. *Mother Wore Tights*, based on a book by Miriam Young, is a musical with a story . . . considerably ahead of the worn-out excuse palmed off in most song-and-dance films. It relies on incident rather than plot and is fortunate in the expertness with which topnotch values are drawn out of material which, in itself, is lightweight. Miss Grable is up to her standard. Dan Dailey, a new leading man for her, does very well and bids fair to register strongly in a role which provides him full occasion to sing and dance." (*Motion Picture Herald*)

"Until it gets involved, but really involved, with a

With Dailey in *Mother Wore Tights*.
With Veda Ann Borg (fifth from left) and chorines in *Mother Wore Tights*.

straggly, sentimental piece of hokum from the typewriter of Lamar Trotti, *Mother Wore Tights* is a pretty fair song and dance show. This new musical . . . displays the shapely gams of Betty Grable whenever it gets the chance, and it must be said that Miss Grable in Technicolor is balm for the eyes. None of the songs is particularly tuneful and the dance routines are just that, but Dan Dailey puts a deal of compensating personality into the tired numbers." (*New York Times*)

"*Mother Wore Tights* is a familiarly styled Technicolor musical opus. Leisurely paced and loosely constructed as a series of undramatic vignettes, picture will appeal to patrons who prefer their nostalgia trowelled on thickly and sweetly. Numerous hoofing sequences featuring Miss Grable and her vis-a-vis, Dan Dailey, also fail to rate the heavy accent put on them by the footage. Chief drawback is rambling story, whose lack of both major and minor climaxes is made glaring by Walter Lang's deadpan direction." (*Variety*)

PRODUCTION NOTES AND COMMENTS

Judging from most of the early reviews of *Mother Wore Tights*, no one really knew how it would sit with Grable fans. Mainstream critics had frequently faulted the star's vehicles for their pat storylines, cardboard characters, and gaudy production values, but trade reviewers—more attuned to public tastes—usually recommended Betty's films without reservation. The unabashed nostalgia and sentimentality of *Mother*, however, unnerved those who thought the leggy star best in stereotypical backstage stories. The casting of Betty as the mother of grown daughters (albeit only in the latter part of the picture) seemed too radical a departure from her established persona, and there was legitimate concern that the show

With Connie Marshall and Mona Freeman in *Mother Wore Tights*.

In old-age makeup for *Mother Wore Tights*.

wouldn't fare as well as Grable's wartime exercises in escapism. Zanuck and the Fox brass shared this concern; the production had cost over $2,727,000, making it the most expensive Grable starrer to date (and, as it turned out, of her entire career).

Remarkably enough, though, *Mother* became Betty's biggest hit, returning $4,026,000 in domestic film rentals alone. Audiences everywhere willingly accepted La Grable as a devoted mother and apparently didn't mind that the legendary, seemingly ageless glamour girl was portrayed at film's end as being nearly 65 years old. Dan Dailey, in his first outing with Betty, showed himself to be a perfect leading man for her, and their numbers together were absolutely the film's highlights. Newcomer Mona Freeman delivered a first-rate performance as the snobbish daughter, Iris.

THAT LADY IN ERMINE
(20th Century-Fox, 1948)

Credits: Producer-director, Ernst Lubitsch (uncredited co-director, Otto Preminger); screenplay, Samson Raphaelson; music director, Alfred Newman; art directors, Lyle Wheeler and J. Russell Spencer; songs, Leo Robin and Frederick Hollander; camera, Leon Shamroy; editor, Dorothy Spencer.

Cast: Betty Grable (Francesca/Angelina); Douglas Fairbanks, Jr. (Colonel/Duke); Cesar Romero (Mario); Walter Abel (Major Horvath/Benvenuto); Reginald Gardiner (Alberto); Harry Davenport (Luigi); Virginia Campbell (Theresa); Whit Bissell (Guilio); Edmund MacDonald (Captain Novak); David Bond (Gabor); Harry Carter, Thayer Roberts, Don Haggerty (Staff Officers); Duke York (Sergeant); Francis Pierlot (Priest); Joe Haworth (Soldier); Harry Cording, Belle Mitchell, Mary Bear, Jack George, John Parrish, Mayo Newhall (Ancestors); Ray Hyke (Albert's Knight).

With Douglas Fairbanks, Jr. in *That Lady in Ermine*.

Songs: "Ooooh, What I'll Do to That Wild Hungarian," "This Is the Moment," "There's Something About Midnight," "The Melody Has to Be Right," "Jester's Song" (Robin-Hollander).

Release Date: August 11, 1948. *Running Time:* 89 minutes.

SYNOPSIS

One night in 1861, at the stroke of midnight in the Italian castle of Bergamo, ghostly ancestors of the Countess Angelina escape the confines of their portraits hanging in the great hall. Angelina is a perfect double for Francesca, the 16th-century countess who saved the castle from Hungarian invaders. The other ghosts wonder if young Angelina could be as brave as her famous ancestor; betrothed to the handsome Mario, she is to be married soon and can avail herself of his protection. As the spirits drift back to their portraits, Francesca whispers parting advice to the sleeping Angelina: real love will be accompanied by the sound of a flute.

On the night of their marriage Mario, now the Count of Bergamo, leaves the castle to defend it against invading Hussars. Later, the Bergamo home is taken by Hungarians led by stern, handsome Colonel Ladislaud Karoly Teglash. Angelina is informed by him that she is a prisoner of war. He notices her resemblance to Francesca, the ermine-clad woman in the portrait, and is told about the earlier Countess and her liberation of the castle.

Mario reenters the castle, disguised as a gypsy, but fails to liberate it and is captured. The spirit of Francesca intervenes, and through her ghostly presence Teglash is convinced to leave the Bergamo castle. Other spectral powers are bought to bear, and before the end of the story Angelina—who has heard the sound of a flute when Teglash was near—has her marriage annulled and weds the handsome Colonel instead, putting Francesca's spirit to rest.

REVIEWS

"The famous Lubitsch touch, that tongue-in-cheek, sly-wink, delightful handling of human foibles on the screen, is indelibly stamped on *That Lady in Ermine*. This Technicolored costume fantasy . . . is a light, amusing fable. [S]killful use of innuendo brings many a chuckle. It is impossible to say whether the film will appeal to all kinds of audiences." (*Los Angeles Times*)

"Effects of the Lubitsch touch in his last film . . . promises in the beginning a rather refreshing fantasy. But unfortunately, as the show progresses, some of the charm disappears as quickly as can the characters in the fantasy. This might very well have been due to the death of Lubitsch while the picture was being made. At any rate, if it's color you want, liberally sprinkled with imagination plus the gorgeous Betty Grable, you'll find it all there. . . ." (*Los Angeles Daily News*)

"Again playing on the human foibles, the late Ernst Lubitsch's trademark has been stamped all over *That Lady in Ermine*. In attempting to inject comedy into the story much of it fails to materialize. However, skilled direction of feather-light dialogue and use of the innuendo will draw many chuckles from audiences." (*Motion Picture Herald*)

"Betty Grable's draw at boxoffice is the factor that will determine financial fortunes of *That Lady in Ermine*. Since star's turnstile powers are considerable, film may be counted upon for at least average grosses. Grable fans, however, will be disappointed. She does a trouper's job with dual role and sings with appropriate gusto. [But] the rest is rambling, episodic and, frankly, dull. Not even the wizardry of the late Ernst Lubitsch is able to inoculate it with laughs." (*Hollywood Reporter*)

PRODUCTION NOTES AND COMMENTS

That Lady in Ermine, the first of Betty's "costume" pictures, was both a critical and commercial washout. Trade reviewers were baffled that Fox put Grable into such a picture, mainstream reviewers lamented the impotence of "the Lubitsch touch" (due to the producer-director's sudden death and his subsequent replacement by Otto Preminger, a director not known for his light touch), and moviegoers wondered why Betty didn't show more of her famous legs.

Originally bought by Fox in 1942 at the behest of Lubitsch, and announced as a starring vehicle for Irene Dunne, *Lady in Ermine* went into production as *This Is the Moment*, the title of one of its songs. The titular garment, which had a three-foot train, was composed of 900 pure, unbleached, golden-white Russian ermine skins (the average coat used about 200 skins), and cost

With Reginald Gardiner in *That Lady in Ermine*.

With Ceasar Romero in *That Lady in Ermine*.

With Fairbanks in *That Lady in Ermine*.

$28,000. Grable danced while wearing the coat in the "There's Something About Midnight" number, but the hot studio lights needed for the Technicolor cameras made it an unpleasant experience.

There were others. In Fairbanks' first scene with Betty, he was to carry her through double doors into a vast hall, then pause for a kiss before whisking her up a flight of stairs. She was wearing a gold-encrusted white silk dress with hoops six feet wide. On the first take, Fairbanks carried her through the doors, caught the $1,000 garment on a door jam, and ripped it off his surprised co-star. Later on in the production schedule, she developed a bad cold and high fever. Lubitsch shot around her for two days, and she still didn't feel quite up to snuff when she returned to the studio. Then, when Lubitsch died of a heart attack on November 30, 1947, with the picture only half finished, he was replaced by Otto Preminger, a stern taskmaster with whom Betty scarcely got along.

Preminger waived any directorial credit, possibly out of respect to Lubitsch, possibly because the film turned out poorly and he didn't want to be linked to it. Grable turned in her usual workmanlike performance, and even had a couple of nice musical moments, but she was clearly out of her metier. The public thought so, too, and the film didn't rack up anywhere near the grosses of its immediate predecessor, *Mother Wore Tights*. In fact, with domestic film rentals of $1,414,000 (against a negative cost of $2,484,000), *Ermine* was Betty's first money-loser since 1942's *Footlight Serenade*.

WHEN MY BABY SMILES AT ME
(20th Century-Fox, 1948)

Credits: Producer, George Jessel; director, Walter Lang; writer, Lamar Trotti, based on the play *Burlesque* by George Manker Watters and Arthur Hopkins, adapted by Elizabeth Reinhardt; art directors, Lyle Wheeler and Leland Fuller; music director, Alfred Newman; songs, Mack Gordon, Josef Myrow, Andrew B. Sterling, Harry von Tilzer, Alfred Byran, Joseph McCarthy, Fred Fisher, Buddy De Sylva, Lew Brown, Ray Henderson, Billy Rose, Ted Lewis, Bill Munro, M.C. Brice, and Walter Donaldson; camera, Harry Jackson; editor, Barbara McLean.

Cast: Betty Grable (Bonny); Dan Dailey (Skid); Jack Oakie (Bozo); June Havoc (Gussie); Richard Arlen (Harvey); James Gleason (Lefty); Vanita Wade (Bubbles); Kenny Williams (Specialty Dancer); Robert Emmett Keane (Sam Harris); Jean Wallace (Sylvia Marco); Pati Behrs (Woman in Box); Lee MacGregor (Call Boy); Charles Tannen (Interne); Noel Neill, Lu Anne Jones, Joanne Dale, Dorothy Babb (Specialty Dancers); Hank Mann (Man); Edward Clark (Box-Office Man).

Songs: "When My Baby Smiles at Me" (Sterling-Lewis-Munro), "By the Way," "What Did I Do?" (Gordon-Myrow), "Oui Oui Marie" (Bryan-McCarthy-Fisher), "Don't Bring Lulu" (Rose-Brown-Henderson), "Birth of the Blues" (De Sylva-Brown-Henderson), "The Daughter of Rosie O'Grady" (Brice-Donaldson).

Release Date: November 23, 1948. *Running Time:* 98 minutes.

SYNOPSIS

Skid and Bonny Johnson are carefree, young marrieds playing the burlesque circuit during the Roaring Twenties. Bonny, keenly aware of Skid's weakness for booze and broads, realizes that he has the potential to be a great stage comedian. The Johnsons are working in a small touring company when Skid gets an offer from famed theatrical impresario Sam Harris to play the comic in one of his stage extravaganzas. Bonny tries to convince Skid that he should take the job, but he hesitates. Their pal Lefty, the stage manager, deliberately fires Skid in order to force him into accepting Harris' offer.

While Bonny continues touring in burleycue houses, Skid registers a big hit in the Harris show. Success goes to his head, however, and when Bonny reads that he's about to do a show with her former rival, Sylvia Marco, she fears he'll surrender to the temptations of demon rum and high living. She talks to Skid, who promises he'll use his influence to remove Marco from the new show. He takes the sultry Sylvia to a speakeasy, hoping a casual social situation will soften the blow. When the joint is raided,

Striking a pose for *When My Baby Smiles at Me.*

With Dan Dailey and James Gleason in *When My Baby Smiles at Me.*

photographers snap Skid and Marco together and plaster the picture in the newspapers. Bonny gets the wrong idea and, believing Skid unfaithful, institutes divorce proceedings. Meanwhile, she's courted by an old admirer, wealthy cattleman Harvey Howell, who sees her impending split as his big opportunity.

Skid agrees to the divorce, but he is devastated by the breakup and decides to drown his sorrows. Back in New York prior to marrying Howell, Bonny finds out how far Skid has fallen. She enlists the aid of their old friend Lefty, who gets Skid dried out and back in show business. But, with his self-confidence in tatters, he starts drinking before curtain time on opening night. Bonny, who has come to the theater to see him, suspects what's happening and goes on stage to guide Skid through his old routines. Buoyed by his ex-wife's presence, Skid straightens up and goes through his paces with the old panache. The Johnsons are thus reunited and continue their careers together.

REVIEWS

"Betty Grable is making another of her periodical excursions into the songs and dances and fripperies of a Technicolored burlesque queen. This time the excursion is under unusually superior auspices. She is given ample opportunity to chant a fast song or croon a weepy one in discreetly revealing costumes, tossing in an occasional dance." (*New York World Telegram*)

"If rigid adherence to formula still pays off on the screen, then the year's most successful picture should be *When My Baby Smiles at Me*. That is assuming your reaction to Miss Grable swinging her hips and singing a couple of old song hits is slightly above the whistling stage." (*New York Times*)

"Grable and Dailey, co-stars of the memorably successful *Mother Wore Tights*, are together again, and again congenially matched, in this George Jessel production in Technicolor of the stage play *Burlesque*. Song, dance, nostalgia and sentiment are combined with sparkling presentation, glib dialogue, plentiful humor and able supporting performances to round out an attraction sure to rank well up among the year's musicals. [T]he numerous brilliant production numbers come along as integral narrative ingredients rather than as interpolations. The end result [is] more satisfying than that achieved by most musicals." (*Motion Picture Herald*)

"Producer George Jessel wisely dug into the file for the play *Burlesque* to make certain of a happy collaboration of stellar talent, story, and musical interpolation. Sure, the old wheelhorse creaks a bit at the edges, but what it lacks in high-powered melodramatics is more than compensated for in its flip manner, frank nostalgia, corny jokes and the superlative 'burley' atmosphere that Jessel reads into its presentation. Betty Grable, vivacious and curvaceous, is all that her fans could want. She wiggles into the burlesque costumes with the charm that is peculiarly Betty's, and more recommendation could not be made." (*Hollywood Reporter*)

PRODUCTION NOTES AND COMMENTS

For purposes of screen adaptation, the popular George Manker Watters-Arthur Hopkins play *Burlesque,* which made a star of Barbara Stanwyck in its Broadway run, was already a shopworn item when 20th Century-Fox bought it from Columbia in August, 1947. It had been filmed twice by Paramount—as *The Dance of Life* (1929, starring Nancy Carroll and Hal Skelly) and *Swing High, Swing Low* (1937, with Carole Lombard and Fred MacMurray)—before being purchased in 1939 by Al Jolson, who intended it to be a comeback vehicle that would reunite him on screen with wife Ruby Keeler. The couple's divorce later that year scotched Jolson's plan, and he most likely sold the play to Columbia around the time that studio filmed his biography, *The Jolson Story* (1946).

In any event, the property was given to producer George Jessel to develop as a starring vehicle for Grable, who had just finished the disappointing *That Lady in Ermine.* Jessel engaged Dan Dailey, Betty's *Mother Wore Tights* co-star, to play the male lead. Dailey, himself a former burlesque hoofer, threw himself into preparation for the part, tirelessly rehearsing his dance numbers for nearly a month before the start of filming—and losing 30 pounds in the bargain.

Grable, still soured by *That Lady in Ermine,* demanded that scrupulous attention to period costuming be overlooked somewhat in favor of outfits designed to show off her figure—which she well knew to be one of her principal assets. She was delighted to work with Dailey again, and a press release issued after the close of production claimed she requested he be assigned to at least one of her two yearly pictures for Fox.

Savvy reviewers, particularly those of the show-business trade papers, commented upon the plot's threadbare nature but agreed that, as a Betty Grable vehicle, the picture more than lived up to expectations. Audiences agreed. Seen today, however, *When My Baby Smiles at Me* impresses as a showcase for Dailey rather than his distaff co-star. His high-octane dancing and genuinely charming portrayal of a stereotypical show-biz character actually overshadows Betty's typically ener-

With Dailey in *When My Baby Smiles at Me.*

getic but one-note performance. The production cost nearly $2,361,000 but, with domestic film rental totalling $2,997,000, it still turned a respectable profit for Fox.

THE BEAUTIFUL BLONDE FROM BASHFUL BEND

(20th Century-Fox, 1949)

Credits: Writer-producer-director, Preston Sturges; based on the story by Earl Felton; art directors, Lyle Wheeler and George W. Davis; music director, Cyril J. Mockridge; songs, Mack Gordon, Josef Myrow, Don George, Lionel Newman, Meta Orred, and Annie F. Harrison; camera, Harry Jackson; editor, Robert Fritch.

Cast: Betty Grable (Freddie Jones/Hilda Swandumper); Cesar Romero (Blackie Jobero); Rudy Vallee (Charlie Hingleman); Olga San Juan (Conchita); Sterling Holloway (Basserman Boy); Hugh Herbert (Doctor); El Brendel (U.S. Marshal); Porter Hall (Judge O'Toole); Margaret Hamilton (Elvira O'Toole); Emory Parnell (Mr. Hingleman); Chris-Pin Martin (Joe); J. Farrell MacDonald (Sheriff Sweetzer); Marie Windsor (LaBelle Bergere); Esther Howard (Mrs. Smidlap); Chester Conklin (Messenger Boy); Mary Monica MacDonald (Freddie at age 6); Snub Pollard (First Hanger-On); Frank Moran (Hood); Joseph Turkel, George Lynn (Reporters); James Joseph O'Neill (Patrolman); Len Hendry (New Yorker).

Songs: "Beautiful Blonde From Bashful Bend" (George-Newman), "Everytime I Meet You" (Gordon-Myrow), "In the Gloaming" (Orred-Harrison).

Release Date: May 27, 1949. *Running Time:* 77 minutes.

SYNOPSIS

Freddie, a cute little blonde about 20 years old, is an orphan whose granddad has taught her how to protect herself in the tradition of the Old West. She's been a crack marksman—or markswoman—since the age of six and, even though blossomed into womanhood, she still holds her own with a six-gun. As the story begins, she's stuck in the local clink because she got mad at her boyfriend, Blackie, took a shot at him, and ended up hitting the local judge in the posterior. When Freddie tries to plead her case, Blackie puts in an appearance and the fight starts again. Freddie gets mad, grabs a gun, and fires. She hits the judge again . . . in the same place.

Needing to leave town quickly, Freddie and her girlfriend Conchita swipe a couple of train tickets and head for Snake City. When the train pulls into town, both the good and the bad elements are out to greet who they think is Miss Hilda Swandumper, the new schoolmarm. One look at the faces of Old Man Basserman and his two boys, and Freddie realizes why it's been tough for Snake City to keep a teacher. She's more than willing to assume the role temporarily, and when the Basserman boys get out of hand she demonstrates her shooting expertise, making the difficult students her abject slaves.

Without warning, Blackie shows up in town, ready to apologize to Freddie. The Bassermans, out to protect their beloved teacher, suspect Blackie of dark motives. They dress up as Indians and conk him over the head with a rock. He comes to and blasts at them with his own six-shooter. Old Man Basserman, convinced his boys are dead, starts a raging gun battle in town. In the middle of the ruckus, the boys show up hale and hearty, and their pa shamefacedly calls for a truce. Blackie and Freddie patch up their quarrel and all is forgiven.

With Rudy Vallee in *The Beautiful Blonde From Bashful Bend.*

REVIEWS

"Betty Grable's strength at the box-office faces something of a challenging test with her latest attraction. [It] is a dubious endeavor in low comedy and broad acting spinning on a one-gag pivot strictly out of burlesque. It's all bewildering for noise and clamor and astonishing for the dragnet which [writer-director Preston] Sturges puts out in search of belly laughs. Sturges resorts to the painfully archaic device of having Miss Grable lose her skirt and wiggle what's exposed squarely into the Technicolor camera." (*Motion Picture Herald*)

"Why 20th feels it must keep Miss Grable's most valuable assets covered under long skirts, give her as few songs and dances as possible and expect top results is a major mystery. Despite the fact that this attempt at horse-opera burlesque was produced by Preston Sturges—a master at sophisticated comedy—it still doesn't come off." (*Fortnight*)

"[A] cock-eyed comedy with several excruciatingly funny scenes, some saucy dialogue and artful performances by Betty Grable and an interesting supporting cast. The Preston Sturges production, however, is clearer in intent than in materialization. What starts as an amusing variation on the Annie Oakley legend evolves into a fragmentary, episodic story that is nothing more than a succession of comedy episodes . . . . La Grable . . . troupes the show with her customary vigor. She is on screen most of the time, which is all to the good since the boxoffice fortunes of the piece will be largely the result of her boxoffice appeal." (*Film Daily*)

"There are intermittent flashes of period satire and wit in this steam-rollered travesty on pioneer days, but they are mighty few; and the amount of fine talent dragged into the picture and then ignored or wasted is appalling. Betty Grable—singing, dancing, or just plain acting—does a capable job with the messed-up material provided her." (*Cue*)

PRODUCTION NOTES AND COMMENTS

Hollywood has always had a penchant for allowing highly feted artists to occasionally run amuck without supervision or accountability; it didn't begin with *Heaven's Gate.* Preston Sturges, a prominent screenwriter who specialized in literate screenplays with sharp wit and pungent dialogue, had earned a reputation as a can't-miss comedy craftsman while tenured at Paramount, where he wrote and directed several classics—including *The Lady Eve, Sullivan's Travels* (both 1941), *The Palm Beach Story* (1942), and *The Miracle of Morgan's Creek* (1944)—before leaving the studio after pro-

With Al Bridge (left), El Brendel, Cesar Romero, Olga San Juan, and Chris-Pin Martin in *The Beautiful Blonde From Bashful Bend.*

tracted conflicts with management. Darryl Zanuck wooed Sturges over to Fox, where he was to be given total autonomy in the selection, development, and production of his films . . . along with a handsome salary.

After the huge box-office success of *Mother Wore Tights*, Zanuck reasoned that Grable needed more tailor-made properties and less mindless musicals. He importuned Sturges to make his first Fox film a Betty Grable vehicle. Not necessarily thrilled about working with Betty, but hoping to win Zanuck's favor and guarantee his total freedom with front-office interference, the writer-director agreed to flesh out an Earl Felton treatment, *The Lady From Laredo*. Zanuck claimed to love Sturges' early draft of the script and okayed the production.

Production was delayed for several reasons, firstly because there was some doubt as to whether or not the picture should be made in color. Sturges insisted on so doing, having reasoned that Grable's popularity derived from the Technicolored depictions of her charms. The rising costs of color cinematography and prints, coupled with temporary but crippling taxes imposed on American pictures by the British market—where Zanuck hoped to recoup much of his investment—forced a postponement.

Grable went into *That Lady in Ermine*, and Sturges began working on a project much closer to him, *Unfaithfully Yours*.

A brilliant if morbid black comedy, *Unfaithfully Yours* in finished form made Zanuck uneasy (with good reason:

With Sterling Holloway in *The Beautiful Blonde From Bashful Bend.*

A gag still taken during production of *Beautiful Blonde From Bashful Bend*.

With Mature in *Wabash Avenue*.

the film flopped). He began to doubt Sturges' judgment. When *Beautiful Blonde* finally rolled in late 1948, the Fox honcho deluged Sturges with memos and suggestions. The writer-director had little enthusiasm for the project, and helmed it with something less than his usual level of expertise. Grable, not particularly happy with the script or the character, performed in her customarily spirited manner, but grew to dislike Sturges and, by the end of shooting, refused to speak to him.

Unfaithfully Yours failed to achieve much success. When *Beautiful Blonde* was released, critics generally excoriated the writer-director over whom they had once fawned. They called the picture a laborious, one-joke farce—and they were right. Even the public, which up to this point had supported Grable's pictures enthusiastically, was taken aback by their favorite's latest offering. The film flopped, earning only $1,489,000 in domestic film rental, though it cost $2,260,000. Angry over what she felt was her betrayal by studio management, Grable started grumbling. For his part, Zanuck fired Sturges, whose career never recovered.

WABASH AVENUE
(20th Century-Fox, 1950)

Credits: Producer, William Perlberg; director, Henry Koster; screenplay, Harry Tugend and Charles Lederer; art directors, Lyle Wheeler and Joseph C. Wright; music director, Lionel Newman; songs, Mack Gordon, Joseph Myrow, Bert Kalmar, and Joe Cooper; camera, Arthur E. Arling; editor, Robert Simpson.

Cast: Betty Grable (Ruby Summers); Victor Mature (Andy Clark); Phil Harris (Uncle Mike); Reginald Gardiner (English Eddie); James Barton (Hogan); Barry Kelley (Bouncer); Margaret Hamilton (Tillie Hutch); Jacqueline Dalya (Cleo); Robin Raymond (Jennie); Hal K. Dawson (Healy); Colette Lyons (Beulah); Charles Arnt (Carter); Walter Long, Bill Daniel (Dancers); Marion Marshall (Chorus Girl); Percy Helton (Ship's Captain); Henry Kulky (Joe); Alexander Pope (Charlie); Dick Wessel (Electrician); Peggy Leon (Hairdresser); Bill Phillips (Attendant).

Songs: "Down on Wabash Avenue," "Walking Along With Billy," "Baby, Won't You Say You Love Me?", "Wilhelmina," "May I Tempt You With a Big Red Rosy Apple?", "Clean Up Chicago" (Gordon-Myrow), "I've Been Floating Down the Old Green River" (Kalmar-Cooper), "I Wish I Could Shimmy Like My Sister Kate" (Armand J. Piron-Peter Bocage).

Release Date: April 29, 1950. *Running Time:* 92 minutes.

SYNOPSIS

Likable con man "Uncle Mike," having cheated his partner Andy Clark out of his money, opens up a successful music hall along Chicago's Wabash Avenue during the 1892 World's Fair. His star performer and favorite heartthrob is Ruby Summers. Andy, having tracked Mike to Chicago, tries to get his money back and make a play for Ruby at the same time. Both efforts fail.

Then Andy hits upon a scheme. By faking the death of a stumblebum named Hogan, he threatens to implicate Mike and thus blackmails himself into the business as a full partner. Together they open a swank club on the Fair Grounds. Andy, who believes Ruby to be too coarse, convinces her to subdue her performing style. The "new" Ruby soon becomes a big success, winning a Broadway contract—and falling for Andy as well. But Mike breaks up their planned marriage when he discovers that Hogan's "death" was a hoax and exposes Andy as a fraud.

Both Ruby and Andy leave Chicago hurriedly; she

becomes a Broadway star and he winds up playing piano in a Bowery theater. Mike, ultimately realizing that Ruby is unhappy without Andy, gives up his claim on her and convinces her to find Andy and marry him—which she does.

REVIEWS

"This breezy filmusical takes full advantage of the shapely Grable gams as well as the many other of Betty's talents—not that the male contingent in the audience will pay much attention to the latter. [T]here is Technicolor photography, a laugh-infested script, catchy tunes and the inevitable nostalgic guy-meets-dame plot characteristic of tune-and-fun films that plumb the past for genesis. Such stereotyped source material and the fact that a vacillating pace slows the overall tempo are the picture's only shortcomings." (*Boxoffice*)

"*Wabash Avenue* presents Betty Grable, Victor Mature and Phil Harris in another of those backstage song-and-dance dramas that Miss Grable seems to enjoy, even if no one else does. Mr. Mature and Mr. Harris battle for Miss Grable's affections. Their struggles appear about as genuine as the grapplings of professional wrestlers." (*New Yorker*)

"*Wabash Avenue* isn't on the screen more than three minutes before Betty Grable is performing a shimmy dance in a cut-down costume that affords onlookers the best view of the Grable torso that they have enjoyed in some time. Henry Koster's direction, as it inevitably does, finds beguiling human qualities in the script and performances . . . thus giving more realistic dramatic substance than the usual shallow, tinselled musical." (*Hollywood Reporter*)

"Betty makes a substantial comeback in her first release since *Beautiful Blonde From Bashful Bend*—and of bashful memory. Histrionically, distinction is decidedly lacking. But the Grable chassis, being neither lacking nor wanting, makes up for a good deal. [F]ilm is

With Reginald Gardiner and Victor Mature in *Wabash Avenue*.

With chorus boys in *Wabash Avenue*.

With dancer in *Wabash Avenue*.

often routine and dull, but decidedly a Grable staple."
(*Motion Picture Herald*)

PRODUCTION NOTES AND COMMENTS

Fox was anxious to put Grable back into an old-fashioned backstage musical after the relative failures of *That Lady in Ermine* and *The Beautiful Blonde From Bashful Bend*. Taking no chances, producer William Perlberg revamped one of the star's best vehicles, *Coney Island*, changing the story's time frame and locale but little else. The *Wabash Avenue* title was originally slated for Fox's treatment of the romance between songwriter Gus Kahn and his wife Grace, the rights for which were purchased by the studio in 1946 for June Haver.

Perlberg mounted a lavish, eye-popping production (negative cost: $2,115,000) that encompassed the construction of a two-block replica of the 1892 World's Fair midway, several blocks of Wabash Avenue, and New York's Victoria Theatre. Hundreds of period costumes were designed or rustled up by the costume department, including 14 outfits for Grable alone.

In preparation for his role as Andy, the con man who

winds up playing piano down on the Bowery, Victor Mature actually learned how to tinkle "Baby, Won't You Say You Love Me?" on the ivories. Initially, Henry Koster wanted him to dance with Grable in a number, but the bulky Mature demurred, lifting his size-12 1/2 shoes for the director to see.

In working out her numerous dance routines, Grable was reunited with dance director Billy Daniels, who'd drilled her for production numbers in her Paramount films of the late '30s.

Domestic film rental amounted to $2,039,000.

MY BLUE HEAVEN
(20th Century-Fox, 1950)

Credits: Producer, Sol C. Siegel; director, Henry Koster; based on the story *Storks Don't Bring Babies* by S. K. Lauren; screenplay, Lamar Trotti and Claude Binyon; music director, Alfred Newman; songs, Harold Arlen, Ralph Blane, Walter Donaldson, and George Whiting; art directors, Lyle Wheeler and Joseph C. Wright; camera, Arthur E. Arling; editor, James B. Clark.

With Dan Dailey in *My Blue Heaven.*

Cast: Betty Grable (Kitty Moran); Dan Dailey (Jack Moran); David Wayne (Walter Pringle); Jane Wyatt (Janet Pringle); Mitzi Gaynor (Gloria Adams); Una Merkel (Miss Gilbert); Louise Beavers (Selma); Laura Pierpont (Mrs. Johnson); Don Hicks (Young Man); Irving Fulton (Specialty Dancer); Billy Daniels (Dance Director); Larry Keating (Doctor); Minerva Urecal (Miss Bates); Mae Marsh (Maid); Noel Reyburn (Studio Employee); Phyllis Coates (Woman); Barbara Pepper (Waitress); Myron Healy (Father); Lois Hall (Mother); Frank Remley (Orchestra Leader).

Songs: "My Blue Heaven" (Whiting-Donaldson), "Don't Rock the Boat, Dear," "Friendly Islands," "Halloween," "Live Hard, Work Hard, Love Hard," "I Love a New Yorker," "It's Deductible," "What a Man" (Arlen-Blane).

Release Date: September 15, 1950. *Running Time:* 96 minutes.

SYNOPSIS

Beloved radio stars Kitty and Jack Moran take a big chance and bring their considerable talents to television, hoping to click in the new medium. Not surprisingly, they become a smash hit and their show a must-see program.

With Dailey, David Wayne, and Jane Wyatt in *My Blue Heaven*.

Yet, for all their success, Kitty and Jack are still denied the one thing that would make them truly happy: a child. Then, at last, Kitty learns that she is "expecting"—finally! Returning home one night after a party celebrating her pregnancy, Kitty is badly injured in a car crash. She loses the baby and is told by doctors that she won't be able to have any more. Bitterly hurt and initially depressed, Kitty and Jack are bolstered by the happiness of their friends, Walter and Janet Pringle, who have many children. They elect to adopt a child, only to find that it isn't as easy as it sounds. After a number of disappointments, however, the Morans finds themselves adopting *two* children simultaneously. Even more miraculously, Kitty learns that, doctors' predictions to the contrary, she's pregnant again!

REVIEWS

"Miss Grable and Dailey [are] unfortunately involved with an overly sticky plot, but it doesn't get in the way enough to keep this from being anything but a top money-grabber among the long series of 20th's ultra-commercial color musicals . . . . the real eye-catcher of the pic is a lush, brunet youngster making her initial screen appearance . . . Mitzi Gaynor. In addition to a pert and saucy face and the kind of figure boys don't forget, she's long on terping and vocalizing." (*Variety*)

"Don't be surprised if this Betty Grable-Dan Dailey Technicolor musical out-grosses its predecessors by a substantial margin, for it's got everything the others had plus a rare thing musicals are not even expected to have. It's got a story that could stand alone. The subject of adoption, often and usually quite unsatisfactorily used as picture material, receives in this musical the most authentic and engrossing treatment it has had on the screen." (*Motion Picture Herald*)

"*My Blue Heaven* . . . apparently is angled at that audience which presumably gurgles and glees at the most

Dailey and Mitzi Gaynor in *My Blue Heaven*.

With David Wayne in *My Blue Heaven*.

elementary banalities that occur on the video screen. [I]t is probably the gooiest and guckiest musical film from 20th Century-Fox in years. Let us not dwell too closely . . . upon the incredible spectacle of Mr. Dailey kicking up his heels and acting like an infantile looney when he learns that he is to become a pop, [or] of Miss Grable gulping sadly and turning her tearful face aside when she learns that she cannot be a mother." (*New York Times*)

PRODUCTION NOTES AND COMMENTS

Extremely interesting with its background of radio stars performing on television—the new medium that posed the greatest threat to Hollywood since radio was invented—*My Blue Heaven* also broke musicomedy tradition by flirting with tragedy and pathos in its depiction of Grable's tragic car accident and her subsequent attempts to adopt children. In fact, that aspect of the plot seems to have disturbed some of the film's critics, who called the film overly sentimental and manipulative of audiences' feelings.

This film is also notable in that, for the first time since *The Dolly Sisters*, reviewers praised two supporting players nearly as much as they did Grable. Almost all of them commented on Mitzi Gaynor, whose small but highly visible supporting role portended a starring career of brief duration. David Wayne also elicited kudos from the scriveners, and with good reason: He got many of the picture's best lines. In one scene, commenting on the numerous children his wife has provided him, he says dryly, "It's gotten so now that I'm even afraid to shake hands with her."

As usual, Grable performed vigorously and displayed her fabled gams prominently. The critics, however, judging from their glowing reviews of Gaynor and Wayne, were plainly tiring of Grable. The drop in public support was less apparent, though; *My Blue Heaven* managed to pull in some $2,805,000 in worldwide film rentals on an expenditure of $2,135,000, and while its profit margin wasn't as high as that of earlier Grable pictures, it was still more than respectable—especially given the new competition from television.

CALL ME MISTER
(20th Century-Fox, 1951)

Credits: Producer, Fred Kohlmar; director, Lloyd Bacon; screenplay, Albert E. Lewin and Burt Styler, based on the play by Harold J. Rome and Arnold M. Auerbach; songs, Mack Gordon, Sammy Fain, Jerry Seelen, Earl K. Brent, Frances Ash, and Harold J. Rome; art directors, Lyle Wheeler and Joseph C. Wright; camera, Arthur E. Arling; editor, Louis Loeffler.

Cast: Betty Grable (Kay Hudson); Dan Dailey (Shep Dooley); Danny Thomas (Stanley); Dale Robertson (Capt. Johnny Comstock); Benay Venuta (Billie Barton); Richard Boone (Mess Sergeant); Jeffrey Hunter (The Kid); Frank Fontaine (Sergeant); Harry Von Zell (General Steele); Dave Willock (Jones); Lou Spencer, Art Stanley (Dance Team); Bobby Short, Bob Roberts (Singers); Jerry Paris (Brown); Ken Christy (Chief of Staff); Dabbs Greer (Colonel's aide); John McGuire (Andy); Harry Lauter, Jack Kelly, Paul Burke (Soldiers); Geraldine Knapp (Canape Girl).

Songs: "I Just Can't Do Enough for You, Baby," "Love Is Back in Business," "Japanese Girl Like American Boy" (Gordon-Fain), "Lament to the Pots and Pans" (Seelen-Brent), "Going Home Train," "Call Me Mister," "Military Life" (Rome), "I'm Gonna Love That Guy" (Ash).

Release Date: January 31, 1951. *Running Time:* 95 minutes.

With Benay Venuta in *Call Me Mister*.

SYNOPSIS

Highly decorated First Sergeant Shep Dooley, stranded in Tokyo after World War II, can't wait to get back to Broadway, where he was a top song-and-dance man. Short of ready cash, he reluctantly elects to sell his prized dancing shoes, but isn't having much luck doing so. He runs into his wife Kay, from whom he has been separated for many years. She joined CATS, the Civilian Actress Technicians, and entertained troops during the war. Seeing Shep with dancing shoes in hand, Kay figures he danced his way through the conflict without having served in combat.

Kay still loves Shep, but they mix about as easily as oil and water; after another misunderstanding, she volunteers to go with handsome Captain Johnny Comstock to Kyoto, where she puts on a show for the American soldiers stationed there. Shep shows up in full dress uniform and combat ribbons, and while Kay realizes she's misjudged him, she still remains somewhat aloof. He fears she's in love with Comstock.

Returning to Tokyo, Shep learns that his outfit has sailed back to the States. Then, writing false orders assigning him to detail in Kyoto, he joins the show in hopes of wooing Kay back to him. A jealous Comstock tries to keep them apart, but eventually the couple reunites. Then Shep learns that his outfit, having arrived back in America, has been mustered out of the service. That means he's now a civilian, so, he says, call him "mister."

REVIEWS

"Fox has a sock filmusical in *Call Me Mister*. Drawing but lightly on its Broadway revue namesake for book and songs, it is smooth, easy-to-take screen entertainment that promises to register smoothly at the ticket windows. Footage sparks along through songs, dances and a skeleton story framework with an infectious zip. The two stars are excellent and Danny Thomas scores a solid personal success with his sympathetic type of comedy." (*Variety*)

With Dan Dailey and dancers in *Call Me Mister*.

"[A] most pleasant musical comedy—handsome in its plush Technicolor production and stunning in its array of top flight talent. Lloyd Bacon's direction skillfully highlights the comedy values and pushes the action along at a tempo that is particularly breezy and effective in the second half. Betty Grable socks across the grand score and plays her part of the trouper in characteristic yestful style." (*Hollywood Reporter*)

"Let it be said that the movie version [of *Call Me Mister*] is a good musical despite its patent misrepresentation. Editorials could—and should—be written about how movie companies buy stage properties for their titles alone—and then ignore the guts of the show that made the titles important. In the movie we miss such sock tunes as 'South America, Take It Away,' but by nylon! we've got Betty Grable's legs. Miss Grable, as you might expect, looks great throughout the production." (*Los Angeles Daily News*)

"[A]side from the title, one skit, and a couple of songs, all of this bears little relation to the excellent Broadway revue of a couple of seasons back. The Fox version of *Call Me Mister* is essentially a vehicle for the pulchritudinous Miss Grable, and neither script nor camera overlooked a single angle that might help accentuate her endearing young charms—which makes it perfect for Grable fans." (*Saturday Review*)

With Dailey in *Call Me Mister.*

With Dailey in *Call Me Mister.*

PRODUCTION NOTES AND COMMENTS

In November, 1947, 20th Century-Fox paid $200,000 for the screen rights to the 1946 Broadway smash *Call Me Mister*—at that time a phenomenal amount for such a transaction. Yet the studio all but discarded the play's book and lyrics when it came time to fashion a screen adaptation. Scripting chores were assigned to ex-infantrymen Albert E. Lewin and Burt Styler, whose military experience presumably qualified them to concoct a story about armed-services life. Updated to correspond with topical events, the Lewin-Styler screenplay set the movie in Japan during the early days of the Korean War. Only three of Harold Rome's original songs were interpolated into the film, and many reviewers—especially the New York-based ones, who were familiar with the original property—expressed disbelief that Fox would so cavalierly treat the material that had secured box-office success for the play. This, in fact, became the main point of criticism, for there was little else to fault in such a superbly constructed filmusical (and Grable's last first-rate starring vehicle).

Director Lloyd Bacon and dance director Busby Berkeley, reunited for the first time since 1933's *42nd Street*, shared reminiscences of "the good old days" for Fox publicity scribes, and Berkeley was quoted in one press release at saying that he knew Betty Grable would one day be a big star when he pulled the 13-year-old out of a chorus line to feature her in a production number for *Whoopee!* (1930).

With Signal Corps Major Robert B. Randle as a Technical Advisor, a second-unit crew was dispatched to Japan to shoot backgrounds of U.S. army installations and establishing shots of Tokyo side streets and Kyoto parks.

Studio production went reasonably smooth, although Berkeley was still very much the stern taskmaster of his early Hollywood days. Grable figured in several great production numbers (especially "Japanese Girl Like American Boy," dancing with the Dunhill Dance Trio), and performed brightly with favorite leading man Dan Dailey, but the lion's share of pre-release publicity focused on Broadway favorite Benay Venuta. (Another soon-to-be-famous New Yorker, cabaret singer Bobby Short, warbled "Going Home Train.")

Call Me Mister came in for $1,900,000, the first Grable picture to cost less than $2,000,000 since 1944's *Pin-Up Girl*. It returned worldwide film rentals of $2,697,000.

MEET ME AFTER THE SHOW
(20th Century-Fox, 1951)

Credits: Producer, George Jessel; director, Richard Sale; screenplay, Mary Loos and Sale, based on a story by Erna Lazarus and W. Scott Darling; songs, Jule Styne and Leo Robin; art directors, Lyle Wheeler and Joseph C. Wright; music director, Lionel Newman; choreography, Jack Cole; special effects, Fred Sersen; camera, Arthur E. Arling; editor, J. Watson Webb, Jr.

Cast: Betty Grable (Delilah); Macdonald Carey (Jeff); Rory Calhoun (David Hemingway); Eddie Albert (Christopher Leeds); Fred Clark (Tim); Lois Andrews (Gloria Carstairs); Irene Ryan (Tillie); Steven Condos, Jerry Brandow (Dancers); Arthur Walge (Joe); Edwin Max (Charlie); Robert Nash (Barney); Gwen Verdon (Dancer); Max Wagner (Doorman); Al Murphy (Process Server); Rodney Bell (Dr. Wheaton); Harry Antrim (Judge); Lick Cogan (Man); Billy Newell (Stage Manager).

Songs: "Meet Me After the Show," "I Feel Like Dancing," "Bettin' on a Man," "It's a Hot Night in Alaska," "No Talent Joe," "Let Go of My Heart" (Styne-Robin).

Release Date: August 15, 1951. *Running Time:* 86 minutes.

SYNOPSIS

Broadway producer Jeff is justifiably proud (and possessive) of his wife, musical-comedy star Delilah, whose talents he molded, Pygmalion-like, as she climbed the ladder of stardom. Their seven-year marriage has been trying from the start, but Delilah finally decides to call it quits after Jeff apparently throws her over for wealthy Gloria Carstairs, the backer for his latest show. Suing Jeff for divorce, Delilah gets both her decree and a handsome $2500 monthly alimony, thanks to the show's success.

Later, after leaving the show, Delilah flees to Miami, a town with many happy memories for her. Jeff follows her there in hopes of patching things up, but there are additional complications: two of them, to be exact. Both her Broadway co-star, Christopher Leeds, and an amorous muscleman, David Hemingway, are vying for her attentions. Delilah, meanwhile, secretly hopes she can effect a reconciliation, and feigns amnesia. She gets her old job back, singing in the small-time dive where Jeff first discovered her.

Amazingly, Jeff himself becomes an amnesia victim after being conked on the head. A worried Delilah, hoping she can restore his memory, returns to the show. Jeff regains his memory after seeing his ex-wife in her familiar star spot, and the tempestuous couple is reunited.

REVIEWS

"[T]here's no denying that the sight of this curvaceous, platinum-topped dynamo, sprayed in Technicolor and

With Macdonald Carey in *Meet Me After the Show.*

With dancers in *Meet Me After the Show*

With Rory Calhoun and Macdonald Carey in *Meet Me After the Show.*

singing and hoofing as though she were having the time of her life, is still something for anybody's sore eyes. A blessed good thing, too . . . the new production [is] the old business about the jealous backstage bickering between a musical-comedy star and her producer husband. The musical numbers—rain on the desert—are, as usual, handled quite nicely." (*The New York Times*)

"[S]trictly in the tradition of 20th Century-Fox musicals—meaning Technicolor, elaborate and lively production numbers, and a plot that will not test an audience's I.Q. but suffices as material to fill in between songs and dances. . . . Varied music and dance numbers, all starring the gyrating Betty, are distributed before, during and after flimsy but easy-to-take plot incidents. Miss Grable really turns on the charm in this one . . . ." (*Los Angeles Times*)

"[A] not-too-robust thread upon which to string the Grable pearls, but that is not too essential in this instance. The point is that when you have Grable to sell, you sell Grable, and not dramatic content. [There are] elaborate and effective production numbers and plenty of movement and motion to keep things lively." (*Motion Picture Herald*)

"20th-Fox has another money-making musical in *Meet Me After the Show*, a light, bright entertainment that moves swiftly along its 86-minute course. Marquee weight of Betty Grable and Macdonald Carey and a slick Technicolor dressing add to its appeal. Pleasing score and eye-filling production numbers round out the film's assets although the finale number could be trimmed to provide an even better windup. . . . Fact that it was brought in for less than the usual Grable musical is another feather in [producer George Jessel's] cap." (*Variety*)

PRODUCTION NOTES AND COMMENTS

Producer George Jessel, who had already overseen numerous Grable vehicles, came through with another handsome package in *Meet Me After the Show*. He

With Gwen Verdon (left) and dancer in *Meet Me After the Show*.

assigned scripting and directorial chores to former pulp writer and novelist Richard Sale, who had previously worked on two 1950 Fox pictures: *I'll Get By* (a remake of *Tin Pan Alley*) and *A Ticket to Tomahawk*. Sale brought in his wife, writer Mary Loos, to help with the screenplay.

It was Sale who came up with the idea of having Betty put on a "lucky garter" whenever she goes out—a ploy designed to expose the star's gorgeous gams. "We never show off Betty's legs," Sale commented with tongue-in-cheek, "unless they have a place in the story." Then, he added wryly, "Sometimes we have to do a lot of thinking to find a reason."

Jessel's production maintained the sumptuous standard set by previous Grable starrers without costing quite as much. The film's quarter-million-dollar backgrounds included 92 sets in all, including replicas of New York's 21 Club and Florida's Flamingo, Palm Island Casino, Starlight Room, and Tropic Room night spots, in addition to an 800-seat theater set.

For the first time in 10 years, Betty appeared on screen in a swim suit, a two-piece white satin number covered with pink fishnet. It revealed that the classy chassis was still in first-class condition, although by now Betty was forced to diet fairly strenuously to dispose of unwanted poundage she picked up between pictures.

Metropolitan Opera star Robert Weer was engaged as a vocal coach to Macdonald Carey and Eddie Albert, both making rare singing appearances. Carey actually surprised Sale and Jessel with his robust baritone, which he'd never before used in a film. Reportedly, Darryl F. Zanuck himself was extremely pleased with Carey's interpretation of the director (whose characterization, the actor said later, was modeled after Elia Kazan), and Fox signed him to do two pictures a year.

Negative cost of *Meet Me After the Show* was $1,825,000. Worldwide film rentals totalled $2,606,000.

THE FARMER TAKES A WIFE

(20th Century-Fox, 1953)

Credits: Producer, Frank P. Rosenberg; director, Henry Levin; screenplay, Walter Bullock, Sally Benson, and Joseph Fields, based on the novel *Rome Haul* by Walter D. Edmonds, and the play by Frank B. Elser and Marc Connelly; music director, Cyril Mockridge; songs, Harold Arlen and Dorothy Fields; choreography, Jack Cole; art directors, Lyle Wheeler and Addison Hehr; camera, Arthur E. Arling; editor, Louis Loeffler.

Cast: Betty Grable (Molly Larkin); Dale Robertson (Daniel Harrow); Thelma Ritter (Lucy Cashdollar); John Carroll (Jotham Klore); Eddie Foy, Jr. (Susanna); Merry Anders (Hannah); May Wynn (Eva); Noreen Michaels (Amy); Ruth Hall (Abbie); Mort Mills (Floyd); Gwen Verdon (Abigail); Gordon Nelson (Race Official); Ed Hinton (Boater); Emile Meyer (Cargo Master); Lee Phelps (Bartender); Ted Jordan (Driver).

Songs: "We're in Business," "On the Erie Canal," "We're Doing It for the Natives in Jamaica," "When I Close My Door," "Today I Love Everybody," "Somethin' Real Special," "With the Sun Warm Upon Me," "Can You Spell 'Schenectady'?" (Arlen-Fields)

Release Date: June 12, 1953. *Running Time:* 81 minutes.

SYNOPSIS

Molly Larkin, whose late father was a well-known Erie Canal boatman, is a prize-winning cooking-school graduate who now wrangles grub on "Old Hickory," a canal boat owned by hard-boiled, hard-drinking Jotham Klore. He's a frequent fighter with railroad men—the natural enemies of canal boaters—who have designs on Molly. She refuses his advances, more vigorously when Klore hires good-looking Dan Harrow to be his new driver. Dan wants to work his way to Buffalo, where he's to meet his sweetheart Susanna Weaver, daughter of a farmer for whom he once worked.

The clever, irrepressible Molly schemes to get Dan for herself. She manages to delay the trip to Buffalo long enough that, by the time they finally do arrive, Susanna has left for Illinois, where her family now lives. Dan decides to stay around "Old Hickory," and when Klore is jailed for brawling, Molly convinces him to leave with her, renovate her dad's old boat, "Sarsey Sal," and operate it as partners. Later, Dan hears that Susanna has married an Illinois farmer, and he proposes to Molly. His plan is to enter "Sal" in the yearly boat race, win the cash prize, and buy a farm. But Molly, who has no interest in being a farmer's wife, resents his trying to make her one.

Determined to prove that she can't be molded to someone else's desires, Molly borrows money to bail out

With Dale Robertson (center) and John Carroll in *The Farmer Takes a Wife.*

Klore so he can enter the race against Dan. She even agrees to ride with Klore. During the race, heated words are exchanged and the hot-tempered Jotham leaps from his own craft onto "Sarsey Sal." Dan whips him in a fair fight, pitching him overboard into the river, then goes on to win the race and claim a chastened Molly for his bride.

REVIEWS

"Setting and period are the most attractive features of *The Farmer Takes a Wife*, which strives to be both picaresque and picturesque. But like its score . . . the film seldom seems to gain a footing above the waterline for long. Miss Grable is as saucy and leggy as ever . . . . Everybody breaks into song at intervals, even under the most improbable circumstances." (*Los Angeles Times*)

"Betty Grable, off the screen for some time, needs a much more auspicious vehicle than this mediocre musical for her return. The entertainment values are only so-so at best and the grossing prospects are of like calibre. Henry Levin's direction . . . fails to add any punch that would keep up interest . . . ." (*Variety*)

"[T]he attempt to convert into musical comedy what was originally good comedy-drama, both on the stage and screen, doesn't quite come off. The music is uninspired, without there being an outstanding tune, and the dance routines are unimaginative. [T]he film ambles on in rather listless fashion." (*Hollywood Reporter*)

"The stage play of Frank Elser and Marc Connelly has been transformed to make a huge screen musical whimsy, and jammed full of tuneful, cheerful and lilting songs. The audience pleasure results less from Betty Grable or Dale Robertson . . . than from the lavish, detailed, quite superior sets . . . and from the seven songs by Harold Arlen and Dorothy Fields . . . ." (*Motion Picture Herald*)

With Eddie Foy, Jr. in *The Farmer Takes a Wife*.

With Thelma Ritter in *The Farmer Takes a Wife*.

With Carroll and Robertson in *The Farmer Takes a Wife*.

PRODUCTION NOTES AND COMMENTS

The Farmer Takes a Wife is probably the weakest film in Grable's oeuvre, owing mostly to its mundane screenplay and turgid, uninspired staging. The star herself is clearly uncomfortable, perhaps because she'd fared poorly in period pieces. Dale Robertson is young and handsome, but his chemistry with Grable is almost non-existent. And the score represents a low point in the careers of Harold Arlen and Dorothy Fields, who'd heretofore contributed some of the most memorable songs in movie musicals.

Walter Edmonds' novel *Rome Haul* had been dramatized in 1934 as *The Farmer Takes a Wife,* and the stage production had starred Henry Fonda, who came to Hollywood to reprise the role in Fox's 1935 film version (which cast him opposite Janet Gaynor, playing the role taken by Grable in the musical remake). The first movie had been fairly popular, launching Fonda as a film star, and Fox obviously thought it could resuscitate Grable's career as well as give a boost to up-and-coming Dale Robertson.

The remake's failure wasn't due to any lack of time or effort. A practical set of locks, duplicating part of the Erie Canal, was built on a 35-acre patch of the Fox backlot; the basin at Rome, complete with docks and waterfront buildings, was constructed on a 20-acre section nearby. The crew mounted a 30-foot camera crane atop a barge for some shots, a difficult and time-consuming process. One of Betty's numbers, part of a dream sequence, required a month of rehearsal, took a full week to shoot, and ran a full reel (nearly 10 minutes) when cut together. In it Grable swung a bullwhip, mastered after several days of practice during which she gave herself numerous painful welts.

The Farmer Takes a Wife essentially finished Grable's solo starring career. Modestly produced—judged alongside her earlier pictures, anyway—for $1,860,000, it took in a mere $1,220,000 in domestic film rentals, making it the star's worst money-loser since *That Lady in Ermine*.

One trivia note: Grable took her second movie bath in *Farmer* (the first was in *Sweet Rosie O'Grady*).

HOW TO MARRY A MILLIONAIRE
(20th Century-Fox, 1953)

Credits: Writer-producer, Nunnally Johnson; director, Jean Negulesco; based on plays by Zoe Akins, Katherine Albert, and Dale Eunson; music directors, Alfred Newman and Cyril Mockridge; camera, Joe MacDonald; editor, Louis Loeffler.

Cast: Marilyn Monroe (Pola); Betty Grable (Loco); Lauren Bacall (Schatze); David Wayne (Freddie Denmark); Rory Calhoun (Eben); Cameron Mitchell (Tom Brookman); Alex

With Marilyn Monroe in *How to Marry a Millionaire*.

With Cameron Mitchell, Monroe and Lauren Bacall in *Millionaire*.

D'Arcy (J. Stewart Merrill); Fred Clark (Waldo Brewster); William Powell (J. D. Hanley); Tudor Owen (Mr. Otis); Emmett Vogan (Man at Bridge); Charlotte Austin (Model); Richard Shackleton (Bell Boy); Eve Finnell (Stewardess); Benny Burt (Reporter).

Release Date: Nov. 4, 1953. *Running Time:* 95 minutes.

SYNOPSIS

Three glamorous models, Pola Debevoise, Loco Dempsey, and Schatze Page, pool their limited resources and rent a lavish New York penthouse with one aim: to land wealthy husbands. A chance encounter introduces handsome young millionaire Tom Brookman to Loco and Schatze; he's immediately taken with the latter, who believes him to be a wage slave and brushes him off. She instead pursues aging oil tycoon J. D. Hanley, who seems genuinely interested in her.

Loco accompanies well-to-do Waldo Brewster to what she thinks is a convention in Maine. Instead, she's taken to his lodge in the wilderness. She comes down with measles while staying there, which temporarily thwarts Waldo's amorous advances, and later meets a good-looking forest ranger named Eben.

Pola, meanwhile, heads for Atlantic City, where she is to meet the mother of J. Stewart Merrill, a likely prospect. But the near-sighted blonde, who's reluctant to wear her glasses, gets on the wrong plane. By coincidence she meets her landlord, Freddie Denmark, whose own financial future is at risk due to the machinations of a crooked accountant.

From that point on, everything seems to happen at once. Schatze agrees to marry Hanley. Loco, accompanied by the rugged Eben, arrives on her wedding day. Pola shows up with Freddie in tow. Tom Brookman's arrival and Schatze's reaction to him convinces Hanley that it's the younger man she really loves. He calls off the wedding, and Schatze resigns herself to marrying for love rather than money. But when the three couples go to dinner at an expensive restaurant, Tom shocks them all into senselessness by producing a thick wad of bills to pay for the meal.

REVIEWS

"The cast is a marquee mechanic's delight and an exhibitor's bonanza bait. Take a look: Marilyn Monroe, Betty Grable, and Lauren Bacall are three delicious little babes from Model-land, prettily predatory creatures if ever you saw some. It's fun every bit of the way, with the running time tearing by unheeded, and an occasional 'oh' and 'ah' as magnificent scenic effects unfold via Cinema-Scope." (*Motion Picture Herald*)

"The picture, in Technicolor, is adorned by a beauteous trio of feminine stars who play their roles so smartly and ingratiatingly that they keep the audience in a state of hilarity all through the running of the comedy. Betty Grable, Lauren Bacall and Marilyn Monroe give off the quips and cracks, generously supplied by Nunnally Johnson, with a naturalness that adds to their strikingly humorous effect, making the film the funniest comedy of the year." (*New York Daily News*)

"*How to Marry a Millionaire*, CinemaScoped simultaneously at the Globe and Loew's State Theatres, is an extremely entertaining film, and it would be that, like its predecessor, *The Robe*, no matter what its condition of width, height, and depth . . . . Betty Grable and Lauren Bacall go through their paces with all the expected aplomb . . . . It is particularly noteworthy that Marilyn Monroe has developed more than a small amount of comedy polish of the foot-in-mouth type." (*New York Post*)

PRODUCTION NOTES AND COMMENTS

A more or less "official" remake of *The Greeks Had a Word for Them* that also borrowed elements from *Moon Over Miami*, *How to Marry a Millionaire*, the second film to utilize the CinemaScope widescreen process, certainly must have given Grable fans an eerie feeling of *deja vu*. She lost first billing to Marilyn Monroe, whose

With Monroe and Lauren Bacall in *How to Marry a Millionaire*.

turn in Fox's *Gentlemen Prefer Blondes* just a few months before had been successful enough to make her one of the studio's biggest assets. That, coupled with Grable's own decline (hastened by the failure of *The Farmer Takes a Wife*), could have made for a particularly difficult shoot, but Betty actually befriended Monroe and defended the younger actress against co-star Lauren Bacall's habitual complaints about her tardiness.

Grable was at the end of her rope as far as 20th Century-Fox was concerned. She knew it, and everyone else at the studio knew it too. Her box-office pull, while weaker than it had been only a couple of years previous, still counted for something, and as Fox was still unsure whether or not Monroe could draw on her own (*Gentlemen* had co-starred Jane Russell, then at the peak of her popularity), Grable was pressed into service. But most of the publicity surrounding the production was geared toward Marilyn, as were the stories "leaked" by press agents to influential columnists. Actually, Grable delivered one of her best performances as one of the film's predatory females, and had the picture been released two years earlier it might have given her career a much-needed boost.

As it was, *Millionaire*'s grosses filled Fox's coffers to overflowing, bringing the studio worldwide film rentals of $8,000,000—quite a profit for a production with a negative cost of $1,870,000.

THREE FOR THE SHOW
(Columbia, 1955)

Credits: Producer, Jonie Taps; director, H. C. Potter; screenplay, Edward Hope and Leonard Stern, based on the play *Too Many Husbands* by W. Somerset Maugham; assistant director, Earl Bellamy; music director, Morris Stoloff; music arranger, George Dunning; choreography, Jack Cole;

songs, George and Ira Gershwin, Gene Austin, Roy Bergere, Hoagy Carmichael, Harold Adamson, Lester Lee, Ned Washington, and Bob Russell; art director, Walter Holscher; camera, Arthur E. Arling; editor, Viola Lawrence.

Cast: Betty Grable (Julie); Marge Champion (Gwen Howard); Gower Champion (Vernon Lowndes); Jack Lemmon (Marty Stewart); Myron McCormick (Mike Hart); Paul Harvey (Colonel Wharton); Robert Bice (Sgt. O'Hallihan); Hal K. Dawson (Theatre Treasurer); Charlotte Lawrence (Girl); Willard Waterman (Moderator); Gene Wesson (Reporter); Aileen Carlyle (Mother); Rudy Lee (Boy); Eugene Borden (Costume Designer).

Songs: "Someone to Watch Over Me," "I've Got a Crush on You" (The Gershwins), "How Come You Do Me Like You Do" (Austin-Bergere), "Down Boy" (Carmichael-Adamson), "Which One" (Lee-Washington), "I've Been Kissed Before" (Russell-Lee).

Release Date: February 24, 1955. *Running Time:* 93 minutes.

SYNOPSIS

Marty Stewart, Broadway musical comedy writer and performer, was reported killed in action in Korea. His wife Julie has since married Marty's former partner and collaborator, Vernon Lowndes. But the Army was mistaken: Marty wasn't killed, and after having been missing for two years, he returns to New York to rejoin his wife. When he learns what has happened he's furious. When Vernon learns of his rival's return *he's* furious. The only one who enjoys the mixup is Julie, who loves the idea that both

With Gower Champion (left), Jack Lemmon, and dancers in *Three for the Show*.

With Lemmon, Marge and Gower Champion in *Three for the Show*.

With dancers in *Three for the Show*.

men want her as a wife. The Army admits it is to blame for the curious situation, and Julie feels somewhat justified in having both a husband and a (legally bound) lover.

Marty and Vernon demand that Julie choose between them, a sentiment echoed by Gwen, who worked with all of them in a nightclub act and loved each man at different times. Julie plays the men against each other, with the result that both of them finally walk out on her. To salve their outraged feelings, they write a musical about their experience and call it *Too Many Husbands*. As added revenge, they cast Gwen in the starring role as a thinly disguised Julie.

When advance ticket sales fail to measure up to anticipated levels, producer Mike Hart tells Marty and Vernon that they'll need a strong marquee name to lure theatergoers. Both men agree that Julie is the only logical choice, but neither is willing to swallow his pride and ask her to join them. Eventually, Gwen and Mike persuade Julie to come into the show. She confesses that she still loves Marty but also has strong feelings for Vernon and doesn't want to hurt him. During rehearsals, however, Vernon realizes he truly loves Gwen, leaving Julie free to reconcile with Marty. With the confused interrelationships finally untangled, the foursome makes *Too Many Husbands* a hit show.

REVIEWS

"If it's still true, as it used to be, that among folks who like musicals it's Grable two to one, this could be one for the money. [I]t hangs almost entirely on the exuberant personality of that veteran money-making star. It is a loud, brassy, ribald musical strung on a very thin but bawdy plot, interrupted from time to time by extraordinarily lavish production numbers . . . . [A]t times [picture] seems too unsubtle to appeal to sophisticated audiences and too Broadwayish to be appreciated in the corn country." (*Motion Picture Herald*)

"The principals in this slight but cheerful item . . . make a fairly successful effort to be brisk, cute and cooperative, but their materials, Technicolored and widened to CinemaScope size, are woefully thin. However, *Three for the Show* does serve to bring Betty Grable back to the screen. Luminously blonde and shapely enough to give the megrims (*sic*) to most of the readers of fan mags, Miss Grable proves she can fill a musical assignment as neatly as she does her revealing wardrobe." (*New York Times*)

"The entire score is super . . . the cast is knockout . . . [but] you can stir all this together, add Technicolor, add

Rehearsing a scene with Lemmon (back to camera) and Champion under the watchful eye of director H.C. Potter (at right).

Below: The scene as shot.

CinemaScope—and it all comes out as not too much, when the plot is old and tired. The production numbers . . . are, definitely and honestly, worth the price of admission. So you just go to see them, and ignore the plot when it pops up." (*Los Angeles Examiner*)

PRODUCTION NOTES AND COMMENTS

Making her first film away from Fox since *The Day the Bookies Wept* in 1939, Grable was up to her usual standard in *Three for the Show*, winning favorable personal reviews from critics otherwise not overly impressed with the enterprise. Columbia, temporarily sans its resident top female star, Rita Hayworth (who would have been equally good in the role of Julie), signed Grable for this updated version of its non-musical 1940 hit *Too Many Husbands*, which had starred Jean Arthur, Fred MacMurray, and Melvyn Douglas. Based on the Somerset Maugham play *Home and Beauty,* it utilized already familiar farcical situations, well dusted and polished.

Unfortunately, the musicalized remake wasn't nearly as successful in the dusting process. Moreover, the addition of risque flourishes and dialogue aroused the censorial ire of the Catholic Legion of Decency, which informed Columbia that it would slap a "C" (for "Condemned for Viewing by Adults or Children") rating on the picture unless its "frivolous treatment" of marriage and marital vows—along with suggestive situations and costumes— was toned down. Columbia did some judicious trimming, ultimately squeaking past the influential Legion with a "B" (Morally Objectionable in Part for All) rating.

Interestingly enough, the film's musical highlight did *not* go to the star: It was Marge and Gower Champion who took honors in that department, with their elegant dancing to the Gershwins' beautiful "Someone to Watch Over Me."

HOW TO BE VERY, VERY POPULAR
(20th Century-Fox, 1955)

Credits: Producer-director-screenplay, Nunnally Johnson; based on a play by Howard Lindsay, a novel by Edward Hope, and a play by Lyford Moore and Harlan Thompson; assistant director, Ad Schaumer; music director, Cyril Mockridge; song, Jule Styne and Sammy Cahn; choreography, Paul Godkin and Sonia Shaw; music director, Lionel Newman; art directors, Lyle Wheeler and John DeCuir; camera, Milton Krasner; editor, Louis Loeffler.

Cast: Betty Grable (Stormy); Sheree North (Curly); Bob Cummings (Wedgewood); Charles Coburn (Tweed); Tommy Noonan (Eddie); Orson Bean (Toby); Fred Clark (Mr. Marshall); Charlotte Austin (Midge); Alice Pearce (Miss Syl); Rhys Williams (Flagg); Andrew Tombes (Moon); Noel Toy (Cherry Blossom Wang); Emory Parnell (Chief of Police); Edmund Cobb (Policeman); Hank Mann (Newsvendor); Leslie Parrish (Girl on Bus), Milton Parsons ("Mr. X").

Songs: "How to Be Very, Very Popular" (Styne-Cahn), "Shake, Rattle and Roll", "Bristol Bell Song" (Ken Darby-Lionel Newman), "Bunny Hop" (Ray Anthony).

In *How to Be Very, Very Popular.*

With Orson Bean, Sheree North, Robert Cummings, and Emory Parnell (in hat) in *How to Be Very, Very Popular.*

Release Date: July 22, 1955. *Running Time:* 89 minutes.

SYNOPSIS

After singing and dancing in a San Francisco night spot, Stormy Tornado and Curly Flagg go off to change and accidentally witness the murder of a fellow burlesque performer. When the murderer warns them that if they're around to identify him, they'll get the same treatment, the two strippers throw coats over their scanty costumes and head for the hinterlands.

The money they have takes them as far as a small college town where, to get out of a downpour, they inadvertently wander into a fraternity house and make the surprised but delighted acquaintance of Fillmore Wedgewood, Eddie Jones, and Toby Marshall. Eddie, in an attempt to hypnotize Toby, succeeds in putting Curly

under his spell instead. He doesn't know how to bring her out of it, but she is subservient to his will and dances whenever she hears the word "Salome." While under the spell she also finds some fascination in kissing the timid Toby, and does so at every opportunity.

The next morning—Commencement Day—a front-page newspaper headline announces "Bald Barber Sought in Strip Slaying," and the accompanying story reveals to Stormy, Curly and their new friends that the murderer is a madman. In answer to a telephone call from Stormy, Curly's father (who is bald) arrives at the campus. Toby's father (also hairless) and a disguised San Francisco cop named Moon (another bare-headed man) also show up.

Marshall and Flagg are arrested because of their baldness but released in time to attend the commencement exercises that night. During the ceremony, someone mentions the Battle of Salamis, and it sounds enough like

With Robert Cummings and Orson Bean in *How to Be Very, Very Popular*.

"Salome" to send Curly into her dance. The real murderer, "Mr. X," takes a pot shot at her, but the police—tipped off that her life could be in danger—swarm in and take him prisoner. At the police station, all the bald men are sorted out, explanations are made, and everyone heads for San Francisco in a bus, by this time happily paired off.

REVIEWS

"It's a long time since a picture as completely wacky as *How to Be Very, Very Popular* has graced the screen. Along its rowdy route on the road to zaniness, it makes absolutely no sense and it's doubtful if producer-director-writer Nunnally Johnson intended it to. Sheree North, who has been getting a tremendous publicity buildup, has her first important role as the dancer. Betty Grable plays her cohort. Besides Miss North's dance and the opening title selection, there are no other songs or dances in the film, which is rather surprising considering the cast." (*Motion Picture Herald*)

"The result is funny—the pace lively, the acting cutely comical, the lines bright, amusing and occasionally sparkling. The cast does a beautiful job of juggling the farcical nonsense along the CinemaScope color screen—led by celluloid sizzlers Betty Grable and Sheree North [who] knows how to handle her lines, as well as her figure . . . ." (*Cue*)

"Miss North wisely submitted this performance to the editors of the *Harvard Lampoon*, asking to be nominated the worst actress of the year. She may have been a little hasty, however, for Betty Grable . . . manages to outdo Miss North in the same category . . . . The impression one gets is that Nunnally Johnson . . . may

unknowingly be a victim of California smog. If so, it's more dangerous than we suspected." (*Saturday Review*)

PRODUCTION NOTES AND COMMENTS

Betty Grable's cinematic swan song, while hardly her worst film, certainly doesn't rate with the pictures of her peak period in the '40s, or even some of her early '50s efforts. Moreover, while Grable does at least get top billing, she's hardly the focal point of the enterprise. Sheree North, a recent addition to Fox's contract roster, was the recipient of a big buildup from the studio; she got the best number—the show-stopping "Shake, Rattle and Roll," the first rock 'n' roll song used in any movie—and most of the critical attention. North replaced Marilyn Monroe, originally announced to star in the production but who, in January of 1955, refused to take the part. It's more than likely that Fox didn't sign Grable until Monroe balked; the picture needed a star name, and North lacked both the experience and the fan following to carry it on her shapely shoulders.

Writer-producer-director Nunnally Johnson, whose association with Zanuck dated back to the days of Twentieth Century Pictures, cobbled together the book *She Loves Me Not* by Edward Hope, the play adapted from it by Howard Lindsay, and another play, *Sleep It Off* by Lyford Moore and Harlan Thompson, to form the plot of *How to Be Very, Very Popular*. He might just as well have started from scratch with an original treatment, because the finished film betrayed its patchwork literary origins in several places. Nonetheless, it was helped along by the zestful performances of the stars, and the nearly middle-aged Grable gave a good accounting of herself in scanty costume and vigorous dance numbers.

The production was a troubled one. During rehearsals before shooting began, Grable pulled ligaments in her right leg and showed up for wardrobe fittings on crutches. On the first day of shooting, while filming the downpour sequence, North's head got so thoroughly soaked that the cerise scarf she wore ran its color into her dyed hair, turning it shocking pink and delaying further shooting for the day. Later she sprained her sacroiliac, and again held up production. Both Grable's and Cummings' children came down with the measles at different points in the schedule, and one of the featured players dropped out of the picture due to ulcers, necessitating recasting of his role and reshooting of his scenes.

How to Be Very, Very Popular, brought in for $1,565,000, was far less expensive than the peak-period Grable films of the late '40s and early '50s, but still didn't earn nearly as much. Domestic film rental, at $1,656,000, was far below what the studio had once expected from Betty's films.

APPENDIX: SHORT SUBJECTS

Researching the short subjects in which Betty Grable appeared is a difficult, frustrating task—largely because many of them either no longer survive or are unavailable for reappraisal. Moreover, credit listings gleaned from infrequent trade-magazine reviews are maddingly incomplete, and in a few cases—the early Educationals—Grable isn't billed at all, either under her own name or that of Frances Dean, a non de plume she reportedly adopted to escape detection by Samuel Goldwyn, to whom she was contracted in 1931. Nonetheless, we have elected to print what information we could find on these tantalizing titles, along with review excerpts, strictly for the edification of Grable completists.

1. CRASHING HOLLYWOOD (Educational, 1931).

Director: William Goodrich (aka Roscoe "Fatty" Arbuckle). Screenplay: Ernest Pagano and Jack Townley. Photography: Dwight Warren. Cast: Eddie Nugent, Phyllis Crane, Rita Flynn, Bryant Washburn, Virginia Brooks, Wilbur Mack, George Chandler. *Release Date:* April 5, 1931. *Running Time:* 20 minutes.

"A bright and snappy comedy with Hollywood as the locale, and the story of three girls endeavoring to crash the studios. It gives the lowdown on how girls exist while trying to make the screen, all done from a mighty humorous angle. There is a swell sequence where they frame a 'rough' party to kid a girl from Iowa. She thinks it is the real thing, with doubles of a lot of famous stars present. These doubles include Charlie Chaplin, Greta Garbo, and many others, and they do their stuff in a manner that will tickle all the fans. Modern, nicely paced, and with some snappy comedy dialogue unusual in shorts." (*Film Daily*)

"A wow. Oh, boy, here's a pippin'. Bringing the country cousin from Iowa to see Hollywood and then finding her not so meek and reticent is the gist of the story, but the party where the cousin is to get a different slant on studioland is a corker." (*Motion Picture Herald*)

2. EX-SWEETIES (Educational, 1931).

Producer: Mack Sennett. Director: Marshall Neilan. Screenplay: John A. Waldron, Earle Rodney, Walter Weems, and Ewart Adamson. Cast: Harry Gribbon, Marjorie Beebe, Wade Boteler, Betty Boyd. *Release Date:* April 12, 1931. *Running Time:* 21 minutes.

"Marshall Neilan directed Harry Gribbon and Marjorie Beebe in this one, but the comedy pair does not come up to the standard they have set in previous efforts. The lines are not half bad and the plot idea is fair enough, but the old stuff makes the short drag too much to be really effective. Gribbon and Wade Boteler fall for Marjorie, until the appearance of Betty Boyd [could this be Grable?], who steals the spotlight. The husband steps up with a revolver and Gribbon disappears. Harry plays, as usual, the clumsy stupid lad. Betty Boyd is attractive and appealing. Slow, but fair enough entertainment." (*Motion Picture Herald*)

3. LADY! PLEASE! (Educational, 1932).

Producer: Mack Sennett. Director: Del Lord. Cast: Arthur Stone, Dorothy Granger, Helen Mann, Walter

Long, Bud Jamison. *Release Date:* February 28, 1932. *Running Time:* 20 minutes.

"Falls flat. This one won't arouse much laughter or enthusiasm. The story is weak and the dialogue commonplace. Arthur Stone, as an amateur detective, starts out to solve a robbery and, through no fault of his, returns the stolen jewels and receives a large reward. The theme has been done many times and to better advantage." (*Film Daily*)

"A Sennett comedy effort, which possesses a few laughs even though the lines are anything but new and the situations have been done and done again." (*Motion Picture Herald*)

4. HOLLYWOOD LUCK (Educational, 1932).
Director: William Goodrich. Screenplay: Ernest Pagano and Jack Townley. Cast: Virginia Brooks, Rita Flynn, Frances Dean, Clarence Nordstrom, Fern Emmett, Lynton Brent, Dennis O'Donnell, Addie McPhail. *Release Date:* March 13, 1932. *Running Time:* 21 minutes.

"The three Hollywood extra girls—Rita Flynn, Virginia Brooks and Frances Dean—still trying to crash into the studios. They dig up a newcomer who through dumb luck accomplishes more than they have been able to do in months. The offering is bright and moves along at a fast pace, with the three girls proving to be good comedy combination as well as a pleasing eyefull." (*Film Daily*)

"Comedy bits that stood out were these: the upsetting of the girls by the gusts from the whirling propeller of a plane, the acquisition of a complete breakfast by high financing with a 'borrowed' bottle of cream, and a steam roller's trip over a trunk in which was supposed to be one of the girls who was let down via a bedsheet from the window." (*Motion Picture Herald*)

5. THE FLIRTY SLEEPWALKER (Educational, 1932).
Producer: Mack Sennett. Director: Del Lord. Screenplay: John A. Waldron, Earle Rodney, Harry McCoy, John Grey. Cast: Arthur Stone, Lee Kinney, Wade Boteler, Dorothy Granger, Patsy O'Leary, Joe Young, Bobby Young. *Release Date:* March 13, 1932. *Running Time:* 21 minutes.

"Mechanical. Arthur Stone is the chief comic, assisted by Wade Boteler, Dorothy Granger, and Patsy O'Leary. The two men are golf pals, and Stone arouses the unreasoning jealousy of his friend over the latter's wife. The principal gag involves a sleepwalking scene with Stone entering the bedroom of his friend's wife with the usual

Frame blow-up from *Hollywood Bound.*

developments. They resort to the old stuff of hanging on a broken fire escape over the street far below for thrills." (*Film Daily*)

6. HOLLYWOOD LIGHTS (Educational, 1932).
Director: William Goodrich. Screenplay: Ernest Pagano and Jack Townley. Cast: Virginia Brooks, Rita Flynn, Tut Mace, Fern Emmett, Ted O'Shea, Lynton Brent, Jack Shaw, Bert Young. *Release Date:* May 8, 1932. *Running Time:* 20 minutes.

"The three girls in Hollywood trying to break into the studios are again featured—Rita Flynn, Virginia Brooks, Tut Mace. This comedy follows the usual routine, but is snapped up at the end with a lively sequence where one of the girls doubles for a western hero by jumping from a roof at a fire. She lands on the hero's horse instead of in the fire net with disastrous consequences to the horse." (*Film Daily*)

"More than a little slapstick in this comedic effort, centering about three girls who are vigorously in search of extra work in Hollywood to make the price of train fare. Only a fair effort." (*Motion Picture Herald*)

7. AIR TONIC (RKO Radio, 1933).
Producer: Lou Brock. Director: Sam White. Screenplay: Joseph Fields and Walter Weems. Cast: Ted Fio Rito and His Orchestra, Betty Grable, Leif Erickson. *Release Date:* December 22, 1933. *Running Time:* 21 minutes.

8. LOVE DETECTIVES (Columbia, 1934).
Producer: Zion Myers. Director: Archie Gottler. Screenplay: Edward Eliscu and Archie Gottler. Cast:

With Frank Albertson in *Love Detectives*.

Frank Albertson, Betty Grable, Gloria Warner, Tom Dugan, Red Stanley, Armand Kaliz. *Release Date:* March 6, 1934. *Running Time:* 19 1/2 minutes.

9. FERRY-GO-ROUND (RKO Radio, 1934).
Producer: Lou Brock. Director: Sam White. Screenplay: Joseph A. Fields and Johnnie Grey. Cast: Gene Austin and His Stooges, Candy and Coco, Betty Grable. *Release Date:* November 23, 1934. *Running Time:* 20 minutes.

10. THIS BAND AGE (RKO Radio, 1935).
Producer: Lou Brock. Director: Sam White. Screenplay: Ewart Adamson and Jack Cluett. Cast: Ted Fio Rito and His Orchestra, Betty Grable, Marjorie

With Walter King in *The Spirit of 1976*.

Boothe, Irma Richardson, Monte Collins, Bob McKenzie. *Release Date:* January 25, 1935. *Running Time:* 20 1/2 minutes.

11. THE SPIRIT OF 1976 (RKO Radio).
Producer: Lee Marcus. Director: Leigh Jason. Screenplay: Joseph A. Fields. Songs: Val Burton and Will Jason. Cast: Walter King, Betty Grable, Virginia Reed. *Release Date:* February 12, 1935. *Running Time:* 20 minutes.

"Leigh Jason has been turning out some pips for Radio. So good that the danger is they'll be stopped to divert Jason to full-length productions. These shorts stand head and shoulders above the contemporary one- and two-reelers because they rest on the solid foundation of a comic idea. It's a mixture of Gilbert and Sullivan and 'Of Thee I Sing' in the case of *Spirit of 1976*.

"For 20 minutes [the short] spoofs the droll thought of a futuristic president, who abolishes work 100 percent only to have a strike against loafing. Workshovels are bootlegged and other absurdities of human nature are exploited for giggles. Story is unfolded half in dialog and half in lyrics. Both are excellent.

"Cute blonde, Betty Grable, was more than the customary painted figurehead, giving a lubricated and intelligent assist." (*Variety*)

"There is entertainment in this novelty comedy, in which a year far ahead finds all play and no work the keystone of the country's activity. Told largely in musical fashion, with clever lines, is the story of the candidacy of Elmer Green for president, on a platform of all play, all wealth divided equally. A nonsense idea, it is entertainingly put across." (*Motion Picture Herald*)

12. DRAWING RUMORS (RKO Radio, 1935).
Producer: Lee Marcus. Director: Ben Holmes. Screenplay: Joseph A. Fields. Cast: Joey Ray, Betty Grable. *Release Date:* July 12, 1935. *Running Time:* 17 minutes.

"Featuring Joey Ray and directed by Ben Holmes, another 'Headliner' has just been finished. Ray sings 'You Opened My Eyes,' which is the song hit from Wheeler and Woolsey's *The Nitwits*, a chorus of 'Star Dust,' and 'Be Still My Heart.' This short offers another attraction in a specialty dance by Betty Grable, who appears for the first time [sic] as a leading leady with Wheeler and Woolsey in *The Nitwits*." (*Film Daily*)

"This introduces Ray, a good looking young man with fair voice and good song selection; and Betty Grable,

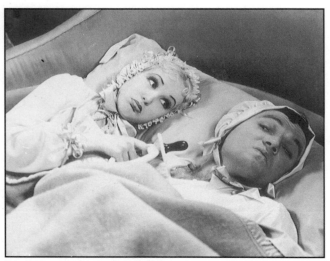

Frame blow-up from *Hollywood Bound.*

whom Radio features frequently these days—and she is good-looking. Comedy concerns producer of night-club show who falls out with Ray, his master of ceremonies. But Ray appears in producer's new show on chance he may win back girl, also in show, with whom he had quarreled. And he does." (*Philadelphia Exhibitor*)

13. A NIGHT AT THE BILTMORE BOWL (RKO Radio, 1935).

Producer: Lee Marcus. Director: Alf Goulding. Screenplay: Joseph A. Fields. Cast: Jimmy Grier and His Orchestra, Betty Grable, Grady Sutton. *Release Date:* June 21, 1935. *Running Time:* 17 1/2 minutes.

"In addition to presenting Jimmy Grier's orchestra and specialty entertainers, this subject has been vested with something of a plot revolving around Betty Grable's idea to send her party guests on a treasure hunt, with everybody to meet at midnight at the Biltmore Bowl, and the loser to pay the check. This gives the two-reeler a bit of suspense aside from its substantial entertainment qualities in the musical line. Actual shots made in the Biltmore rendevous include glimpses of various film stars. There are a few touches of comedy also. All in all, a subject that looks big from a production standpoint and holds a good measure of varied enjoyment." (*Film Daily*)

14. A QUIET FOURTH (RKO Radio, 1935).

Producer: Lee Marcus. Director: Fred Guiol. Screenplay: Leslie A. Goodwins and Jack Townley. Cast: Betty Grable, Edgar Dearing, Jack Rice, Margaret Armstrong, Earl Blackwell. *Release Date:* August 9, 1935. *Running Time:* 18 1/2 minutes.

"A family comedy, done on the style of the old Edgar Kennedy shorts, with the father siding with the boy friend whom daughter likes in preference to the rich snob that mother has picked her to marry. They go on a Fourth of July outing for a quiet picnic in the woods, but find that they have picked the spot that a U.S. Army artillery troop is using for target practice. There is a lot of noisy comedy that results in the discomfiture of the unwanted suitor." (*Film Daily*)

15. SCREEN SNAPSHOTS #15-11 (Columbia, 1936).

Casual footage of film folk including English actors playing cricket in Hollywood, an afternoon tea, and a costume party at the Knickerbocker Hotel. Cast: C. Aubrey Smith, Montague Love, Betty Grable, Jackie Coogan, Lily Pons, Jeanette MacDonald, Anita Louise, Dick Powell. *Running Time:* 9 1/2 minutes.

16. SCREEN SNAPSHOTS #16-7 (Columbia, 1937).

Casual footage of film folk including scenes at a circus, intercollegiate races, and a party at Fred Stone's estate. Cast: Chester Morris, Gene Autry, James Gleason, Marlene Dietrich, Anita Louise, Pat O'Brien, Mae Clarke, June Travis, Patricia Ellis, Paula Stone, Ruby Keeler, Betty Grable. *Running Time:* 9 1/2 minutes.

17. SCREEN SNAPSHOTS #16-10 (Columbia, 1937).

Casual footage of film folk including a swimming meet at the West Side Club. Cast: Edward Everett Horton, Doris Dudley, Stubby Kreuger, Johnny Weissmuller, Cesar Romero, Olivia de Havilland, Joe Penner, Betty Grable, Olsen and Johnson, Claire Trevor. *Running Time:* 8 1/2 minutes.

18. SCREEN SNAPSHOTS #18-4 (Columbia, 1938).

Casual footage of film folk including Hollywood football game. Cast: Dick Foran, Johnny Mack Brown, Mickey Rooney, Frankie Darro, Jackie Coogan, Wayne Morris, Cary Grant, Phyllis Brooks, George Raft, Bing Crosby, Joe E. Brown, Betty Grable. *Running Time:* 9 1/2 minutes.

19. SHOW BUSINESS IN WAR (20th Fox, 1943).

"This is a tribute to the entertainment world telling the world at large of the great part it plays in the present conflict. Viewed are the contributions of the screen, stage, and radio towards the upkeep of morale of enlisted men and officers. A few of the personalities to be found include: Tyrone Power, Clark Gable, Hedy Lamarr, Dorothy Lamour, Carole Lombard, Walt Disney, John Ford, Darryl Zanuck, Irving Berlin, Loretta Young, the Ritz Brothers, Jack Benny, Mary Livingstone, Edgar Bergen and Charlie McCarthy, Deanna Durbin, Al Jolson, Fred MacMurray, Rita Hayworth, etc. In addition there are shots of WAC leaders, trade papers, trade heads, etc., and this results in a marquee attraction, one which will do the indsutry a lot of good, and one which should be given the most intensive backing." (*The Exhibitor*)

20. ALL-STAR BOND RALLY (20th Fox, 1945).

"A special two-reel all-industry effort made for the Seventh War Loan, this features Vivian Blaine, Jeanne Crain, Bing Crosby singing 'Buy a Bond,' Linda Darnell, Betty Grable singing 'I'll Be Marching to a Love Song,' June Haver, Bob Hope, Harry James and His Orchestra, Faye Marlowe, Harpo Marx, Fibber McGee and Molly, Carmen Miranda, and Frank Sinatra singing 'Saturday Night Is the Loneliest Night of the Week.' It has entertainment as well as a vital message for the theatregoers, and it also pays tribute to the theatre managers in whose houses the public is urged to buy bonds. Excellent." (*The Exhibitor*)

21. HOLLYWOOD BOUND (Astor, 1947).

Compilation film made up of RKO shorts *Ferry-Go-Round*, *A Night at the Biltmore Bowl*, and *Spirit of 1976*.

"The pattern here is the same as used in a similar film devoted to Bing Crosby, and some old Grable shorts have been linked together with a thread of astory. While the Grable appeal isn't that of a Crosby, this should fit into the lower half, provided that it isn't oversold. The styles are dated, but throughout the numbers are such figures as Gene Austin, Joy Hodges, Walter Woolf King, Jimmy Grier, Lucille Ball, Preston Foster, and Edgar Kennedy. Grable hasn't too much to do, and only delivers one song." (*The Exhibitor*)